PENGUIN BOOKS

KIDS HAVE ALL THE WRITE STUFF

Sharon A. Edwards won a 1990 Good Neighbor Award from State Farm Insurance Companies and the National Council of Teachers of English for starting the Writing Box project with her students. She is a demonstration teacher at Mark's Meadow School, which is jointly operated by the Town of Amherst and the University of Massachusetts at Amherst. Multicultural education and curriculum innovation, which are central to Sharon Edwards's teaching of five-, six-, seven-, and eight-year-olds, have helped stimulate her interest in children's writing.

Robert W. Maloy, Ed.D., is the director of a nationally recognized tutoring program called the TEAMS Project, which pairs college undergraduates with linguistically and culturally diverse students in public schools throughout the Pioneer Valley region of western Massachusetts. He has worked with teachers, students, and schools as continuing education manager and adjunct associate professor at the University of Massachusetts at Amherst for much of his career in higher education, and his teaching and writing focus on school improvement and educational change.

Kids Have All the Write Stuff

INSPIRING YOUR CHILDREN TO PUT PENCIL* TO PAPER

Sharon A. Edwards and Robert W. Maloy

PENGUIN BOOKS

or Crayon or Felt-Tip Marker or Computer

PENGUIN BOOKS
Published by the Penguin Group
Viking Penguin, a division of Penguin Books USA Inc.,
375 Hudson Street, New York, New York 10014, U.S.A.
Penguin Books Ltd, 27 Wrights Lane,
London W8 5TZ, England
Penguin Books Australia Ltd, Ringwood,
Victoria, Australia
Penguin Books Canada Ltd, 10 Alcorn Avenue, Suite 300,
Toronto, Ontario, Canada M4V 3B2
Penguin Books (N.Z.) Ltd, 182–190 Wairau Road,
Auckland 10, New Zealand

Penguin Books Ltd, Registered Offices:
Harmondsworth, Middlesex, England

First published in Penguin Books 1992

10 9 8 7 6 5 4 3 2 1

LIBRARY OF CONGRESS CATALOGING IN PUBLICATION DATA
Edwards, Sharon A.
Kids have all the write stuff: inspiring your children to put
pencil* to paper: *or crayon, or felt-tip, or computer/ Sharon A.
Edwards and Robert W. Maloy.
p.   cm.
Includes bibliographical references.
ISBN 0 14 01.5972 X
1. English language—Composition and exercises—Study and
teaching—United States.   2. Education—United States—Parent
participation.   I. Maloy, Robert W.   II. Title.
LB1576.E32   1992
649'.68—dc20   92–3777

Printed in the United States of America

Set in ITC Garamond Light with Dom Casual
Designed by Beth Tondreau Design

Contents

Acknowledgments

We want to thank the children and parents who joined our Writing Box Project during the past four years. Their willingness to explore writing at home has made the promise of this book a reality.

Support for our work with families came from a research grant from the University of Massachusetts at Amherst, several manufacturers of writing supplies, and the State Farm Insurance Companies with the National Council of Teachers of English, who recognized Sharon's efforts with their "Good Neighbor Award."

Byrd L. Jones, professor of Education at the University of Massachusetts, and Mary M. Kitagawa, demonstration teacher in the Amherst Public Schools, gave much appreciated feedback and support throughout the writing of the book. Each shared his or her vision of the unlimited potential of children supported by homes, schools, and communities. Their clear thinking and insights made us pursue relentless exactness in our writing.

We have benefited from the thoughtful reading and suggestions by Michael Morgan, Mike Munley, Janet Edwards Giliberti, Donna Lynch, Debra Jacobson, Marna Bunce-Crim, Joanne Manning, Susan Lehtinen-

Chodorow, Karen Sabers Dalrymple, Sandra Wilde, and Charles Parham. We thank Harvey B. Scribner, Esther Terry, Peter Elbow, Mary Melonis, Melanie Reuter, Patricia Gordon, Mark "Pres" Pieraccini, Andy Hamilton, Sheryl Jablonski, and Dawn M. Bond for their helpful comments and support. We have learned about school improvement and parent involvement in education from Richard J. Clark, I. E. Seidman, Miriam Williford, Michael Greenebaum, John Fischetti, Dorothy Watson, Susan Benedict, Kathleen Holland, Dwight Allen, Tom DeBello, Atron Gentry, Boreth Sun, David Bloome, Bill and Nancy Gibson, Sue Fletcher, and Jack Heffley.

Leah Mermelstein provided invaluable assistance in researching titles for the Young Writers' Bookcase. Christine Kubin was instrumental in helping us assemble the first version of the Writing Box and its accompanying guide for parents.

We also want to thank our editors at Viking Penguin, Kathryn Court, senior editor, Caroline White, associate editor, and Robert Castillo, production editor; and our agent, Edward Knappman, who believed in this project when it was just an idea and a dream.

Finally, we thank our parents, Flora and Roy Edwards, and Peg and the late Bill Maloy. They continue to inspire us to put pen to paper and express our ideas.

This book is dedicated to young writers and the powers of their intellect and creativity.

A Bill of Writes

1. *I write to please myself.*

2. *I decide how to use my Writing Box.*

3. *I choose what to write and know when it is finished.*

4. *I am a writer and a reader right now.*

5. *I have things to say and write every day.*

6. *I write when I play and I play when I write.*

7. *I can write about my experiences and my imagination.*

8. *I enjoy writing on computers and typewriters.*

9. *I spell the way I can and understand spelling as I write.*

10. *I learn as I write and write as I learn.*

A Note to Parents

Kids Have All the Write Stuff shares the remarkable stories of youngsters ages two to nine who are writers at home. Young children
accomplish far more in written language than most of us realize.
Given their own writing materials and encouragement from adults, children convey their curiosity and new ideas through writing. Early marks
and scribbles evolve into readable symbols as children express their
thoughts through drawings, words, and stories. Communicating through
symbols promotes children's image of themselves as skillful, confident
learners. Writing is not a special ability or innate talent that only certain
youngsters possess. It is an area of personal growth that parents, grandparents, aunts and uncles, teachers, and other interested adults can inspire
in young children.

WRITING IS FUNDAMENTAL:
FUN-FROM-THE-MIND

Most adults do not connect writing with young children. They ask, "Why would you do this with a child?" "How is it beneficial?" "Aren't two-, three-, and four-year-olds too young?" "Shouldn't they learn to write in school when they're ready?" "Why push something they won't need to know till they get older?"

Our response is that writing is fundamental—"fun-from-the-mind"— and a key to a child's current and future learning. Whether you realize it or not, your child is a writer right now! That fact leads our list of compelling reasons for making writing an essential part of your child's life today.

1. Writing Opens a New Gateway to Learning

Young children write spontaneously and enthusiastically. Infants and toddlers want to pick up pencils and crayons to make marks and lines on paper. These are "baby steps" in their development of using written language.

Preschoolers' scribbles are their approximations of symbols. Their oral stories, often rich in fantasy, are explorations of words, characters, and plot that evolve from their experiences and imaginations.

School-age youngsters' drawings and unconventional spellings communicate their ideas and emotions. Their interest in fiction and nonfiction generates a wide range of choices and styles for topics and text.

When writing is a natural feature of children's lives, their concentration on it is total and their enjoyment is great. They demonstrate that they have something important to say. A cycle of successful learning is created between adults and children that stimulates the latter's interest in language, reading, math, science, history, and many other topics. Encouraging a young child's writing promotes the development of a positive self-image as a capable learner and, in countless enjoyable ways, builds the foundation for future success.

2. Writing Is Fundamental to Reading

In a society dependent upon understanding print, reading is fundamental to learning. What is not as yet clearly understood is that encouraging children's writing is an effective way to develop reading skills. Children think of themselves as successful at anything they find easy to do. Their early interest in print and how they can express their own ideas with symbols gives adults continual opportunities to answer questions, provide information regularly, and write together. Through reading their own writing, children begin to understand the purposes and pleasures of written language. An explanation of what reading is and why people do it becomes tied to the personally satisfying experience of conveying one's own thoughts to others through writing.

Children write for the same reasons that they listen to stories or read books: to be entertained, to share events and ideas, to figure something out, and to try something new. Pleasure, learning, and experimentation are strong motivators for writing, just as they are for reading. As children read their scribbles, they behave as readers, conveying their meaning through text. Authoring and reading a text gives a child a sense of competence with print, which encourages further interest in writing and reading.

3. Writing Will Be Essential in the World of Tomorrow

Today's children will graduate from high school in the first decade of a new century and can anticipate productive lives beyond the year 2050. They face a lifetime of choices. Most will change their careers five to eight times, competing for complex new jobs, half of which we cannot yet imagine. Their ability to communicate—to write, read, compute, and solve problems effectively—will determine their success in twenty-first-century careers.

The advent of an information age has begun redefining the nature of work and everyday life in the United States. The number of professional, managerial, and technical jobs now exceeds those on assembly lines, in construction, and on farms. Eighty-five percent of new jobs in the 1990s and beyond will require not only a high-school diploma but some postsecondary education as well. By the turn of the century perhaps half of all jobs will involve computers or other forms of information technologies.

Communicating effectively in a complex future world seems a distant goal for many people in our country today. There are 27 million illiterate Americans and only 3 million teachers and tutors. One out of every five adults in the United States has difficulty completing a job application. In Massachusetts alone, 600,000 adults have not progressed beyond a fifth-grade level of writing or reading proficiency. In this country, reported Jonathan Kozol, "twenty-five million American adults cannot read the poison warnings on a can of pesticide, a letter from their child's teacher, or the front page of a daily paper. An additional 35 million read only at a level which is less than equal to the full survival of our society."[1] In 1988 the Hudson Institute forecast that fewer than 1 in 4 new workers entering the labor market between 1985 and the year 2000 will be able to perform seemingly routine reading and writing tasks such as preparing orders, computing price lists, or reading catalogs. Only 5 percent will be able to read professional publications and write technical reports.[2]

In addition to these alarming statistics there are many adults in this country who simply do not like to write because they think they cannot write well, spell correctly, remember all the rules of grammar and syntax, or use a varied vocabulary. Most of us experience at least one of these blocks. Many adults do not view writing as enjoyable or even useful. They may also be embarrassed by their writing, feeling they have few ideas worth communicating or preserving in print. They do not express themselves creatively or work through feelings about a subject or area of concern on paper. And they blame their personal abilities rather than the way they learned to write.

In school, children do not automatically or easily learn to write, nor do they necessarily enjoy the writing they must do. Opportunities to write for authentic reasons or to express ideas are not easy for well-meaning teachers to create in classrooms with twenty-five or more students. Typical writing curriculums assign topics and emphasize memorization of rules. They rarely allow students to experience the pleasure, power, and self-directed learning of writing, revising, and sharing ideas with both adults and peers.

According to a national report on the language-arts proficiencies of fourth, eighth, and twelfth graders, between one half and two-thirds of the tested students were unable to perform a "persuasive," "informative," or "narrative" writing task at the level of "adequate or better." No more than 11 percent of high school seniors earned the highest rating of "elaborated" on any of the three writing assessments, and only 3 percent produced an excellent piece of persuasive writing.[3] Might this be, in part, because children are so often assigned a topic to write about instead of being asked to persuade, inform, or narrate about issues of interest to them?

Part of the literacy problem may be the pervasive influence of television and other media in the lives of children. In one year, an eight-year-old spends 900 hours in class and 1,170 hours watching television. A 1988 study of 26,000 eighth-graders from 1,200 schools nationwide reported that young adolescents "spend only two hours a week on reading outside of school and logged in four times as many hours watching television as doing homework every week."[4] Much of children's TV watching consists of passively viewing programs that offer few opportunities for engagement or personally meaningful activities. Yet when programs are chosen with purposeful learning in mind, television itself can be a powerful source of information about people, places, and the world around us.

In the future, people will need to understand and utilize the power of all forms of communications. They will discuss things using words, gestures, and pictures, through oral, print, and electronic mediums. Writing, the way we describe it in this book, is an enjoyable way for youngsters to develop the communicative talents that they will need to enter the society of tomorrow.

4. Writing Enables Thinking and Reflecting About Ideas, Feelings, and Circumstances

In this era of telephones, television, electronic mail, automated bank machines, and other forms of instantaneous communication, it is easy to minimize the role of writing. Why write when someone can pick up the telephone or fax an article more rapidly and easily? Writing is important for personal growth and reflection as well as disseminating information. It may be even more important in our hectic modern lifestyles because finding time for reflection is usually not built into our schedules. In rereading our own texts, we ponder personal thoughts and beliefs and reflect on earlier ideas or emerging viewpoints.

Putting thoughts into writing helps us make sense of the rush of daily events and experiences. We think our way through, notice patterns, and raise questions to investigate. Many people write down their thoughts before attending meetings or making decisions to get a better sense of all sides of an issue. Many find journals and diaries essential to evoke resolutions or new ideas and solutions. Writing has permanence. Ideas and conclusions that have been written down can be reexamined months—even years—later, in light of new situations. Writing bolsters memory, which may lose or confuse important details.

Similarly, writing is a means of personal reflection and consideration for youngsters. It is a lifelong ability that should be developed in a young child. Children who write confidently at home enjoy learning. They have fun and communicate their ideas through written language. As they mature and enter adolescence and adulthood, they use writing to maintain their stability and sense of perspective in the face of pressures in their lives as well as school assignments.

5. Writing Occasions Children's Decision-Making

As writers, children are active creators rather than passive consumers of information. They use all of their knowledge to determine what to write and for what purposes, as well as how to use the writing materials at their disposal to accomplish their goals. These choices are important: what words will be used; in what order; whether pictures will be included; where the writing will go on the page. As kids consider these issues, they become the chief executive officers of their own learning, seeing how their decisions achieve results. Sometimes with parents, but often by themselves, they choose what to change and what to leave alone in their texts. They consider other people's written communications with greater acuity, assessing what they like and do not like and explaining why.

A WRITING BOX FOR EVERY CHILD

Our thinking about children's writing at home began with questions from our work in schools: How can all children be successful learners? How can adults promote every youngster's full growth and development?

In the 1980s we became interested in the whole language approach to teaching, in which children's own writing serves as the beginning of their learning about language. What we found within this philosophy were concepts that radically changed our beliefs about what even the youngest children can learn and accomplish. In 1988, we combined our knowledge of whole language and "process writing" with the powerful role that parents play in their child's life. We developed and tried out an easy, inexpensive, and effective way to promote successful learning for children that begins with their writing at home. We call it a Writing Box.

Writing Boxes are containers (we use see-through plastic ones) filled with materials for young children to keep at home and use any way they choose. Since that first year, more than a hundred youngsters from Sharon's kindergarten, first-, and second-grade classes, and many more in several other Massachusetts schools, have received Writing Boxes.

A Writing Box might contain:

- white construction paper
- colored construction paper
- lead pencils
- erasers
- scented watercolor markers
- crayons
- colored pencils
- cellophane tape
- glue
- stapler
- scissors
- ruler with shaped template cutouts
- small and large notebooks
- small chalkboard
- white and colored chalk
- pencil sharpeners
- alphabet chart
- top-locking plastic bag
- classroom-made blank books

We chose colorful, child-sized items that appeal to young children, such as a small Swingline stapler that is just right for the size and strength of small hands. Some items grab attention, like the multicolored covers on various sized notebooks. Some are unusual, like a pencil sharpener attached to a small globe. One of three lead pencils has a shiny exterior instead of plain yellow. The C-THRU plastic ruler has small templates of geometric shapes in its center. Fiddle Sticks markers have different scents. The materials are inexpensive, durable, and easy to replace. Paper-covered, child-made blank books for children to write in at home and bring back to school to be typed into "published" cardboard-cover editions are also part of the contents.

Because most parents we encountered found it strange to encourage children to write at home before they learned to read or spell, we wrote a handbook to accompany each Writing Box, in which we suggested strategies for promoting writing, included examples of children's own spellings, and informed parents of the impact of adult involvement on a child's writing process.[5]

The premise of the Writing Box is simple yet profound: Young children like to write and are excited about having their own materials. "It occurred to me that more writing might take place outside the classroom if the materials were readily available," Sharon told parents during the first year of the project. "At this age, the children are discovering all kinds of wonderful things. They use the Writing Box as a partner in those experiences. It lets them express what they're feeling on paper in their own ways."

In 1990 the project gained national publicity when Sharon received the first Good Neighbor Award presented by State Farm Insurance Companies in cooperation with the National Council of Teachers of English for implementing Writing Boxes with her students and their families. The award photograph of Sharon, the children, and their Writing Boxes was advertised in *USA Today*, *Time*, and *Newsweek*, along with State Farm's promotional publications.

"AN EXPLOSION OF WRITING"

Our initial goal had been to spark interest in writing among children and families. Neither of us was prepared for what happened after the Writing Boxes went home. Personal materials in a portable plastic box, enhanced by parental involvement and support, proved to be a more powerful catalyst for children's writing than we ever dared imagine when we started the project.

As we talked with families that first year, we were astonished by what the children did after receiving their Writing Boxes. One mother described "an explosion of writing" by her daughter. Another said that her child used the materials for writing and drawing every day after school till they were completely used up. A third watched her daughter go upstairs, dismantle a small plastic table, move it downstairs, reassemble it in a corner of the living room, put her Writing Box under it and some special objects on top of it, and declare it "My desk!" A note from another parent four days after the materials went home read: "A weekend with the Writing Box is like no other." She described how her daughter had used the materials to teach her younger brother, taken them with her to church, and remained involved with writing for the entire weekend.

Each year similar reports came back to Sharon. At their own pace and in their own way, youngsters explore writing at home. Many multilingual children wrote in two or three languages. We inquired about where kids wrote and found out: the kitchen table, the bedroom floor, a child's desk, a parent's desk, the corner of the living room, or, as one youngster replied, "all over the place." We asked what they wrote, and they replied:

- "I'm writing like crazy at home. I'm writing a book called *Heidi*."
- "A lot of things, scary things."
- "Every kind of thing, animals, my family, robots."
- "Fiction and nonfiction, but more fiction."
- "Jets, warriors, and things."
- "Everything."
- "Hundreds of grocery lists 'cause my mom tells me to."
- "Letters."

When we examined samples of children's writing, we found:

- signs
- grocery lists
- fiction stories
- nonfiction stories
- letters
- dinner menus
- writing games
- poetry
- recipes
- plays
- diaries
- chapter books
- maps
- birthday cards
- captions for drawings
- thank-you notes
- journals
- speech balloons for cartoons
- drawings
- jokes
- newspapers
- notes and messages
- rhymes
- names
- mazes and puzzles
- rules for games
- numbers
- movies
- comics
- words and phrases
- homework assignments
- copying from books or texts
- surveys
- pretend writing
- fictional languages
- riddles

As family routines and interactions expanded to include writing, it became a regular activity the children did on their own and shared with parents. Mothers and fathers who had not thought of their children as writers and had not encouraged their youngster's exploration with written language at home gained new understandings about how they could support their child's learning. They created new conditions for children to explore literacy by providing accessible materials, promoting invented spelling, reading aloud, and responding enthusiastically to children's communications. Younger and older siblings eagerly joined these activities. Some families then needed writing materials for each child.

Encouraging a young child's writing is neither difficult nor expensive. The basic approach is familiar from assisting your youngster to walk, talk, read, play ball in the yard, ride a bike, build models, or conduct home science experiments. Wanting the best for your child, you encourage play, choice-making, risk-taking, and a gradual development of talents that are continually combined in new ways and applied in fresh settings.

Applying these same strategies to writing creates events that are truly exciting. Children discover the power of written communication; gain confidence as readers and writers; increase their chances for success in school; and develop strong images of themselves as competent learners and decision-makers. Parents and other family members interact with children in different ways from watching television, reading aloud, or pursuing a hobby. They become effective promoters and partners in a child's individual growth and development. Writing can easily become the most mutually satisfying activity you regularly engage in with your daughter or son.

1

Understanding Writing

Part 1 discusses key ideas for understanding young children's writing, how to create a Writing Box, ways to implement writing processes fit for children, and specific strategies for adults to use to inspire young writers. These concepts will make writing a child-initiated, adult-supported activity in your family.

1

Watching Young Writers

Young children write everywhere—in family living areas and kitchens with parents, siblings, and friends; in their rooms amidst toys, stuffed animals, and clothes; on a computer or a typewriter; in restaurants and offices as they wait; in cars and buses traveling down the highway; and in schools.

Their writing is spontaneous, playful, creative, self-absorbing, and always expressive. Youngsters choose their own topics and genres. They explore words and their meanings, have fun with shapes and letters, and illustrate their work with drawings—all ways that they communicate with others. And as they cut, paste, and staple pages together, they talk, laugh, and interact with friends.

Kids want to learn about, and try for themselves, all kinds of written communications—recipes, lists, poetry, signs, chapter books, letters, cards, fiction and nonfiction. Writing springs from their curiosity and creativity—the desire to tell a story and to explore different materials. Children discover how to express ideas and feelings on paper and, in so doing, reflect on their changing daily lives.

We introduce many young writers in the chapters that follow. They are youngsters who assume their own ability to write. Their experiences and what we have learned from them are the basis for this book.

Christina, who is now twenty months old, has heard the alphabet song almost daily since she was an infant. As her mother sings the song, she stops to let Christine name the letters: "A, B, C, ___, E, F, ___, H, I, J, K, L, M, N, O, ___, Q, R, S, ___, U, V, W, X, Y, ___."

She sees letters in books and in her home environment. A small alphabet quilt with pockets hangs on her doorknob within easy reach. Each pocket has a letter on it and contains an object beginning with that letter sound. She takes these objects out of their pockets and puts them back in other places on the quilt. Then she begins a "Where's Your Home?" game that her mother has been playing with her since she was a year old. "No no, doggie, not your home!" she sings as she takes the little dog out of the *M* pocket. "No no, yo-yo, not your home!" she continues, and the yo-yo goes back to the *Y*.

She regularly hears stories, observes her parents reading and writing, and receives encouragement to scribble. Her mother points out letters to her and writes her name so she can see it. As Christina makes lines on paper, she occasionally points at her marks and says, "A, C." Even at this young age, she associates letters with writing as a result of her mother's playful approach to teaching her about the alphabet. She is doing what many children do naturally: associating words with objects and letters with words by playing games, singing songs, and listening to stories. One day, busily making lines and squiggles on paper, she proclaimed happily, "Christina writing!"

Since he was three, Kyle has regularly engaged in reading and writing activities in his home: hearing books, composing lists and letters, drawing pictures, and telling oral stories.

From the moment he entered kindergarten at the age of five, he has loved the environment, which is filled with many choices for children's playing and thinking. One of his favorite areas is a writing table where children compose their stories in their own spelling. Another is a read-aloud area where he listens to favorite books.

Always full of questions, Kyle wonders about science and nature and adult activities. By constantly taking apart and reassembling his toy ve-hicles, he investigates his own questions about how their parts and batteries work. Riding home from school with his aunt Sharon one day, he inquired, "How do people write books?" She explained briefly that people write about things that they think are important or interesting. Then their writing is published in books that are sold in bookstores.

That evening Sharon remarked, "Kyle, you are so smart and you learn so fast, you could be anything you want to be when you grow up—a scientist, an engineer." He replied, "I could be a writer."

Six-year-old Carmen would not write or draw when she started school. Listening to stories in English was confusing and difficult for her. She did not know names or sounds of letters, nor how to form them. She could narrate only brief oral stories because of her limited vocabulary. Her attention was short-lived for activities that involved making letters or pictures, but she listened eagerly to songs, especially those in Spanish.

Dramatic changes occurred when she discovered ways to explore writing with the assistance of her teachers. First, she learned to paint her name and then write it on paper. Hearing books, she began recording her oral stories on tape and listening to them over and over again. By the end of the school year, she was writing the lunch menu to read in front of the class and inventing the spelling of signs and messages, including one to warn others away from her projects: "DT TCH" (Do Not Touch).

Writing is now becoming a part of Carmen's home activities through the use of her Writing Box and the involvement of her mother and brother, who read aloud to her at night. She has also begun to "play school" with her brothers and sisters. She told her teacher, "I want to read. Please teach me to read right now!"

Before first grade, Clayton's home writing experiences consisted of making greeting cards for relatives and friends with his mother's help. They have done this together since he was three. He created the illustrations, and while his mother spelled the words aloud, he wrote "Happy Birthday."

Usually a quiet six-year-old, on the day he received his Writing Box at school, he was so excited that he jumped up in the air. Six weeks later, he brought to school his first two stories from home and announced excitedly, "I wrote fiction and nonfiction. This is the first time I ever wrote nonfiction." A month later a doctor meeting him for the first time asked what he liked to do. Clayton confidently replied, "I write!"

He continues to write regularly on his own. His parents do not ask him to; they just watch him from an adjoining room in the evenings as he sits at the kitchen table, his head bent over his paper. With his Writing Box, Clayton writes between one and three stories almost every day at home, more than 150 pages in the first four months. He does not ask for any assistance with spelling or choosing topics. He does not discuss his stories before writing them, but when they are completed, he reads them to his parents. Mother and Father follow his lead and listen attentively, allowing him to stay up late to finish his writing in the kitchen, sharing his writing with friends and relatives, and mailing his cards and letters to family members.

Watching an adult typing his stories at school one day, Clayton observed, "I better slow down. You can't keep up with me." In the spring he proclaimed, "I want to be the boy who writes the most books in the world."

At home and at school, six-year-old Eugenie hardly ever picked up a pencil because drawing and writing were not easy for her. She was rarely happy with the look of her efforts. A dramatic change of behavior—from a long-standing avoidance of paper and pencil activities to satisfaction as a willing author and illustrator—occurred after she received her own materials.

"She didn't dive into the Writing Box right away," said her mother. "She was dragging her feet about using it and liked playing with the materials but not writing with them."

Gradually, with her mother's encouragement and support, she wrote in invented spelling, beginning with grocery lists and short personal narratives. The morning she brought her first two stories to school, she remarked, "Ms. Edwards will be so excited." She became a regular, self-motivated writer. That year Eugenie became the first student in her class to author a chapter book at home.

She wanted to draw the illustrations in the published versions of her stories and voluntarily stayed inside during recess to do so. Her mother, thrilled with her daughter's new attitude about writing and drawing, remarked, "I really believe the Writing Box said to her, 'This is something you can do in your big life.' Picking up a pencil, unless a kid were really interested—what would they do without a base like the Box?"

———

Adults who are unacquainted with young children's writing may think these stories are exaggerated or exceptions. Yet the joy and excitement shown by Christina, Kyle, Carmen, Clayton, Eugenie, and others you will meet in upcoming pages, express what youngsters feel when they write and receive support and encouragement from adults.

YOUNG CHILDREN'S WRITING

What kinds of writing can youngsters do who cannot form letters, spell words conventionally, or punctuate sentences? The answer is ALL KINDS! Children's topics come from their experiences and their imaginations, and they produce remarkably sophisticated communications. From the time they can pick up a pencil or a crayon, children make squiggles, circles, lines, and scoops. This is how they play with symbols—they have fun with materials and discover what happens when they make marks on paper.

Christina's writing at twenty months

As they develop a knowledge of text, their marks represent written language and serve many purposes: exploring symbols, transmitting a message, and pretending to write. Whole words or entire sentences may be conveyed by a single mark or symbol that they read by attributing meaning to it.

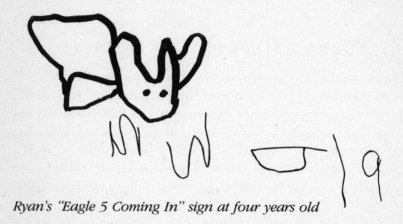

Ryan's "Eagle 5 Coming In" sign at four years old

From their scribbles, youngsters gradually form approximations of letters, and these appear in their writing. The letters may be backwards, sideways, or even upside down. They do not usually represent sounds in words but text in general. The first letters used are often those from a child's name.

Four-year-old Sam's letter to "Big Bear" (with drawing by his mother) [*Dear Big Bear, I love you! Thank you for the treasure hunt. Thank you for the ice cream cones.*]

Toddlers and preschoolers try out some of the same forms of communication that older children use to convey information.

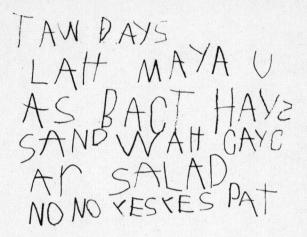

Menu by six-year-old Pat [Today's lunch menu is baked cheese sandwich, cake, or salad bar. No, no. Yes, yes.]

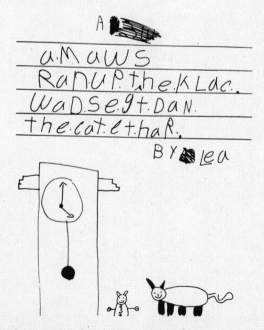

Six-year-old Lea's version of a nursery rhyme [The mouse ran up the clock. When she got down, the cat ate her.]

Young children produce projects by themselves or in collaboration with adults, siblings, or friends. They try imaginative fiction with original plots and characters. Stories vary in length from one page to more than a dozen.

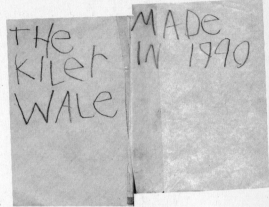

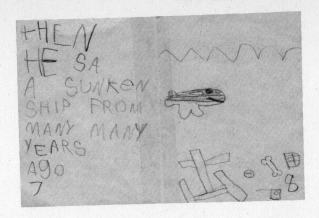

"The Killer Whale," an adventure story by six-year-old Alain [One day Killer Whale said: "I want to go for a walk." Killer Whale ate many fish. Then he saw a sunken ship from many, many years ago. He saw a strange fish. Then he went back home. The End]

Young writers compose different forms of communication that express their ideas and feelings.

Seven-year-old Charles's characters using an alphabet stencil (stencil was backwards when he traced the letters)

Opposite: *Eight-year-old Emily's letter to Sharon after Christmas [Dear Sharon, How is your book coming? I can't wait till I see you again. How are you? I'm babysitting a cat. His name is Sam. When are you coming to see me again? Go onto back. I got a Nintendo set from Santa. I was so happy. I have to go now. Bye. Love, Emmy. P.S. What do you get when you cross a worm with a prickly porcupine? Answer: Barbed wire.]*

NOTES:

Dear Sharon,
How is your Book
Coming? I can't wait
Till I see you again.

How are you?
I'm babysitting
a cat His name
is Sam. When
are you coming
To see me again
go onto back →

I got a Nientendo
Set from Santa.
I Was so happy.
I have to go now
Bye ☺ Love
      Emmy

PS. What do you
     get when
     you cross a
worm with a
Prcly Porcipine
Answer...
Bar Bed wire

Gabriela
MS EbW CaceS
fouND FouWes At Thø LittiL
ILøND iN Thø ParkiHg
thø caløfs at thø FouWes
Wear Wiet and PørPiL
We Weht
OUT ON firSt
day O7 SøPriHg

Gabriella's newspaper story [Ms. Edwards's class found flowers at the little island in the parking (lot). The colors of the flowers were white and purple. We went out on the first day of Spring.]

Young writers also begin considering the responses of their intended readers. Six-year-old Eugenie wrote her first chapter book after hearing an oral story told to her by an Egyptian friend of her mother. Telling Sharon about her own written version, Eugenie commented: "I don't think the kids will understand one part. It's about the moon." She explained that there were mummies in the story, and she was not sure that all her classmates knew about mummies. This shows that Eugenie was thinking as an author and that she was concerned about her readers: Did they possess enough information to understand her ideas and make the story as effective as she wanted it to be?

Here is her text, in its entirety:

The Golden Mummy
Written and Illustrated by
Eugenie
made in Amherst, Massachusetts
1989

Chapter 1
Death
My mommy has an Egyptian friend. She says her grandmother died when she was a kid.

Chapter 2
Danger in a Metal Pyramid
Did you hear about the mummy?

Chapter 3
Mystery
Dad and some men and me are going to the pyramid at night. The moon was full. So it was not such a good idea. We got there at midnight and we saw one hundred mummies. The golden one she said was her grandmother. I was not afraid. The mummies were three-headed. I asked for the Queen of mummies. She said that the mummies were good.

The End
About the Author
I like to swim, ski, and skate. I like dogs, too.

THE NATURALS

In the 1984 film *The Natural*, Roy Hobbes, a mysterious drifter played by Robert Redford, joins a struggling baseball team. After languishing on the bench, he is pressed into action as a pinch hitter because the manager has no one left to put in the game. Hobbes steps up to the plate and hits a majestic game-winning home run. Soon he is a star—hitting home runs and carrying his woebegone team to the top of the league. How does he play baseball so easily, so effortlessly, accomplishing these magnificent feats? Roy Hobbes is a natural.

The story is a legend, but its message is unmistakable: Some individuals are gifted—naturals at what they do. They seem born with the ability to do what others cannot. Most of us accept and marvel at what we think of as their special talents. We assume that people who perform especially well in a certain area have an innate facility that the rest of us do not possess.

This assumption is inaccurate.

All young children are naturals at learning, as parents know very well. They have a seemingly limitless potential for accomplishment. Their talents flourish when actively supported by home, neighborhood, and school. Having studied how infants, toddlers, preschoolers, and elementary-grade students grow and learn, psychologists and educators consistently reinforce this message. As the late educator and philosopher John Holt eloquently noted:[1]

> Children are passionately eager to make as much sense as they can of the world around them, are extremely good at it, and do it as scientists do, by *creating* knowledge out of experience. Children observe, wonder, find, or make and then test the answers to the questions they ask themselves. When they are not actually *prevented* from doing these things, they continue to do them and to get better and better at it.

After more than forty years of research on how people learn, psychologist Benjamin S. Bloom has concluded that "what any person in the world can learn, *almost* all persons can learn." They need "*favorable learning conditions*" that spark their interests and enable them to express their talents freely. In the case of young children, it is adults—usually parents and sometimes grandparents, older siblings, friends, and teachers—who provide those necessary conditions. They encourage children by creating a climate of learning and discovery: They give time, resources, and energy to promote a child's interests from an early age. They read to children, allow them to explore and act independently, and praise their attempts to try new things.[2]

True, some individuals' accomplishments exceed those of the rest of us. Exceptional athletes, artists, musicians, scientists, writers, teachers, and members of every field achieve their successes not solely because of their capabilities. They reach their potential through a long period of practice, hard work, and intense learning—encouraged and supported by others. In Bloom's studies of world-class performers in science, sports, and the arts, he's found that "no one reached the limits of learning in a talent field on his or her own."[3] Most people who write for a living work regular hours at a desk, struggling to arrange ideas into a coherent form. They go through draft after draft of each composition. Like anyone who must convey ideas through writing, they are constantly learning how to better communicate.

With consistent encouragement and support, the possibilities for what any child can accomplish are wide open. Every child already possesses what it takes to think, ask questions, learn, and create, although children have different learning styles. Some prefer diving into hands-on activities, while others want to observe and assess before trying something out. When children can choose an approach to learning that matches their interest, they accomplish more than adults usually expect from individuals so young.

What does a view of children as natural learners mean for the development of their writing? It has generally been assumed that young children who write freely possess innate talents or are more intellectually gifted than those who do not write as much. Such views overlook the writing capabilities of young children. "My first message, then, is that children can write sooner than we ever dreamed was possible," remarked writing researcher Lucy Calkins, reaffirming what Maria Montessori found in her work with impoverished Italian children a hundred years ago.[4]

Children acquire information and ideas about writing from everything they do: seeing words all around them, watching people read and write, listening to comments and conversations. They ask questions, hypothesize what written words say, and formulate their own answers. They identify products and places by recognizing pictures and symbols. For example, young children who watch television or who have eaten a "Happy Meal" know what the "golden arches" signify: They read that symbol as "McDonald's." Similarly, they recognize the "No Smoking" symbols displayed in public places, the message on a stop sign, and the meaning of the colors on a traffic light. Children are surrounded by symbols and continually accumulate knowledge of print in this text-filled society.

Young writers produce ideas for text as they talk, draw, and compose symbols and letters. They want to write and will do so on their own in their pretend play. They have the desire and ability to produce written expression for their own purposes long before they know the conventions of handwriting, spelling, and punctuation. Sometimes they also want adults to read and understand what they have written.

When assured that what they are doing is valued by adults, virtually all young children between the ages of two and nine regularly engage in activities normally associated with much older writers:

- reading their marks as text
- composing their own stories
- creating characters and plots
- working on stories and drawings for sustained periods of time
- understanding fiction and nonfiction
- experimenting with genres: poetry, letters, journals, stories
- switching roles from writer to reader
- utilizing punctuation and standard spelling
- writing more than one draft of a composition

A FORMULA FOR SUCCESS

Play + Choice + Approximation + Risk taking = Children's Learning

To discover the formula, we simply observed how parents successfully contribute to all of their children's learning. We concluded that the strategies that promote crawling, standing, walking, talking, and other milestones of human growth and development can be readily applied to writing. Adults support children's play, decision-making, gradual learning, and experimentation through encouragement, direct involvement, and modeling behaviors for youngsters to imitate.

Play

Children grow and learn through play. It is a constant feature of their daily experiences—beginning with an infant's responses to rattles, songs, and adult affection, and developing into older children's make-believe. Babies learn through activities that stimulate their senses: putting things into their mouths, making sounds in response to what they hear, and grasping objects. Preschoolers and school-aged youngsters learn from activities that involve the use of their creative imaginations: playing with trucks, wooden blocks, musical instruments, and paper and pencils.

Adults expect children to play and support it by allotting time and providing materials. Through play, children's creativity and risk-taking flourish. Everything they know and are learning in their daily experiences helps to inspire their play, which imitates life—playing store, school, or baseball.

Although this sounds contradictory, play is a serious activity. In play, children exercise their freedom to experiment, and sometimes to fail. Since the outcomes usually do not involve punishment for making mistakes, play activities encourage much risk-taking and learning. Moreover, making mistakes and learning from them is part of the experience. In baseball, for example, errors, wild pitches, and strikeouts are part of the excitement about the game. Baseball would be no fun if the batter or the pitcher succeeded every time. So too in children's play. The uncertainty of success in new situations sustains interest and propels youngsters toward greater levels of awareness and accomplishment.

"The basis of learning is the ability to pretend. Making something out of what is at hand," says television's Mister Rogers. Vivian Gussin Paley, a teacher, author, and MacArthur Grant recipient, also asserts the importance of play as a way for children to understand the world around them: "In play, the child says, 'I can *do* this well; I can *be* this effectively; I *understand* what is happening to me and to the other children.'"[5]

Choice

Personal choice is a powerful motivator for learning. Children continually determine what they want to accomplish through their activities. They concentrate intensely on things they are doing. We have all heard youngsters say "I can do it my own self!" and have watched children who are too young to talk express their opposition in screams or cries when forced to leave their choices.

Parents discover early that they must follow a youngster's decision about when to crawl, stand, walk, and talk by letting their child choose when to begin and how to proceed. Adults can assist the child's progress, but they cannot decide the pace. Parents may introduce their own goals, such as daily naps, foods to try, and when toilet training begins; yet to succeed, all of these require the child's cooperation. Some youngsters do not like to nap, will not eat certain foods, and are not toilet-trained when parents want them to be.

With children, the tricky spots are usually the transitions between stopping one activity and beginning another. How do you create a transition for a youngster who's happily brushing her teeth and playing with the water in the sink and does not want to accompany you outside to do something else? You find ways to make your child feel that the choice is hers—or both of yours together—rather than yours alone. You follow a child's lead, engage her interest, make suggestions, discover what works, and let her learning process evolve over time.

Approximations

Youngsters' attempts to do anything new are usually far from exact. Children rarely succeed fully in anything the first few times they try it: rolling over, holding a bottle, sitting, standing, walking, talking, counting, drawing, writing, or reading. To develop their abilities and capacities, children do the same things over and over, in ongoing approximations, to achieve increased levels of accomplishment. You assist your children's efforts by providing physical and verbal support as long as they demonstrate a need for it. You see the results of children's efforts, for example, as their speech begins to be recognizable and they quickly develop a capacity to repeat or say words they have not spoken before. You respond with pleasure and encouragement, which promotes your child's learning and continued efforts.

Over time, children's approximations become easier for them to do alone and easier for adults to let them do by themselves. With each milestone in a child's development, there comes a point at which they no longer need direct adult involvement because they can perform the activity alone. Adults are confident that children will accomplish all of the skills that most of us achieve in this manner, so they accept children's approximations as natural learning strategies. They expect mistakes to be part of the process and rarely criticize a youngster's efforts to master a new activity. They do not demand instant correctness because that is not how individuals learn. Instead, adults encourage children to do what they can and express delight with their improved performances over time.

Risk-taking

Children are risk-takers because approximations rather than immediate accomplishments are acceptable to them. They will try again rather than give up on something that they want to do. They constantly explore and push against the boundaries imposed by their environment and their own physical skills. If they did not do this, their muscles and brains would not develop and they would not learn. Initially children help their bodies to grow by kicking, jumping, squealing, pulling, pushing, and rolling. As they gain mobility and visual acuity, and their curiosity increases, they initiate new risk-taking behaviors that are requisite parts of learning.

When toddlers attempt to stand or walk, they fall down; when they first try to communicate verbally, they are unable to use words in ways that most of us can understand. They do not need to achieve a complete success the first time to feel self-satisfaction from their efforts because they are not afraid to do what is necessary to develop independence. Risk-taking involves continual experimentation. Children try out new combinations of activities to see what results they get. The "evidence" they acquire influences their subsequent responses. For example, hand-eye coordination is learned by piling blocks into towers and buildings or creating three-dimensional maps and features of physical terrain. The same blocks can also form the shapes of letters. Letters lead to words and words to expressions of ideas. Ideas and concepts, achieved through risk-taking, are key to children's more complex accomplishments.

When parents support children's willingness to take risks by complementing their efforts—"Oh, you did it all by yourself!" or "Look what you did!"—independence, creativity, and new behaviors follow. Parental excitement about children's developing capabilities encourages risk-taking and provides a supportive and reassuring message: "Try! We'll pay attention, assist you, and praise your efforts."

APPLYING THE FORMULA TO CHILDREN'S WRITING

With writing, parents usually abandon the formula of play, choice, approximation, and risk-taking in favor of a different formula based on memorization and correctness. They do what was done to them. Parents seldom think of writing as an exciting and interesting way that children choose to communicate ideas and events. Rather they equate it with separate, disconnected skills: handwriting, spelling, punctuation, capitalization, complete sentences, and paragraphing. Adults remember writing experiences in school that emphasized all these skills, and they assume that this is the way children learn to write. Because this is the standard method of teaching, many parents assume it is the only correct way. Not unsurprisingly, many young children dislike these teaching techniques and become turned off to writing.

There is an alternative that accomplishes more learning with less effort. Apply the proven formula to writing, and let it open the door to children's literacy development and their independence as writers, readers, and thinkers. A child can feel successful, confident, inquisitive, self-directed, and motivated from the youngest age.

When introducing writing, keep the following broad ideas in mind.

First, young children between the ages of two and nine are engaging in serious learning when they scribble, pretend, and create their own versions of favorite stories. A youngster's initial efforts at written expression—what are often called scribbling or doodling—is meaningful writing.

Second, any scribble, dot, or line on a page is writing. Do not wait till you see certain features in a child's written communications that are standard or conventional before calling it writing. Left-to-right and top-to-bottom progression of print across the page, legibly formed letters, standard spelling, inclusion of punctuation, and consideration of the intended audience are conventions that children eventually acquire as they explore and experiment with print. It is not necessary for you to be able to read it to understand that your youngster is creating symbols for writing.

Third, be careful when using your own early literacy experiences to guide children's writing. Many adults take for granted the idea that their child will eventually learn to write, in school, *after* learning to read—as most of them did. Yet many adults who learned this way willingly announce that they cannot, do not like to, or will not write. These attitudes frequently result from the teaching method, which is not the only or the best way to learn. Watch what occurs when you introduce writing as something enjoyable and satisfying that children can do. Expect writing from children, engage in collaborative projects with your preschool or school-age youngsters, and read books in which characters write. Encourage alphabet and letter-sound learning, handwriting, and spelling but not at the expense of a child's image of him- or herself as a writer—a person who can already express his or her thoughts and ideas.

Fourth, when encouraged, most children write because they believe that they can. Children who write on their own initiative at a young age do not necessarily have special talents or innate abilities that will develop as they grow older. Adults call a youngster who writes often a "natural writer," just as a child who demonstrates prowess in a sport is labeled a "good athlete" and another who is able to play an instrument well or sing in a fine voice is termed a "born musician." While each child indeed has different abilities and talents, the point to remember is that whatever a youngster does repeatedly and enjoys is something that the child learns about, develops confidence in doing, and feels able to do.

One story summarizes the power of the proven formula for promoting young children's writing. During an interview with one of the families who had a Writing Box, a seven-year-old boy proudly showed a few of the more than one hundred pages he would eventually write at home about the fictional character called a "Mila." His mother and father not only supported his efforts but wrote with him and composed some of their own as well. They said that he sought out adults to listen to his stories.

"Why do you write?" Sharon asked this young writer.

"I don't know," he responded.

"Can you give me a clue?" she continued.

"I will give you two clues," he promptly replied. "It's fun and I like it."

2

Creating a Writing Box

"Today we take our Writing Boxes home!" exclaimed Elizabeth as she entered the classroom one November morning. Her mother said later that she had been talking about her Writing Box for two weeks.

"When are we going to get our Boxes?" Stephen asked at morning meeting.

"Right after lunch," Sharon replied.

At one o'clock, the whole class gathered to hear the directions for packing their Writing Boxes. Twenty-five empty plastic containers were stacked up, awaiting their new owners. On classroom tables were piles of colored paper next to scissors, erasers, pencils, magic markers, glue, tape, and other writing supplies.

The children began talking with one another about which shiny pencil and what color scissors and notebook they wanted. In pairs, they began collecting their materials. Picking up a ruler, John said happily, "My mom has one like this." Finding the scissors, Cindy declared, "Oh, good! I've been waiting a long time for these."

As they gathered their materials, some children made quick choices while others deliberated over their selections. Decisions about a red or

*Eight-year-old Brian's Writing Box note [*Ms. Edwards. I hope we get Writing Boxes on Monday. Brian*]*

blue pair of scissors; a green, yellow, or clear plastic ruler; and different designs on the shiny pencils were important to them. Some reconsidered their choices and exchanged items. When they had finished, everyone wrote and illustrated the title page of their parents' copy of "The Family Guide to Home Writing."

"Thank you for my Box!" declared Jerry as he marched out of the room among the parade of children carrying writing supplies in their arms.

HOW A WRITING BOX WORKS

Sharon recalls longing for colored pencils, watercolor paints, a small stapler, and construction paper when she was six years old. She was fascinated by these materials, which she had only occasionally used in school. At home were crayons and coloring books. No pencils, tape, scrap paper, or child-sized scissors were readily available for her use. She imagined that the materials she did not have would allow her to write, draw, paint, and explore new forms of self-expression. Three decades later, those memories inspired our first Writing Box.

What is it about a Writing Box that propels children's writing? "It gives a child the message: I can write!" Professor Esther Terry, chairperson of the Afro-American Studies Department at the University of Massachusetts at Amherst, said when she first saw the Writing Box. How does a Writing Box convey this message? By providing children with *accessible materials*, *ownership*, and *choice*; these factors, combined with the involvement and support of parents, create the conditions that inspire children to write.

Accessible Materials

Children will use materials more frequently if they have easy access to them. You may remember as a child abandoning your desire to write or draw because finding the things you needed was time-consuming and often fruitless. Pencils were not sharpened or crayons were broken. You could not find paper. The scissors had disappeared or the tape had run out. "Where's the . . . ?" became the anthem of these searches. A Writing Box keeps a child's materials together in one place, making them accessible and easy to find.

Ownership

Part of the appeal of writing for young children is owning their own materials. Although many of the items in a Writing Box are already available in homes, they are usually for general family or exclusive adult use. The warning "these are not to be wasted" curtails their availability and function. When children own them, they have the freedom to create without worrying that they are wasting something. In most families these materials are thought of exclusively as art or drawing supplies. Renaming materials often proves to be an important catalyst for writing activities. Calling them writing tools for children suggests new purposes and expands their possible applications.

Choice

Because the materials are open-ended, they encourage a child's creative thinking and choice-making as part of the writing process. Youngsters decide, take risks, make mistakes, and write about whatever interests them. They revise and do it again differently. There are no right or wrong answers—only an author's personal assessment of the work.

Different kinds and sizes allow a child choices for different projects. A youngster decides whether to use felt-tip markers or crayons, colored pencils or regular pencils, or some combination of leads and colors. By facilitating a child's vision of how a project will look before it occurs, choice and ownership contribute to investment in the writing and drawing. Sometimes the choice of materials will make no difference when the important thing is getting something on paper. Then, any available utensil will do. At other times choices encourage children to consider which best suit their purposes.

Parental Support

Positive responses from caring adults are crucial to all learning, including written language. When parents provide materials, their message is clearly conveyed in the gift that they care about and value a child's writing. A Writing Box gives adults an easy and direct way to demonstrate their interest: by suggesting writing, including it in family activities, complimenting a child's efforts, and celebrating what has been written by mailing it to others or displaying it in the home and workplace. In these ways parents increase their children's enjoyment, encourage their ideas, and build their confidence that they can communicate through written language.

THE IMPORTANCE OF CREATIVITY AND OWNERSHIP

A Writing Box is very different from commercial coloring books and workbooks. It has no directions or suggestions that tell a child how to use it in a prescribed way. The materials encourage a child to think, choose, and try different kinds of expressions without any prior assumptions about what is right or wrong. By contrast, many popular learn-to-write materials are based on adult conceptions of what will interest and teach a child. These materials do not promote feelings of ownership or control because they are not created from a child's ideas. In coloring books or workbooks, children are expected to follow the directions in order to do the activities correctly: stay within the lines, connect dots in correct numerical order, match pictures to letters, and practice spelling words or forming letters. Because the way to use the materials is predefined, risk-taking and experimentation are discouraged.

Choice is not only restricted in commerical materials, but if children make mistakes or feel they have done something wrong, they cannot make changes unless they can erase their original work. This feeling of not doing something right with the materials not only affects whether or not they enjoy and reuse them, but it influences their opinion of their abilities to do pencil and paper activities successfully. They learn that the only correct way to write or draw is the way presented in a coloring book or workbook.

Why do adults readily assume that children will enjoy and benefit from using commercially made coloring books? These materials have a familiarity that adults understand and want to convey to children. Because of the way adults have been taught, they assume that children's scribbling is meaningless, whereas learning to color within the lines at least helps them to get ready for school expectations. This presumption is based on a faulty premise about how children learn.

Encouraging a child's *own* drawings and written compositions is of central importance to his or her learning. Children invest more time and energy, and return to an activity more often, when they feel they're in control of what they are doing. If they lack the excitement that comes from deciding what and when to write, then it quickly becomes a joyless, difficult, adult-assigned task. The purpose of a Writing Box, or any container that you use to store supplies, is that *what* and *how* to communicate should not be presribed by someone else. Children are free to use their writing materials for themselves.

We cannot predict what might make a Writing Box most appealing to your child, but you can make a good guess. You know your child's interests. You will include items that we might never think of—the very things that your child loves—to connect reading, talking, and playing and having fun with language. We endorse the view of author and teacher Peter Elbow, our colleague at the University of Massachusetts, who urged that each Writing Box include only one instruction to the child using it: *"Don't Let Anyone Tell You How to Use This Box!"*

INDIVIDUALIZING THE CONTENTS

Your youngster's age, interests, and how much you want to spend will determine what you put in a Writing Box. Children can begin their explorations of written language with just pencils, a pen, crayons, scissors, and blank paper. Other materials can be added, an item or two at a time.

We group writing materials for young children into four categories: *containers*, *markers*, *surfaces*, and *supplies*.

Containers

Containers let children store and carry writing materials. They can vary in size from small to large, but their purpose is to provide easy access. They can be very simple: a shoebox, a plastic bag, a basket, or any other item large enough to hold materials and afford extra space in which to save writing:

- box
- basket
- backpack
- pencil box

- bag
- suitcase
- drawer

Our original Writing Box is a 16″ × 10½″ × 5½″ see-through plastic container designed for storing sweaters or other articles of clothing. It is roomy enough to hold many writing supplies, yet light enough for a five- to nine-year-old child to carry easily. The clear plastic makes it possible to see what's inside. An interlocking top keep the contents from spilling out every time it is moved and at the same time provides a flat surface that serves as a small desk.

We include a quart-sized food-storage bag with a resealable top to serve as a portable carrying case for small notebooks, pencils, felt-tip markers, or other items a child wishes to take on a trip or errand. Favorite materials in a portable bag give a child opportunities to write and draw while waiting in restaurants, dentist or doctor's office, at bus stops, on shopping trips, or while riding the subway or in a car. A pencil box in a backpack serves the same purpose.

Your choice of a writing container—plastic bag, cardboard box, drawer, backpack, suitcase,[1] or basket—is determined by what will work best in your family and what will appeal to the child who owns it:

- One family has a basket in the kitchen filled with a collection of writing materials that is available to everyone and restocked regularly.
- Another family keeps materials for everyone's use in a kitchen cupboard's drawers. The parents also constructed a "writing table" in the kitchen to give their three children enough room to work together in the center of family activity.
- A nursery-school teacher in Newport News, Virginia, put a writing suitcase in the classroom. It is signed out and taken home overnight by her students. She includes a hole-punch as one of the materials because the youngsters enjoy it so much that it draws their interest to the suitcase.
- Two university professors in Utah pioneered a "Traveling Tales Backpack" to promote writing at home among first-graders. Each child keeps the backpack, which includes writing implements and some suggestions for parents, for two nights at a time. Parents help their

children write stories to bring to school and read aloud to the class. They are invited to listen or to share in the child's story-reading at school.[2]

- Another mother has a drawer in a coffee table at just the right height for her toddler, in which she keeps writing materials along with some of her daughter's favorite small toys.
- Some children use their desks as Writing Boxes.

Markers

Markers enable children to write on surfaces and to create text and illustrations of different sizes, colors, and textures. Some of these instruments are better suited to older children because of the self-control required to use them appropriately and safely:

- lead pencils
- crayons
- chalk
- pens
- computers
- colored pencils
- felt-tipped markers
- paint and paintbrushes
- stamps and ink pads
- typewriter

Felt-tip markers come in a wide variety of bright and pastel colors that last a long time. Parents may want washable magic markers for younger children. Sanford Corporation's Fiddle Sticks Water Color Pens, each with a different scent—cinnamon brown, blueberry blue, licorice black, mango turquoise, lemon yellow, orange orange, grape purple, mint green, melon pink, and cherry red—are very appealing and durable. Since children sometimes do not replace magic-marker tops, the scented markers present a reason to remember. To keep their scents strong and their color long-lasting, they must have the caps on when not in use.

Colored pencils are an attractive tool. Their lead is usually soft, so they break easily if pressed too hard and are used up quickly if sharpened often.

Ball-point pens are not our first choice for kids because so many leak or smudge, and then there is no way to erase or wash off the ink. Children usually prefer to use colored markers, colored pencils, or lead pencils on a regular basis.

Lead pencils are very useful to everyone, young and old, because they can be erased, but they should be kept out of a child's mouth.

Crayons last a long time, provide many choices of color and size, do not require much hand pressure for infants and toddlers to use, and some are erasable and washable. Chunky or larger-sized crayons are not easier for children, in spite of a long-held belief to the contrary. Regular-sized crayons are appropriate, even though they are more easily broken.

Colored chalk works on a chalkboard or on paper. It smudges and leaves a child's fingers and clothing chalky, but it easily washes off skin and out of clothes.

Paints create colorful images in ways that cannot be easily duplicated by other materials. Exploring with paints is very inviting to most young-sters. One family bought a new watercolor set for their son every month because he used it almost daily.

Rather than avoiding finger or poster paints because of the potential mess, arrange a system for their use. Newspapers, a washable plastic tablecloth, or a large piece of plastic spread under an easel or on a table are the key to easy clean-up. A second space covered with newspapers where wet paintings can dry is a good idea.

Provide a paint smock for your child—a plastic or cloth apron or an old shirt or sweatshirt. The covering provides optimal protection if it extends to a child's knees, otherwise youngsters wipe paint from their hands onto their clothes. After the painting is finished, the smock should be hung in its proper place and brushes and containers rinsed and dried before putting them away. Depending upon age, some or all of these procedures can be done by your child after you have assisted him or her in learning what to do.

Stamps and *ink pads* are exciting to children. There are letter stamps, picture stamps, and combinations of both. You can even have stamps imprinted with your child's name on them. The ink in regular office ink pads does not wash off children's skin or clothes easily, but watercolor ink pads are available and do wash off.

Computers and *typewriters* are increasingly the writing instruments of choice for young children. Preschoolers learn a lot about these machines quickly. Some youngsters write stories, signs, lists, diaries, and letters on a computer or typewriter. Younger children enjoy sitting and typing rows and rows of letters. Sitting at a keyboard with children, observing and talking about what they are doing, is an effective way to give them information by answering their questions and responding to their curiosity.

Surfaces

Youngsters enjoy having many different *surfaces* for writing. (Ask any parent whose toddler has written on the freshly painted walls of a room.) In your child's Writing Box—and all around your house—provide children with a variety of paper, notebooks, junk mail, and other kinds of writing surfaces.

Children write on surfaces in all kinds of positions. There are "stand-up places" and "sit-down places," as Linda Lamme has observed.[3] We would add a third: lie-down places. They sit at a table or desk or lie flat on the floor. They stand and move around while writing and drawing on chalkboards, easels, or large pieces of paper hung on the wall. Attaching paper to a wall or an easel, keeping a notebook on a clipboard, and having a Writing Box in a central location offer your child many places and positions in which to write.

It is impossible to tell which writing surface will catch a child's interest. We gave a preschooler a small bound notebook with lined pages that did not rip out. He liked it so well that he slept with it for a number of nights, but when we suggested that he write something in it, he replied, "It's for my homework" and left it blank. Shortly after that, his mother purchased some pads of white, unlined 2″ by 8″ paper that ripped apart easily. He wrote in these pads, tore off the sheets, and hung his compositions all over the house. The kind of pad made a difference to this youngster's writing.

- paper
- pads
- stationery
- magic slates
- notebooks
- chalkboard
- write-on wipe-off board

An assortment of *paper*—different colors, patterns, and sizes, lined and unlined, bound and unbound—sparks interest and offers choices. Let children use paper you are no longer using: paper bags from the store, cardboard, catalogs, greeting cards, computer paper, and forms in the mail.

Blank and *lined paper* enable children to make their own books of different sizes. At some copy stores, pads of scrap paper are sold cheaply or scrap paper is collected and given away upon request. Purchasing a package of copy paper or newsprint may be less expensive than buying pads of paper for children.

Stationery, *cards*, and *postcards* are writing surfaces that children can easily make their own. Their drawings, the addition of stickers, or the use of stamps and ink pads personalize them. Stationery can be ordered with a child's name imprinted on it: "A Note from Caitlin."

A *chalkboard* is an entirely different surface. It lets children express thoughts, then leave or erase them to start again. A sock placed over a child's hand might be an eraser. One family moved a large school slate-board with them to three different houses because it was used constantly by the six children. Small chalkboards are not expensive. If they are placed in the kitchen, playroom, or child's bedroom, writing between family members develops easily. Friends and other visitors can add their own messages as well. A chalkboard in the kitchen of Sharon's parents' home is never without messages.

Write-on wipe-off boards that come in many sizes and shapes—rectangle, heart, cat, teddy bear—are great for messages. They come with their own pen and erase easily with a wet sponge or paper towel. Magnets affix them to kitchen appliances. They are the latest version of a child's magic slate or chalkboard.

Magic slates have been used by children for years and are still available, sometimes for less than a dollar. Although less durable than write-on wipe-off boards, they appeal to children because the special plastic paper lifts to erase their surface. A new version of this idea is a plastic board with an attached pencil and a handle that moves right to left to erase the surface.

Supplies

Supplies enlarge the scope of children's writing and drawing ideas. More complex projects are possible because of access to more than one kind of material. For example, a child can staple pages together. Illustrations need not be limited to drawings. Cut-outs such as photographs, pictures from magazines, the daily newspaper comics, and other drawings can be affixed to the pages with glue or tape. Pop-ups, flaps, and double pages can be made. Larger-sized writing is possible when pieces of paper are held together. Having more than one choice among supplies assures a child that if one item is used up or lost, another is still available.

- tape
- stapler
- brass fasteners
- hole-punch
- pencil sharpener
- liquid correcting fluid
- address labels and stickers
- rulers
- glue or gluesticks
- blank books
- metal rings
- label- or button-makers
- erasers
- correction tape
- scissors
- alphabets

Cellophane tape is essential to a child's creative efforts. It provides many ways to attach things together. Because it is easy to use, and children cannot accurately anticipate the amount needed, they expend yards of it. Tape can be replaced easily and fairly inexpensively, but avoid buying the cheapest brands. The tape is not as sticky, does not roll off its core as smoothly, and does not rip off the dispensers as easily, so more is needed to keep things together.

Gluesticks and *glue* are nontoxic and have no fumes. The smallest containers of glue are the easiest for youngsters to manipulate. Gluesticks work like a tube of lipstick, rolling up and down. They are less messy than glue, but they can break if a child does not know that only a quarter of an inch should be swiveled up at a time and swiveled down before replacing the cap.

Staplers are very useful to older children. We purchase Swingline's small "Tot 50" stapler because it lasts longer than other models and costs only slightly more. Staple refills are inexpensive and found in many stores. Learning to position the stapler carefully will help prevent children stapling their fingers.

A *hole-punch* and *brass fasteners* offer many creative options. Give a hole-punch to a youngster with enough hand strength to manipulate it and watch all of the ways it is used. Brass fasteners are reusable, come in different sizes, and are sold in art or stationery stores. They fasten papers together so they rotate in circles. Children make books, stories, drawings, letters, posters, signs, and artwork with movable parts. They like paper items that move, which is why pop-up books and flap books are so interesting to them.

Rings can hold homemade books together. They come in many sizes, are inexpensive, and open and close easily so pages can be added. They bind thicker surfaces together better than other connectors. Rings are sold in art and stationery stores.

Pencil sharpeners are essential tools because pencils without points are useless. Many kinds of small pencil sharpeners will do the job well. We include two in our Writing Boxes: a small plastic rectangular one and another attached to a small globe with a generally accurate map of the world on it that is produced by A. & W. Products. The children love to spin and read the globe.

Erasers on the ends of pencils wear down quickly, so we put extras over the top of the pencils in Writing Boxes. Preschoolers might find a bigger, hand-held eraser easier to use. Attractive ones come in many sizes, colors, and shapes.

Liquid paper correction fluid, *typewriter correction tape*, *address* and *typewriter labels* let children make changes in their writing and drawing. Liquid paper correction fluid should not be used by children without supervision. Address and typewriter labels peel off and self-stick. They can be written on when permanently affixed to a page. To create personalized stickers, children can draw their own pictures on these plain labels.

Safety scissors have a plastic covering over all surfaces except the metal blades. Although slightly more expensive than plain metal ones, they have a superior cutting edge, which makes them easier to use. Left-handed children should have left-handed scissors or models made for both right- and left-handed cutting.

Rulers require hand strength and coordination to make straight lines. Some children do not use them for this purpose, so we chose two others with templates that give more options. The C-THRU plastic ruler has geometric shapes of a circle, square, triangle, hexagon, rectangle, and parallelogram in its center for tracing. The Sterling alphabet ruler manufactured by Sanford has a template of capital letters. Six-inch rulers are easier for children to use when making lines.

An *alphabet poster* with pictures for each letter can be purchased or made at home. You and your child might enjoy making an alphabet picture chart together. Write the upper- and lowercase letters in pencil for your child to trace or print them yourself. Make the letters a uniform size in block-letter print. Your child can draw the pictures to represent each letter's sound, or the two of you can do this together by cutting pictures out of magazines.

Label- or *button-makers* are fun for children. Label-makers punch letters into plastic, self-adhesive strips that affix to paper, cardboard, or cloth. Children make labels quickly, easily, and inexpensively with this device. Button-makers are also inexpensive. Children draw and write their own buttons and attach them to pins. These are great fun for pairs or groups to make together. A version of button- or badge-making uses clear plastic nameplates that people wear at conferences and meetings. Children write on pieces of paper that slide into the plastic holders and then pin them on their clothing.

CARE AND STORAGE OF MATERIALS

It is not inevitable that young children will ruin or waste writing materials. They can learn routines and procedures for use and storage. Assist children to do so, depending upon their ages and capabilities, by choosing appropriate items, utilizing a protector under the workspace, and providing clear guidelines. These contribute to a child's feeling of success with writing and drawing—and to your relaxation when pencils, pens, crayons, markers, and paints are being used. Here are general suggestions for utilizing materials so that writing can commence with happy results for parent and child.

Establish Simple Rules and Routines Together

Simple procedures that you and your child establish together are a key to reducing accidents and preventing problems. When parents tell us that they must take crayons or paints away from children because the rugs, furniture, walls, or floors have been marked, we ask whether any rules or routines have been established for the use of these materials.

One helpful item is a lapboard, a portable desk, or other protector to place underneath a child's drawing, painting, coloring, or writing. A piece of cardboard, a large clipboard, brown grocery bags, a plastic tablecloth, or a placemat will suffice. Whatever you choose needs to be larger than the child's writing surface and readily available. If your child forgets, put the protector underneath the work and remark, "Remember, this is so nothing gets marked but your paper."

Youngsters of all ages need reminders and assistance with clean-up routines: putting tops on markers and glue, replacing the materials in their containers, and throwing away or recycling scraps. Older children who can do these routines independently still appreciate your compliments about their care of the materials. A two-year-old we know never replaces marker tops. Her family puts the tops on at the end of the day if they remember. They replace the markers when necessary.

Decide which items are safe for your child. Children too young to keep things out of their mouths should not have them. Lead pencils, scissors, and staplers require adult supervision till a child can handle them independently and safely. Also, children apt to mark any surface indiscriminately need your attention.

Children younger than four years old usually have not developed the necessary hand strength to tear tape easily from a dispenser. Cut pieces of it to hang on the edge of a table or chair so your youngster can have it. Because of thickness or texture, cloth, string, ribbon, and cardboard are difficult for most children to cut. Do the cutting if your child cannot.

Clean-up Time Can Be Fun Time

Children want to be able to find their materials and have them ready. Establish procedures to ensure that they associate cleaning up with future use and enjoyment. Assisting and complimenting a child's efforts helps make putting away a painless routine.

Toddlers as young as fourteen months might help you with clean-up time. Giving them a toy or book to put on a shelf or in a container is a way to introduce them to the process and include them in it. Children can learn to be responsible for helping little by little. Your guidance and consistent expectations set a family routine in motion and keep it running smoothly.

Other factors important to helping children learn clean-up routines:

- Keep the tasks appropriate to the age and capability of the child.
- Create a consistent routine that you can participate in patiently and finish quickly.
- Make easy-to-reach storage places for things that the child is responsible for putting away.

Employing Logical Consequences

Every parent faces the dilemma of what to do when a child does something they were told not to do—for example, writing on the walls of a room or leaving colored chalk on a rug. Do you reprimand the child or take the materials away?

An approach known as "logical consequences" provides a proven way of responding to a child's behavior. Logical consequences specify that your actions fit the circumstances of the situation and reinforce the patterns you want to establish in your family.

When one youngster picked up a pencil or pen, her mother would ask, "Where's your paper? Let's get your paper." From a very young age, this child associated writing utensils with a piece of paper. This did not stop her from writing on the vacuum cleaner when she was a little over a year old or on herself between the ages of one and two. But she did not write on furniture or walls. Her mother used logical consequences in response to both occurrences. Deciding that the drawings on the vacuum cleaner were harmless, she let her daughter draw them. But each time her daughter wrote on herself, her mother washed her off, while singing, "Pen, don't write on Kirsten's leg. Write on the paper. Write on the paper."

If a child writes on an inappropriate surface, then it is logical to explain that this is not okay and show the appropriate place for writing. If she continues marking where you said she should not, it is appropriate to have the child's writing or drawing activities temporarily limited to times that you are in close proximity and can supervise. When you are preparing a meal, she can be at the kitchen table. When you are reading or paying the bills, she can be close by, using a desk or protector under her work.

If materials are consistently misused, remove them till you feel that it is appropriate to try them again. Tell your child that you have put the items away but you will return them when you see other materials being used properly.

Compliment her appropriate use of the materials each time that you see it. This is as important as setting limits. When you think that enough practice has occurred for her to know which surfaces are for writing and which are not, tell her that you see she is using the materials carefully and seems ready to have a wider range of choices about when and where to use them. This way you give her the responsibility of how to act when she writes and draws again. Watch what she does then and continue to compliment her use of materials.

An important logical consequence is the reward of periodically receiving new items. Items abound that appeal to children. For instance, if you have not put sticky note pads into the writing materials, these are a treat for a child. Or when you purchase plain white or colored paper and envelopes, your child can choose stickers or stamps and a stamp pad to decorate the paper in her own way. Rewarding correct handling of the materials and the environment is a key to a child's independence with them.

YOUR CHILD'S EVER-EXPANDING LEARNING CENTER

Exploration, play, and fun are children's self-chosen activities. Use them with a Writing Box to create an ever-expanding learning center for youngsters in your home. In this way a Writing Box becomes a magnet for literacy learning and many different writing and reading activities. A Writing Box places literacy learning at the forefront of regular family activities. Children need encouragement and interest from adults, a sense of fun to use the materials regularly, and to connect writing and drawing with reading, talking, singing, and playing.

A Writing Box becomes a home-grown alternative to expensive fads, constant television watching, pressuring a child to learn, or waiting till school entrance to assist her writing and reading activities. Using the foundation for learning created by a Writing Box, expand the kinds of materials your child enjoys at home. Books, records, audio and video tapes, a personal computer, a music keyboard, and many other items may all fit the interests of particular youngsters. Special toys can be added to the Box, such as a teddy bear to whom the child reads, a child's tape recorder to record oral storytelling, or a folder of letters from friends and relatives. The net result is a solid foundation of support for a child's curiosity and desire to learn.

Following are some ideas for using the Writing Box to create a child's learning center.

Place Materials Throughout Your Home

Writing materials distributed throughout the home—a chalkboard and magnetic letters in the kitchen, a write-on wipe-off board in the bathroom, a drawer with paper and pencils in the living room—make writing easy for everyone to do. When tools are everywhere, children and adults use them more often. Some families facilitate their children's writing by providing space in the middle of family areas—under the couch (perhaps on a piece of cardboard that slides in and out as a portable desk), under a child's bed, on a table or counter in a specially designated writing area.

As youngsters produce lots of writing, keeping it together in one place may be difficult. To preserve writing, some families have drawers in which children put their papers, others have a desk in a child's bedroom. The success of any system depends on children being able to find their writing. Plastic boxes, a pocket folder, or expanding cardboard file provide storage and easy access. Keeping everything is not necessary. Put children's writing in a drawer and, as it fills up, sort through, asking the children to decide what to save, send to relatives and friends, or throw away.

Customize to the Age and Interests of Your Child

Writing Boxes can be outfitted for children of all ages. Youngsters between the ages of two and four need only a small-sized starter version: perhaps crayons, pencils, tape, scissors, and notebooks in a handy container. More items can gradually be added to this collection. As they get older, children profit from the choices and decision-making offered by a more extensive set of materials.

Create a traveling version to take along on errands and trips. It can stay in the car or go in and out of the house easily and quickly in its own small carrying case. Your child chooses what to have in the traveling

Writing Box. A clipboard, pad with a cardboard backing, or a Trapper-Keeper binder provides a flat, hard surface for writing.

Customizing a Writing Box is influenced by what you know your child finds enticing. The possibilities are many, but the choice is particular to your youngster: a dinosaur eraser, transportation stencils, books of riddles and jokes, a big pink bow, a plastic lizard, a picture of the family, or puzzles.

The mother of a two-year-old keeps birthday candles and a deck of cards in her child's writing drawer because of her daughter's fascination with these items. This child liked to draw on the playing cards when she was younger. Also in the drawer are catalogs and old greeting cards from Christmas, birthdays, and other occasions because her daughter "prefers to add color to these bright cards than to use plain white paper." This writing drawer capitalizes on the particular interests of her child. As her daughter expresses excitement about other items or loses interest in some that are in the drawer, the contents change to sustain the attraction of the materials.

Use a Child's Interests to Promote Occasions for Writing—and Lots of Other Learning as Well

When a child shows interest in a topic, you have a wonderful opportunity to learn together. Take a child who likes animals to a zoo or pet stores; a child who likes music to a concert; a child who likes to draw and paint to a museum; a child who likes to build to a construction site; a child interested in stars to a planetarium.

One-time events are not the only way to promote a child's interests. Make those interests the basis for a series of learning events. Find information at the library, watch special programs on television, visit people and places connected with the topic, and subscribe to children's magazines. Help your child acquire new information and become an expert at many things. These activities provide opportunities for oral and written language that may inspire your child to write letters, stories, and journals and produce drawings and art projects. The possibilities are vast. Children want information about all sorts of things. A personal interest may continue for long periods of time or change quickly. Whatever a child is wondering about, he will be interested in investigating with you.

Connecting writing to children's interests raises the question about the role and place of television in the home. Most youngsters are intensely interested in TV. Its negative effects are well documented, and many parents and educators believe that turning off the electronic babysitter is the best response. Other positive and active responses might combine children's television-watching with their Writing Box materials and their interest in writing.

TV is a marvelous source of information, and, because words and pictures go together, it can be a catalyst for much literacy learning. Children and parents might choose programs to watch together and discuss what they learned. Public-television shows like "Reading Rainbow," "3-2-1 Contact," or "Where in the World Is Carmen Sandiego?" might be combined with network documentaries, dramas, and comedies to create a regular viewing schedule focusing on learning. Video versions of books and movies can also provide countless hours of enjoyment, especially when watched with other family members. Writing and reading are logical extensions of these choices, as we will see in Chapter 7.

Add New or Special Items

Every item in a Writing Box is a catalyst for learning. A child fascinated by dinosaurs, cats, trucks, or maps will be drawn to a variety of items: dinosaur paper, stamps, and postcards; cat pencils, erasers, and stationery; miniature trucks, a book in the shape of a truck, a notebook with a truck on the cover; pictures of flags of the world, a globe, and geographic puzzles. Other extras are fun to receive: fancy paper clips, clipboards of different sizes, a bulletin board, a selection of stickers, stationery, or an assortment of greeting cards.

As writing materials are used up and need to be replaced, you might try something new and different or purchase another of the same item. One mother regularly selects unusual things for her child's Writing Box —postcards, stationery, large sheets of paper, tiny notebooks, special pens and pencils, stickers, stamps and stamp pads—because they stimulate her daughter's interest.

Birthday and holiday gifts can be chosen with a child's Writing Box in mind. Children might select or request items that they would like to have or make a list of items they want. As occasions arise for giving gifts, rewards, or treats, something from the list can be purchased. As children accompany you to stores, recycling centers, or garage sales, they may identify items they desire for their Writing Boxes.

There Is No Such Thing as Wasting Paper

Keep paper readily available. Young children use lots of it as they express themselves in writing. Different sizes or types are important; in fact, the more, the better. Some children like particular kinds of paper and write more if they can choose the ones they want.

Many adults were told when they were young not to waste paper, and they repeat the same message to their children. A child's idea of waste is often different from an adult's. Some youngsters do not like to write on the back of a paper unless it is a postcard. When one side of a paper is written on, it is not the same as clean paper to kids. One way for adults to help children get used to using the back of a paper is to have a stack of scrap paper always on hand for family use. This scrap paper can be cut up and used as note pads. Friends who work in offices may have paper to recycle that they would give to you.

Compliment and Display Your Child's Writing

From the very youngest ages, children need your compliments and praise. They gain confidence in themselves when they know that someone values what they do. Their confidence encourages their risk-taking with new activities and new learning. Responding to children's scribbles and invented writing by asking what they have written, declaring that you like their writing, and inviting them to hang it somewhere are all ways of acknowledging their efforts and initiative. When writing is displayed openly and proudly, your child will feel that it is important to other people.

3

Writing Processes Fit for a Child

F
ive-year-old Margarida is the youngest of six children in a Mexican-
American family who have lived in the southwestern United States
for eight years. Her friend and frequent neighborhood playmate is
Sharon's nephew Sam. Spanish, the family's primary language, is spoken
at home, and Margarida is learning English through her play with other
children and conversations with Sam's parents.

When Sharon visited her brother's family she spent time with Margarida
and Sam: reading books, recording stories on audio tape, making up math
games, drawing pictures, writing letters, cards, and signs, and talking about
what they saw as they walked through the neighborhood. Sam's older
brother, Brian, often joined them in these activities.

A few weeks later Margarida asked Sam's mother, Susan, when Sharon
would come back again.

Susan explained that it would probably not be soon and asked, "Would
you like to write a letter?"

"Yes," said Margarida.

Susan gave her pencils, crayons, and paper and then returned to her
own work. She listened as Margarida described what she was drawing.

When the girl had finished, she turned the paper over and wrote "Margarida" and "No." Then she asked how to spell "Sharon." Susan wrote it on the kitchen chalkboard for her to copy.

When Margarida had finished writing, Susan demonstrated how to address an envelope and let her put on the stamp. They went to the mailbox at the end of the driveway, deposited the letter, and flipped up the flag. Walking back to the house, Margarida told Susan that she was going to write some more. She sat down at the kitchen table and continued drawing and writing: two letters for Susan and one for Sam. Handing Susan one of them, she held onto the second and said, "Open this one tomorrow."

"Okay," agreed Susan, "go put it under my pillow." As Margarida ran to the bedroom, Susan hung the first letter on the front of the refrigerator. For many days afterward, Margarida saw her work displayed and proudly commented, "I wrote that."

Margarida and Susan's letter-writing illustrates how adults can encourage and promote a writing process fit for a child. Susan supported Margarida's writing from the initial formulation of an idea to the successful completion of her correspondence—in less than half an hour's time. Susan's conversation with Margarida demonstrates ways in which parents can build a youngster's desire to write while simultaneously promoting a child's self-confidence and self-esteem as a writer through a series of strategies that we highlight and explain in this chapter: *kidwatching*, *inviting*, *trusting*, and *publishing*.

From the outset, Susan showed her sensivitity as a *kidwatcher*. By listening and observing, she gathered information that adults often pay little or no attention to—actions that show what a child already knows. Margarida knew what a letter was and why people write them. She knew what she wanted to describe: the landscape and the neighborhood she had walked through with Sharon and Sam.

Susan issued an *invitation* for writing when Margarida asked about Sharon's return visit, knowing that encouraging responses from an adult might positively influence Margarida's desire to communicate on paper. She suggested writing as an authentic response to the situation and conveyed her confidence in Margarida's capabilities by providing materials and posting the letter.

Susan *trusted* Margarida and did not interfere with her decisions, nor instruct Margarida to do something different or add something more. Margarida's picture and three words on the back of the picture were sufficient. Susan also did not write on the paper to convey the entire message that Margarida had said aloud. She let the whole letter be Margarida's, a legitimate communication in and of itself. She could transmit more information later by phone, or trust that Sharon would understand enough to respond appropriately.

To complete the writing process, Susan *published* Margarida's letter by mailing it. Margarida's eagerness to write more letters on her own initiative showed the success of Susan's strategies.

A child's initial experience with something has the potential for turning her toward or away from it. This was Margarida's first letter, as far as Susan knew, and her experiences would affect her willingness to write again. If she had to struggle with it, she might not welcome future writing invitations. The fact that the letter was different from an adult's conventional correspondence is unimportant in comparison with what happened for her. The happy experience inspired her to write three more letters!

WHOLE LANGUAGE LEARNING

Whole language learning has been called "education's most exciting grass-roots innovation."[1] It is, as its name suggests, concerned with the growth and development of the whole child in every learning endeavor: writing, reading, math, science, geography, and social relationships.

As a philosophy, whole language is "an attitude, a set of beliefs about how children learn," that assumes kids are natural learners who want to succeed.[2] Everything that children accomplish within the context of their experiences, with the help of their families both before and after they enter school, builds a foundation for future learning. Writing, in this view, starts with the communication of personally meaningful ideas rather than with the mechanics of letters, spelling, grammar, form, or neatness.

Many parents use whole language with their children, though they may not know the term. They promote children's communication and learning through whole language when they:

- sing songs;
- recite nursery rhymes;
- read together from children's literature and other sources;
- tell stories about real and make-believe characters or events;

- make up jokes;
- count objects;
- enjoy favorite comic strips;
- write and draw with children;
- become an audience for a child's writing;
- play games;
- act out stories;
- solve puzzles and do science experiments; and
- listen to children talk about concepts and ideas.

Adults influence children's language development through their conversations and interactions with youngsters in everyday situations. The amount of information and reflection that can be exchanged is enormous. Commonplace events are full of learning possibilities. A windy day is an opportunity to involve a child in thinking about the weather, the sky, the idea of cause and effect, how an arctic or desert environment is different, or what storms are called when the wind is so powerful that trees blow over.

The effect of the wind on the trees, on a ribbon, hat, or kite creates images for a child to learn from and enjoy: waving a ribbon, chasing a hat, or flying a kite in the breeze. When a parent connects these activities with oral language—telling a story or singing a song about the wind— or with written language—reading facts, stories, or poems—the resulting experiences add to a child's information, generate further questions, and often occasion requests to hear a story, song, or poem again.

Ideas and language from one discussion begin new conversations. Other windy days present the opportunity to sing the same song or make up a new one, recite the same poem or create one of your own, tell or read the same story or try another. Children connect new understandings with old from considering something repeatedly or from examining a topic in detail.

As adults discuss different topics and ideas with children, even those that we consider simple or commonplace—where are those ants going?—the opportunities to form connections for further learning are virtually endless. *Two Bad Ants*, by Chris Van Allsburg, lets a child see the world from an ant-sized viewpoint. Singing "The Ants Go Marching Two by Two" initiates counting by twos. Seeking more information, adults and children discover that there are more species of ants than most of us might ever guess—8,800 different kinds![3]

A basic premise of whole language is respect for children's thinking, communicating, and learning. Adults respond thoughtfully to a child's statements and expressions of ideas. Children feel free to explore sounds, gestures, and words, to make mistakes, and to take risks without being continually corrected or dismissed for behaving childishly. With adult support, children forge new connections between different experiences as they extend the learning they do naturally in their daily lives.

WRITING AS A PROCESS

"Process writing" or "writing process" describes a way of thinking and learning about writing. Process is very different from the way most of us learned to write. In a traditional approach, independent skills—handwriting, spelling, punctuation, and forming complete sentences—are taught first through memorization and workbook practice, and then in compositions about teacher-assigned topics. It is usually a long while before students are allowed to choose a topic on their own.

Traditional teaching is predicated on a product orientation: You have to complete an assignment and correct it in order to show that you know the rules of writing and standard spelling. Rarely do you write for the fun of it or to express ideas in your own way. Young children are not thought of as being capable till they have learned all of the component skills that adults think they have to know in order to write in standard form. Many adults taught in this fashion do not like to write because they do not believe they can do it well—in other words, they fear not knowing all of the rules.

A process approach emphasizes learning about writing as you write about what interests you. Youngsters think of themselves as writers exploring their own ideas. There is no set beginning or end to the learning a person does. The way to understand writing is by doing it, sharing it with others, listening to their ideas and suggestions, adding to or revising your ideas, and learning the conventions by gradually incorporating them into your texts. In *Writing with Power*, Peter Elbow maintains that all writers can express their ideas with creativity and imagination, without worrying about how it looks or the way it sounds. Once it is on paper, they revise by deciding how best to communicate what they want to say. They improve their communications through writing, writing, and more writing—creating and editing till the product meets with their satisfaction.

As you consider how to facilitate a writing process with children, take advantage of their natural desire to learn new things. As they exercise their creative energies "through art, drama, music, movement, writing, or speaking, they are apt to engage in: (1) idea stimulation and planning, (2) drafting or trying out their ideas, (3) conferring with others, (4) revising and polishing their ideas, and (5) sharing or going public with what has been created."[4]

The chart on the following page, inspired by researcher Donald Graves,[5] outlines a young writer's writing process.

Youngsters write for their own purposes and satisfaction, as they should. They write according to what they know about and how much time and attention they wish to devote to a particular piece of writing. Children (like any author) think about a work in progress over time as it is being composed. They might share their thoughts with you, ask questions about their topic, or even request that you read or hear what they have written.

Children do not rehearse, draft, share, edit, redraft, share, and publish every piece of their writing. They use different elements of the writing process at different times to fit specific purposes and contexts. Young writers consider what they wish to communicate. They draft and edit as they go along. We rewrote this page many times, but young writers do not always function like professional authors publishing commercial books. They may finish a piece of writing in one sitting or work on something over a period of days or weeks, revising it repeatedly.

KIDWATCHING

Kidwatching literally means what it says.[6] Adults can learn about what children know by paying attention to their actions. As the famous baseball player and sometime philosopher Yogi Berra once remarked, "You can observe a lot by watching."[7]

Don't just watch, *kidlisten* to youngsters' conversations, questions, and remarks. Kidwatching and kidlistening offer glimpses into children's

A WRITING PROCESS MODEL

Writing Activity	*Brief Explanation*	*Use by Young Writers*
Rehearsal	Preparing to write by reading, brainstorming, talking with others, or writing one's initial ideas about a topic	Young children rehearse through storytelling, oral language play, conversations with adults and children, drawing, doodling, or listing letters or words.
Drafting	Arranging ideas and written statements into a preliminary or first version of the writing	Some writing by young children remains in draft form, as with notes, lists, signs, or drawings with words added. Some writing is strictly for experimentation and play. Other writing changes through more than one draft. Adults contribute when the child asks for assistance.
Sharing	Letting children or adults read the writing or having them as an audience while the writer reads the writing	Young writers let others see or hear their writing. They gain ideas and encouragement from comments by family and friends.
Revising and Editing	Changing some of what has been written, sometimes adding new material or eliminating existing text, and editing for ease of reading	Young writers look over their text to clarify confusing statements, to add new ideas, to refine what they have written, and to resolve errors in spelling, grammar, and punctuation.
Publishing	Making writing available for others to hear or read in a completed or publicly accessible form	Children publish their writing by reading it aloud, displaying it, mailing it to friends and relatives, or binding it in book form.

thoughts. They provide ways for adults to comprehend their amazing range of inquisitiveness and originality.

Kidwatching and kidlistening do not necessitate special abilities, but they do require that you pay attention to young learners. Kidwatchers thoughtfully observe the displays of knowledge contained in children's writing and reading activities and in their questions and conversations. They gain extraordinary amounts of information from everyday events and interactions that might have been missed otherwise. By using what they have learned during kidwatching, adults discover ways to increase children's knowledge and creativity as learners.

Young children are eager to ask, tell, and find out about the world and just as eager to show what they can do, as in the case of a conversation between a four-and-a-half-year-old boy and his mother at the local library. As they chatted, his mother handed him a small pad of paper and a pen. He began talking aloud while writing: "avocado, strike three, corn, strike four, cake, doughnut." As he wrote, his mother smiled approvingly at her son. Her nonverbal responses communicated support for his playful use of writing.

From this brief episode, an astute kidwatcher might conclude several things. First, the boy thinks he can write. Second, he knows that writing expresses meaning—in this case, some familiar foods (although we are not sure why "strike three" and "strike four" are in the list, they had meaning for him). Third, he likes to write, as evidenced by his obvious delight in composing a list. Fourth, this is a wonderful way for his mother to promote more writing in the future. She could hand him a pencil and pad in other public places or suggest he write more about this topic at another time—perhaps a menu, a recipe, or a story.

Kidwatching provides adults with the opportunity to witness what children are constantly learning. As adults pay attention to what children say and write, they learn ways to incorporate youngsters' knowledge and ideas into a lively and interesting writing process. The summer before Kyle entered kindergarten, Sharon suggested that they do some writing. He said, "I can't write in letters." His comment revealed how his concept of writing had changed from the summer before, when he had unquestioningly created text by making scoops that resembled the letter *U*. A year later he knew that he needed letters and that he could not make all of them. Sharon told him to write the way that he could. Instead of making scoops, he wrote the letters in his name. Because she was sensitive to how he was defining writing, Sharon turned his initial reluctance into a positive writing experience.

Kidwatching engages a different set of adult behaviors for a different purpose from those that many parents have learned. Children want to show and tell what they already know and what they want to know. Two- to six-years-olds often tell part of the story while writing, adding sound effects or actions. Their concentration, comments, and questions indicate what they are thinking, what they know, and how they figure out what they are doing. Listening to the oral story, as Susan did with Margarida, informs an adult about a child's ideas and what the writing is intended to mean. If adults concentrate on listening to what children say and watching what they do, viewing themselves as partners, then every child becomes a competent learner and every adult a facilitator of that learning.

Children's Surprising Ideas

Kidwatchers soon recognize what Harvard psychologist Robert Kegan has observed: that young children have "a host of original and (to our minds) amusingly strange views about nature." Children create meaning for their lives from their experiences within their own particular frames of reference. Their ideas "are manifestations of a distinct, separate reality, with a logic, a consistency, an integrity of its own." For example, a youngster may believe that the moon follows people as they walk or that teddy bears' feelings will be hurt if they do not accompany the family on trips and outings. From their point of view, young children cannot comprehend certain things about the way scientific phenomena work or the reasons why older siblings and adults behave as they do.[8]

Children are perceptive reasoners even when they think along lines unfamiliar to adults. When he was four, Ryan ate snacks at Dunkin' Donuts with Sharon two days in a row. The first day, as they got ready to leave, Ryan threw away his things and noticed the letters on the swinging door of the trash receptacle. He traced the letters with his finger, saying the names of those he knew, but did not ask what the words said. Sharon wondered why but said nothing.

The second day, Ryan again used the same receptacle and stood looking at the letters. This time Sharon decided to tell him the words.

"That says, 'Thank you,'" she said.

"No it doesn't," he replied emphatically. "It says 'Trash Can.' "

Ryan had a clear sense of the purpose of written language. To him, the most sensible thing for words on a trash receptacle to say would be "Trash Can"—not "Thank You."

Another demonstration of a child's notions about writing occurred when Emily first received her Writing Box. After examining the materials inside, she promptly took the markers and a piece of construction paper and wrote the following sign:

Emily's riteing box   Keep out 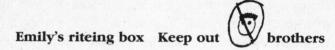 **brothers**

For Emily it made sense that writing should influence other people. Rather than tell her brothers "Do not touch my materials," which she feared would not work, she put the message into print. Although her younger brothers could not read the words, she believed that the power of the sign might keep them from using her items.

Typically adults do not look beyond the humor in statements such as those offered by Ryan and Emily. They laugh at the funny comments but do not recognize the messages they contain about children's thinking. These incidents are more than humorous moments to be remembered and recounted to others. They are opportunities to recognize a child's explorations of knowledge and ideas. These moments present us with a child's interpretation of surroundings or events. Kidwatchers value these situations. They pay attention to what is being said and may use the information later to create stimulating and challenging writing activities.

A News Broadcast That Is Always on the Air

Like a twenty-four-hour cable news station, children continually broadcast the news about their learning. Parents can teach themselves to be informed kidwatchers by tuning in to their child's broadcasts.

Our colleague Debra Jacobson told us about an incident she observed at a motor-vehicle office one day. A young boy and his father were in line together. The boy, three or four years old, was poring over a copy of the driver's manual, occasionally pointing to the text and asking, "What does this say?" The father, preoccupied with the need to get his errand done, answered the questions brusquely.

When the father reached the head of the line, Debra gave a blank registry form and a pencil to the boy, who immediately began filling in all of the lines on the form with little shapes and squiggles. He was totally engrossed in his endeavor when his mother came into the office to join the family. As she approached, he said to her, "Look what I wrote!"

"That's good," she said, and she took his hand to lead him out the door, leaving the writing on the table.

Neither parent had responded to the boy's genuine interest in print and his self-absorbed writing at the motor-vehicle office. They did not treat their youngster's writing as real or important. Most likely they assumed that he was just scribbling. They did not understand the potential impact of experiences like this on his subsequent understanding of reading and writing and his self-image as a successful writer. In their hurry, they failed to hear the broadcast of his interest and knowledge and missed this opportunity to encourage his further explorations with writing.

Children's play with language, like the little boy's scribbling, is an integral part of learning and literacy development. Play is not just something kids do till they are old enough for academic learning in school. It is a serious endeavor for youngsters and one of the ways that they develop new understandings and concepts. Through kidwatching, adults discover how much they can learn from observing what others might call mere child's play.

INVITING

When adults *invite* children to write, either by keeping materials handy or by regularly suggesting writing, they express their belief that written communications are important and meaningful. Kids often write without any suggestions to do so, but invitations reinforce parents' recognition that children are writers right now.

Successful writing invitations cannot be forced. The statement "Now it's time for writing" seldom produces its intended results. A mother told us that she extends invitations for writing gently, so as not to appear too demanding, or her five-year-old daughter will not accept them. Children who are sensitive to suggestions from Mom or Dad may sometimes resist doing something just because a parent wants it to happen.

The best invitations occur when children write for purposes that are authentic. Children indentify authentic writing contexts from observing adults composing or copying lists, notes, recipes, letters, cards, and checks; filling in forms, paying bills, and addressing envelopes; and trying out parent interests and pastimes, such as crossword puzzles, keeping box scores of baseball games, or doing assignments for work or school.

Authenticity also involves following the lead of the child. You may have to wait till a child is ready to write or you might nudge the process along by leaving notes under a child's pillow, in jacket pockets, on a child's placemat, or on the front of the refrigerator. Writing *to* your child invites writing *from* your child. During a parent-teacher conference, one mother told Sharon she had included a note in her son's snack one day and had been amazed by his response. He had written a reply by the time she had arrived home that same day, answering the statements she had written to him.

Writing to others produces surprising and rewarding results. Sending weekly postcards to friends and relatives is a family writing activity that invites everyone's enjoyment of writing. Your child can draw the pictures for the fronts of the cards or you can affix your own photos. Messages take a short time to complete and are a quick way of maintaining regular correspondence.

Every time parents tell a story, they issue invitations for children to tell their own. These can be recorded. Children are eager to hear their own voices on tape and will listen to themselves over and over again. Transcribe stories and put them in an expanding book illustrated by your child.

What Are You Having for Lunch Today?

For many children, the element of play opens communication in ways that they enjoy and will respond to enthusiastically. You can invite writing through conversations as Bob did one day by beginning a series of jokes with Emily, Kyle, and Ryan on the way to lunch. Riding to the restaurant, he announced his order: wormburgers and celery jello. That was all the prompting the children needed to brainstorm their own imaginary lunch menus. Kyle proclaimed that he was having wormburgers on a seaweed bun (they live on Cape Cod). Emily wanted squid and seaweed salad. Everyone took turns announcing their orders and laughing at each other's choices.

When we entered the restaurant, each child requested a separate menu from the waitress. They wanted to read and choose for themselves. While waiting for the food to arrive, the time was ripe for everyone to write a joke menu and read it aloud. Try this with your youngsters. Their funny lunch choices can make a menu of unusual foods to be added to at other times.

Whatever arouses a child's curiosity can become something to write about. If a writing activity is enjoyable and interesting, children will accept your invitations and create others as well.

Setting the Stage for Writing

You set the stage for writing in many ways.

MODEL WRITING

Keep a notebook or small pad in your pocket or purse. Jot down notes about things you want to remember or something your child has said. When you are recording what is important to you, your child will observe your actions and may try this form of writing as well. Demonstrating that writing is pleasurable and useful displays your positive attitude toward written language for your child.

POINT OUT WRITING WHEREVER YOU SEE IT

Read aloud signs, notices, and names in the environment and talk about the fact that someone wrote these. Point out print in the illustrations of books, comics, and ads and talk about the fact that someone wrote these. When you see someone writing, identify the activity and explain the purpose: "She's writing down the numbers on the electric meter. That's how we know how much electricity we have used." "Waiters write your order to remember what different people have asked for."

DISCUSS YOUR OWN WRITING

When children hear adults talking about writing in personal terms, the possibility that they will write for their own interest and enjoyment increases. If your child hears you say that you find something beautiful or interesting and that you want to write about it, he may join in and help you do so. Or you can converse about the topic instead, discussing what you might write and how to describe the idea. When you are interested in a news story or a political issue, mention if you are considering writing a letter to a newspaper or a legislator.

READ ALOUD OR TELL ORAL STORIES TO YOUR CHILD

Stories invite writing. When you discuss the words an author has chosen, ask questions about the characters' responses, or discuss alternate endings for a story, your child considers what she might do if she were the author. Children also talk about things that a story makes them think of—events that really happened or that they have imagined. You can do the same. You and your child may decide to write your own story, poem, song, news article, or comic strip.

Reading aloud and telling stories increase a youngster's knowledge of vocabulary. You may be surprised to hear your child using words from a story or referring to a story in conversations. "Masterpiece" became part of Kyle's vocabulary at four years old after hearing it in a story that he especially liked. He called one of his drawings a masterpiece that same day. A year and a half later, his kindergarten teacher referred to the students' books and drawings as masterpieces. Because Kyle knew this word, he especially appreciated her compliments.

REHEARSE WRITING THROUGH CONVERSATION

Conversation creates opportunities for writing. If you tell jokes, make up rhymes, or sing songs, they can be written down. A joke book is an ongoing project, as is a book of a child's favorite songs. Write and illustrate parts together. Your text will demonstrate standard spellings and conventions of print, and your child's text will show the way he is writing at that time.

Activities that you do together—from taking walks to watching television to reading books—might occasion written text. Create a journal of what you saw on your walk together and record an entry each time you return, even if it is just one sentence. The journal can be read and reread together.

Having time with you as well as experiencing the enjoyment of writing and reading stimulates a child's desire to record thoughts.

Discussing what you and your child might write about provides an oral run-through—a rehearsal for writing. Pretend you are writing about a certain topic and ask, "What would we say if we were writing about this?" Orally edit by changing words, phrases, or sentences. Oral rehearsals and editing are easy ways to familiarize your child with crafting written language.

Children rehearse writing all of the time without realizing it. They sing songs they have made up, talk to parents about incidents that happened during the day, tell information they have learned, ask questions about things they want to know, and discuss subjects that interest them. All of this oral communication provides topics for writing.

TRUSTING

Young children take risks to learn when they feel encouraged and supported by adults. Children want to experience new things and find out about different activities: dancing, horseback riding, karate, skiing, video games, or playing a musical instrument. They continue to learn new things with confidence and unabashed interest when they feel free to make mistakes.

Adults who trust children's desire to learn regard risk-taking and purposeful activities as essential to a writing process. They treat writing as meaningful because it lets children do things they want to do: create shapes and letters, express their own ideas and stories, or communicate with others through print. They realize a child's writing will look different from the standard appearance of written text and will change over time with use, in much the same way that children's speech changes. They expect that a youngster may be completely engrossed in writing one day and ignore paper and pencil for several days afterward.

Some adults, instead of welcoming a child's exploration and invention, feel that they must point out the mistakes in a child's pretend writing or invented spelling. They dismiss what the child is creating because it lacks conventional form. These responses inhibit the willingness of a young writer to take risks with writing. Critical, correcting statements inevitably discourage and dishearten a youngster and impede further risk-taking—

which is true for adults as well. To aid your child's interest in writing and learning about print, show approval and interest in what she does, encourage her writing inventions, and publish her writing. These strategies motivate a youngster to extend her learning through writing in imaginative ways.

"I'm Going to Make My Own Valentines Every Year!"

Eight-year-old Joshua was thinking about what he would write for Valentine's Day. The year before he had created a word-find puzzle for his valentine that included the names of all the students in his class. His mother asked if he wanted to do the same thing again with the names of this year's classmates. He told her that he wanted to do something new. She asked if he wanted her help, but he replied that he was still considering what to do.

Within half an hour he returned to tell her that he had decided to write a poem. He wrote HAPPY VALENTINE'S DAY vertically down the side of a paper, one letter under another, and then composed a sentence beginning with each of the letters. When the poem was complete, he proudly brought it to his mother to read. She was eager to see what he had so confidently set out to do. His decision to write poetry surprised and intrigued her.

As she read the poem, she found herself involved in an inner debate that he was unaware of and that she had not expected. Joshua had used the word "happy" in consecutive lines in the text. His mother immediately recognized the possibility of inserting other words to express the same feeling and improve the sound and the flow of the lines. Judging that he was old enough to understand this concept, she considered whether or not to edit this part of the poem.

Deciding instead to praise his effort and his ingenuity, she delayed the discussion of alternate word choices for another time. He told her how she could help him now: by typing the poem minus the first letter of each sentence, which he wanted to print himself. He chose the color of the paper for the copies and, when they were ready, rolled the valentines up, tied them with ribbons, and took them to school.

His classmates were delighted with his cards. When he brought home their valentines, he expressed his surprise that he had been the only one to make his own. Some of the store-bought cards he had received from classmates were unsigned. His mother suggested that he might want to use the unmarked ones to give out next year.

"I'm going to make my own valentines every year!" he dissented. When she suggested that perhaps his younger sister might like to use them, he added emphatically, "Mom, she's going to make her own valentines, too!"

Joshua's valentine writing illustrates how essential parent trust is to promoting young children's writing. He had an authentic occasion for writing, his parent's support, and a favorable reaction from an audience of classmates. His willingness to take a risk and his confidence in his abilities resulted in his feeling successful. He did not think of writing as difficult or overwhelming or something he needed help in doing. He had no doubt that he could and would write again.

Joshua's mother enabled him to strengthen his risk-taking behavior, feel pride in his initiative, and decide to continue writing—three goals with greater importance than editing text at that moment. She realized that she would have plenty of other opportunities to discuss synonyms with her son: when reading poetry, talking about words, or playing a game to acquaint him with different words that have similar meanings. What was most important at the time was to praise him for trying something new.

Conversations to Promote Children's Risk-Taking

There are many ways to promote children's risk-taking with their writing and drawing, but the best strategies employ a nonjudgmental approach. Honest curiosity expressed through approval and compliments is the invitation for children to talk freely about their compositions.

Thomas Gordon, author of books on parent and teacher effectiveness training, stresses the importance of "I" messages when talking with children.[9] An "I" message straightforwardly presents what an adult is thinking: "I like to see things put away so they do not get lost." This is very different from a "you" message: "You always leave things where they get broken or lost."

"You" messages of this kind place the child in a position where the focus of conversation is his mistakes or inadequacies. A child may try to justify or explain away the situation rather than respond to an adult's

Have a good time.
A real good one
Play with a special friend,
Peculiar time of the year.
You are special.

Very good time to be with a buddy
After that time you'll feel good.
Lucky day for everyone.
Especially people that care.
No one should be alone.
Terrific time to feel good.
Incredibly caring time.
Nice time to feel happy.
Every one should be happy.
Show how much you like someone.

Do a lot on that day.
After that day you'll feel good inside
Ya, thats a real special day and its
valentines day!

Love,
Josh Z.

The original and retyped (facing page) *versions of Joshua's valentine poem*

desire for change. Gordon contends that "I" messages are more effective because they tell a child what an adult is thinking, without judging or demeaning the youngster's intents or capabilities.

Reflective statements, he notes, encourage or invite youngsters to explain or describe their feelings or ideas without implying how they ought to feel or respond: "You look like you're really enjoying that!"

The following statements model ways to communicate the most important message you can give to a young child: that personal thoughts, comments, and writing are valued. These statements assist a youngster to feel safe about taking risks with writing because no criticism is implied.

Conversation openers that acknowledge a child's efforts as actual writing, even a two-year-old's scribbled lines, invite a child to talk with you:

- "What are you writing today?"
- "You look busy with your writing."
- "Look at that! You've done a lot of writing!"

Have a good time.

A real good one.

Play with a special friend.

Peculiar time of year.

You are very special.

Very good time to be with a buddy.

After that time you'll feel good.

Lucky day for everyone.

Especially people that care.

No one should be alone.

Terrific time to feel good.

Incredibly caring time.

Nice time to feel happy.

Everyone should be happy.

Show how much you like someone.

Do alot on this day.

After this day, you'll feel good inside.

Yah! That's a real special day...it's Valentine's Day!

Positive statements acknowledge writing as a worthwhile activity:

- "I see you are writing."
- "It looks like you've been busy with your work."
- "This drawing is very interesting. I'd like to hear about it."

Authentic expressions of interest affirm what the child is doing:

- "What interesting colors! Why did you choose those?"
- "Look at all the details! It looks like a lot is happening in that picture!"
- "You have been busy for so long and have written so much. Do you want someone to listen to your story? I'd like to listen if you do."

You may enjoy this paper and pencil game that promotes risk-taking. Write a conversation with a child. Pose questions for him to respond to and read whatever text he cannot read. For instance,

- "Did you see something interesting outside?"

He writes his answer and reads it to you if you cannot read his text. The game continues—you question and he answers. Of course, you may also alternate roles: He writes the questions and you write the answers.[10]

PUBLISHING

Walking past an open office door, we saw a child-made sign above a desk that said "I Love You Mom." The parent who hung it was publishing her child's writing by putting it in public view. *Publishing* is an easy and effective way for parents to celebrate and share their child's writing. Youngsters enjoy sending their stories or drawings to relatives and friends, seeing them displayed in their homes or their parents' workplaces, and having them transcribed into homemade books. They are happy to know that others see and hear what they are doing.

Publication formally acknowledges adult respect for children's efforts, celebrates the completion of an activity, and gives young authors a sense of closure with a piece of writing. Donald Graves[11] stressed:

> Publication is important for *all children*. It is not the privilege of the classroom elite, the future literary scholars. Rather, it is an important mode of literary enfranchisement for each child.

The writing of youngsters who are using symbols, strings of letters, or invented spelling is published as soon as it is hung, mailed, given, framed, or slipped into an album, whether or not the text resembles standard form. These communications require no revision before sharing with an intended audience. Other writing is published immediately because of its purpose and context: lists taken to the store or on an errand, placecards with names at the dinner table, notes or signs.

Letters and postcards are published when they are mailed; child-made programs of events are published when distributed to their intended audience. Fiction and nonfiction stories, poems, songs, newspapers, and chapter books often remain in first draft but might be changed and edited for distribution to wider audiences. An adult helps a child edit and publish by typing, copying, bookbinding, framing, distributing, or mailing the child's writing.

Revision may be part of publishing. When writers revise, they change their text to make ideas and information reflect what they intended to communicate to readers. They rewrite, add new material, and modify or delete parts of the text. The revision process might begin when authors read their draft and decide to change something. Or it may happen after they share the text with readers or listeners who make suggestions. When parents, siblings, and others hear a child's writing they may ask questions or comment about something that they particularly enjoyed. They might be even more specific and suggest that the text would be easier to understand if the author added a word or rearranged the sentences. The purpose and the context of the message determine whether or not an author might want to revise according to audience suggestions or personal preferences.

Generally we let young writers have decision-making power over whether or not to use ideas for revision. It is easy for adults to become verbal correctors—editors and proofreaders of their children's writing long before it is necessary—usually before the child wants or needs specific assistance with writing conventions. Insensitive responses can diminish enjoyment and impede risk-taking. We prefer that no parent intervention affect a child's writing if it moves a child's thinking quickly to a conventional idea of how a text ought to look or sound. The learning process needs to be child-led in order to make it useful and self-fulfilling for youngsters.

At the same time, by the third or fourth grade, children need to present more closely edited papers to their teachers. We discuss helping children to learn conventions of print in Chapter 9. There you will find many ideas for making editing interesting and enjoyable through the use of what we call an Editing Kit. Teach conventions by occasionally pointing them out in books, text, and environmental print, answering questions, and encouraging your youngster's curiosity. A child learns a great deal through these methods, including a personal excitement about using writing for purposeful activities.

Editing occurs after revisions for clarity of ideas and intentions because it attends to the surface features of a text: punctuation, spelling, paragraphing, and other conventions. Proofreading is the final step. The purpose and context of the writing determine the extent of a writer's revising, editing, and proofreading.

Not every piece of writing needs to be shared with others or edited to an exact publication standard. Youngsters write for many reasons: to explore the meaning of print, to play, to have fun with friends. You may not see all of the writing a child does. Some is private. Some is for play. There will always be writing to celebrate publicly when you encourage it.

Publication is partially determined by the materials and the time available for the activity. Below are some of the ways you can help the process.

HIGHLIGHT WRITING WHERE OTHERS CAN SEE IT
Put the writing and drawing in a prominent place in your home or workspace. Some parents use children's work to make stationery and cards.

READ YOUR CHILD'S STORIES ALOUD
Read the writing to guests and reread it often to your child. The affection for writing is clearly demonstrated when it is reread.

ORAL PUBLISHING
You and your child have many ways to publish orally. Singing a song, sharing a riddle, or retelling a story create audiences for words.

CREATE AN AUTHOR'S SHELF IN YOUR HOME
Designate a section of a bookcase for child-authored books, stories, and drawings. Or you can put the writing in a storage box that can be easily transported from place to place.

UTILIZE AN AUTHOR-ILLUSTRATOR BULLETIN BOARD
A bulletin board located where your child can pin her writing to it becomes an ever-changing display of creative activity. You can title the bulletin board "Kayla's Writing and Drawing" or "Authors and Illustrators at Work."

USE A PHOTO ALBUM TO COLLECT WRITING
Arrange a child's writing by months or years in a photo album or a looseleaf notebook. The collection can be added to the author's shelf and taken along when visiting friends and relatives.

FRAME YOUR CHILD'S SPECIAL WRITING
A story, poem, or drawing can be framed for the home or office and sent as a gift to relatives and friends.

HOLD FAMILY AUTHOR'S CIRCLES

A Family Author's Circle is a forum in which family members read their writing aloud to an interested and supportive audience. This gives everyone the opportunity to answer questions, listen to comments, and receive support for their writing. After reading, the child decides whether or not a piece of writing is ready to be published in book form.

PUBLISH CHILDREN'S BOOKS AT HOME

Child-made books are an exciting part of publishing. When preparing books for home publication, there is a question about whether it is best to change a child's text from the original to a conventional form. The publishing process at school often changes a child's own invented spellings to conventional spellings and adds proper spacing and punctuation. Changing from the child spelling to conventional spelling in a standard format is meant to make the text accessible to all readers and to give the author the importance associated with having a book published. Reading the published version is easier for some children, but more difficult for others who are only able to read it in invented spelling.

There is another way to approach publishing to make reading it comfortable for everyone. Children decide whether to have their own writing appear on the page with the standard printed version, or whether to have only the standard version. This way they can choose to have both—ensuring that everyone can read the text. See pages 289–294 for ways to publish children's own gorgeous books at home.

4

Inspiring Young Writers

Five-year-old Emily had just baked a batch of cookies with her mother when we arrived for a visit. After she had offered some to us, we asked her for the recipe [cookie batter, raisins, m and m's]. She jumped up, ran across the room, grabbed a pencil and paper, and wrote:

KKE BTR RZN MM

Her only question to us was "How do you spell m and m's?"

How had Emily acquired her knowledge about the uses of writing? She had not attended daycare or preschool. Even after she entered kindergarten three weeks before her fifth birthday, the activities at school had not included writing in her own way to communicate ideas and information. She had developed the confidence to write and gained knowledge of print from her experiences at home. Her mother read to her, played games and sang songs with her, told her letter names and sounds, and turned on "Sesame Street" daily. Emily looked at books, asked questions, and talked with adults and children. Although her mother had not specifically encouraged Emily to write anything other than her name, she had responded positively to her scribbles and drawings.

Home activities provided Emily with the information she needed to invent her system of writing words. When she did not know how to represent the "em" sound with a letter, she assumed that there must be something more to learn and asked for our help. Her writing incorporated the conventions she knew about: progressing across the page from left to right and top to bottom and separating words with spaces. She used letter sounds to create words, representing each consonant and the vowel that she heard.

Lines, scoops, squiggles, shapes, letters, numbers, and invented spellings like Emily's are young children's ways of writing. These marks that adults call scribbles are youngsters' representation of print. Like Emily, children gain knowledge of writing from the environment around them, from answers to their questions about letters and words, from conversations they hear and are part of, and from stories and text that adults or others tell or read to them. The difference in children's writing over time results from their growth in physical and intellectual capabilities and their increased knowledge about written language gained from seeing, hearing, and exploring it themselves.

This process is similar to children's speech development, which depends upon the active involvement and encouragement provided by supportive families. Youngsters' babbling sounds evolve into approximations of standard pronunciation and then into understandable speech through physical and cognitive development and daily use of oral language. Just as parents, adults, and family members are crucial to the nurturing of a child's oral language development, they are also indisputably important to a child's written language development. Children who have heard stories learn how written language entertains and conveys information. Their experiences build knowledge of words, ideas, and characters and inspire their desire to communicate on paper.

WRITERS ARE READERS, TOO!

Children become acquainted with the activities called reading and writing as soon as they make marks on paper or look at books. At eighteen months, Christina saw a photograph of two young girls with crayons and blank paper on the cover of Judith Newman's book *The Craft of Children's Writing*. She exclaimed, "Babies. Writing." From her personal experiences she associated the picture with the word "writing." Her mother called her crayon marks writing, so she inferred that the girls were about to do the same thing. When she sits with a book or listens to her mother read to her, she says, "Busy, busy. Reading, reading." When she scribbles, she says, "Christina writing."

Although not unique or unusual, her experiences are contrary to the commonly accepted belief that young children cannot read and write. This view prevails in many homes, daycare centers, preschools, and elementary classrooms where reading is based on correct word recognition, while writing is thought of as something people do when they have learned how to use a composite set of skills that begin with handwriting, letter sounds, and spelling. Yet for parents and teachers who view children's capabilities and interests as integral to their learning, reading is far more than phonic structures and identifying words; writing is not rote memorization of skills and rules but a process of conveying ideas through symbols. From a whole language perspective, writing and reading are integrally connected parts of learning about written language.

It is difficult to determine which develops first: writing or reading. Youngsters communicating with their own symbols may appear to be learning about writing first because they scribble before they say whether or not they recognize symbols in print. Babies, toddlers, and preschoolers who have been read to look at books and create meaning for themselves by reading the pictures.

Readers do many things simultaneously. They create understanding from the illustrations and language of a story, and they draw from any knowledge they already have about a topic. They correct themselves when their interpretation does not make sense. It is not sufficient just to recognize words; a reader must construct meaning in a context. Most adults recall reading unfamiliar topics and finding the text mainly a jumble of words. For instance, instructions for assembling a gas grill seem incomprehensible to many consumers. Although the individual words are familiar, without knowledge of a particular context for using terms and materials, neither subject, verb, nor object appears in a natural relationship. Like adults reading unfamiliar material, children need a context of understanding to make sense of words in a new setting.

Often it is easier for young children to encode—assign meaning to their own writing—than to decode—read and interpret someone else's text. Through encoding their own communication, they begin to figure out things about decoding books, letters, notes, or environmental print without having to first learn letter sounds, a sight vocabulary, or correct identification of words.

Beginning readers derive a huge amount of information by interpreting sources other than text. Consider how many things children "read" in the environment around them: pictures, colors, numbers, a person's facial expressions, the weather, the colors of a traffic light, and symbols such as the golden arches of a well-known fast-food restaurant. How are they able to do this? Children have learned to read by remembering the social context that ascribes a certain meaning to a sad face, a green light, or dark clouds and thunder. Children recognize many things, and they associate a certain meaning with those things long before they enter school.

Youngsters see print everywhere. Product labels for food, toys, games, and entertainment are associated with their experiences and television commercials. Signs—STOP, No Smoking, Shell gasoline, K-Mart, the local supermarket—are easily recognizable for children who see them often and have been told what the words say. They read print in their homes: their own and their siblings' names, the name of the family pet, and other words such as "mom," "dad," "love," "cat," "dog."

Children retell favorite stories that they hear often—sometimes exactly as the text is written—from memory, guided by cues of pictures and text length. This is why it is wise to respond positively to requests for hearing the same story over and over so youngsters can repeat their favorites. The language, the storyline, or both entertain them. Familiar words and phrases inspire their imagination, enrich their thinking, enlarge their concepts, and encourage their images of themselves as readers.

READING BUILDS WRITING

When asked how someone becomes a writer, children's author and poet Aileen Fisher replied: "Read, read, read. See how different writers use words to make things happen or to point up a thought or a feeling."[1] Author William Faulkner told aspiring writers: "Read everything—trash, classics, good and bad, and see how they do it. Just like a carpenter who works as an apprentice and studies the master. Read! You'll absorb it. Then write."[2]

Many parents read aloud to their children and promote independent reading as entertainment, vocabulary development, and a pleasant way in which to share information and foster a love of books. Few parents recognize that reading also provides children with knowledge they need for writing.

The innumerable things children learn from hearing and seeing stories, poems, songs, comics, sports pages, magazines, letters, notes, maps, and nonfiction books provide information that youngsters draw on to create their own writing. The greater familiarity children have with words, concepts, and genres, the easier it is for them to think of topics and ideas to write about for themselves. Written language provides models of sentence structure, conversation, plot, characterization, story line, detail, and suspense.

Keep reading aloud to children even after they read independently. The pleasure of listening to a good story does not diminish with age. Children's determination to learn to read is fueled by their interest in and affection for stories. Catherine Snow and Anat Ninio, who researched the book-reading behavior of young children and their mothers, states: "Books are a source of enchantment and wonder. This message might, after all, turn out to be the most important contribution of picture-book reading to the acquisition of literacy."[3] Without an affection for stories and written language, why would a youngster eagerly pursue the process of figuring out how to decode someone's writing? Reading aloud opens vast new worlds of information and enjoyment that your child could not access alone. It introduces different authors, writing styles, and vocabulary. Learning about words, characters, and themes are important to children's development of concepts at any age.

In Great Britain Gordon Wells conducted a longitudinal study of thirty-two children from toddler age to sixth-grade, all from lower socioeconomic backgrounds. He found that the children's oral vocabulary was well suited to social communications. An important factor lacking when they entered school turned out to be story vocabulary and knowledge of story structures. Children performed below the level of other children on school reading and writing assignments throughout the primary grades if they had not heard stories or had stories read to them.

Wells recommends that children not spend time developing oral vocabulary separately from hearing stories. Storybook language differs from conversational language. It models expressive ways of communicating that capture children's ears and imaginations. Children need familiarity with the elements of story creation: settings, plot, characters, and vocabulary in context, all of which are acquired through hearing books read to them. As young readers and writers, children gain the most from conversations in which they speculate about facts and outcomes. They begin with a "what if" question and go on to compare and contrast situations, details, and the way characters behave in different situations. These experiences show them how to use language symbolically and inspire their story creations.[4]

Children choose topics and vocabulary for their writing from words and story language that they know and from their experiences and imaginations. The more they know from hearing stories, participating in conversations, and discussing concepts and fantasy, the more variety they will express in their writing. Learning new words and expressions is essential to a child's becoming a confident and effective writer and speaker. When you read aloud, tell oral stories, or converse about topics and ideas that your child wants to know about, you build a love of stories, a fascination for finding things out, and an interest in words.

Children who know many words use them in their daily conversations and interactions. During a Fourth of July fireworks display, six-year-old Emily remarked about her younger brother's absence: "Oh, he's missing all of this marvelous entertainment!" Fresh ideas and unique expressions are communicated by children without their intentionally trying to do so. Talking at bedtime when Emily was eight years old, Sharon remarked to her, "You are so smart." Without a moment's pause Emily replied, "Nobody is stupid if they can open the door to non-stupidity."

As children become familiar with accounts of human interactions, they begin to recognize particular ways in which humor, tension, sadness, or happiness are communicated by words. Discuss with your child how authors express ideas or feelings. She may try some of these same things in her own writing. The goal of pointing out features of style and vocabulary in books is to put the power of words and language into a child's hands. Show how authors use words to create pictures in the minds of readers and assure her, "You are a writer too, with many ways to express what you are thinking."

INTRODUCING A YOUNG WRITERS' BOOKCASE

Every year excellent children's books are published that feature writing as a main theme or a central part of the story line. As children read or hear these books, they connect reading with writing as an activity. In some they are exposed to different writing genres. They see characters who write poetry, diaries, journals, postcards, letters, fiction, and nonfiction.

A wide array of styles and formats invites children to explore genres, topics, and ideas in their own writing. For example, a child hearing or reading *The Mouse's Diary*, by Michelle Cartlidge, may decide to keep her own diary. Ludwig Bemelmans's *Madeline* books invite readers to consider what Madeline might write in a journal about her day's adventures. To introduce poetry, read Leo Lionni's *Frederick*, in which a mouse recites poetry he has written to cheer other mice in the midst of winter. Lee Bennett Hopkins's books of poetry for young readers, *Surprises* and *More Surprises*, demonstrate humorous uses of language in short verses. *Kate Heads West*, by Pat Brisson, shows Kate writing letters to friends while traveling.

"A Young Writers' Bookcase," which begins on page 257, lists many options for promoting writing through children's literature. These books introduce different kinds of writing. They:

- show central characters engaged in writing;
- model writing genres; or
- introduce new writing ideas and possibilities.

They include multicultural themes, characters, and authors and depict life in urban, suburban, and rural communities. Because of the importance of these issues, we have sought books that are free from gender-bias and that feature nonviolent resolutions of problems.

Read some of these books with your daughter or son. Books offer a jumping-off point for fascinating discussions about plot, characters, scenes, vocabulary, and many other elements of writing. For example, the popular *Where's Waldo?* series invites discussion about history and puzzles and opens the way for you and your child to create your own versions. Similarly, reading fiction presents wonderful opportunities to describe adventures and fantasies, either orally or in writing.

INVENTIONS TO CONVENTIONS

Encountering your child's scribbles and invented spellings, you might ask: "Why should children be allowed to invent writing in unique ways when they could instead be learning to write conventionally?" You may also wonder, "If I encourage inventions, will invented forms evolve into standard writing?"

Many adults remember learning to write in school by practicing spelling and penmanship—without much attention to ideas. Because of those experiences, you may be concerned about allowing your child to write in invented forms. You suspect that she may not learn how to spell correctly, compose complete sentences, construct paragraphs, or develop a piece of writing that has an identifiable beginning, middle, and end.

Investigators of children's reading and writing development explain that invented writing is part of a process of personal intellectual discovery on the part of children that is a powerful motivator of learning. When children invent, experiment, and question, the discovery that they understand something they had not previously known heightens their desire to discover more. As the cycle develops, youngsters' curiosity about print propels their observations and theories about it. Everything they understand they incorporate into their writing, little by little over time, continuing their cycle of discovery, excitement, and use of new words, characters, and genres.

Spelling researcher Sandra Wilde has noted that when individuals understand conventions, they use them to create new inventions. When children can form letters, they incorporate more letters and fewer symbols into their writing.[5] As youngsters learn standard spellings and conventions of print, they use them to convey their ideas. Wilde explains that sometimes children produce spellings based on other words they know, like the child who wrote "crowshade" for "crocheted."

Four messages by Toby over a nine-month period show what we mean by progression in a child's writing from invention to convention. They become more conventional as he develops his knowledge of written language through his own writing. Neither spelling nor handwriting practice were features of his first-grade classroom experience.

Children use their knowledge of print as their base of information for invented spellings. These are as individual as the children who create them because spelling constructions are determined by each child's

ΓOBY SAEBY   TO SAE DBY

LOVE MS   EDWARDS BOO
LOOK HERE SEE YOU
TOBY

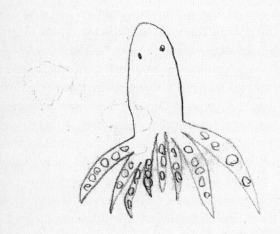

Toby's correspondence:

1. A note to himself [Toby needs to remember his shoes]

2. A Christmas greeting card [Love Ms. Edwards. Boo Look Here See You]

3. A birthday card for a friend [Happy Birthday, Lei-wei. You are a great kid. I hope you like my present.]

4. A letter to Sharon [Dear Ms. Edwards, How is your finger? It's too bad that you got eight stitches. I hope you are feeling good, too. My new class is wonderful. I am having a good time. I hope you can come over one of these nights. This is a made-up creature. Love, Tobin]

HAPPY BiRTHDAY Lei-wei.
YOU Are A GRAT KiD. I HOP
XOU LIKE MY PRASIT.

DEAr M.S EDWARDS HOWe is
Your FINGGRE EiS TO BAD
THAT YOU GAT EahaT
STICH iSS I HOWP YOU
Are FELING GOOD TO.
MY NEW CLASS iS
WADRFLL iAM HAVEiNG
A GOOD TiME.
I HOPE YOU CAN KiM
OEVER ONE OF THAS
NiHst.

THiS iS A MADe uP
KRECHER. LOVE TOBiN

knowledge of letter sounds and English conventions. Here are four spellings of the word "collection" by six- and seven-year-olds, including two youngsters for whom English is a new language:

clacshing calacshin coletion calecshin

The idea that children's writing inventions will lead to their use of conventions is new for many adults who do not remember doing this with their own writing. What adults generally recall about early writing —and none too fondly—are spelling tests, vocabulary lists, handwriting, ditto sheets, and other ways of practicing segmented writing skills. Many adults left those experiences with negative feelings about writing and about themselves as writers. Skills alone do not give someone a sense of herself or himself as a writer. Practicing skills in isolation, without benefit of writing about topics of interest, has little relationship to a writer's purpose of communicating ideas over time or across distances.

When adults insist that children learn to write through constant repetition, practice, and drills, inspiration for writing diminishes. Some children who are writing regularly at home have stopped entirely when their teachers defined writing as a spelling and handwriting program in the classroom. Adult directives that do not take a child's interest into consideration take the enjoyment and self-choice out of writing. When the fun is gone, so is a child's incentive to play, to wonder, to investigate, to make mistakes, and to write about what is important. When a youngster is no longer free to invent, the mandate is to learn how to write "right."

There are important reasons for asking children to write the way they want to write. First, youngsters look for assurance that their writing is accepted and valued. They are aware that there is a right way to spell that they do not know, and like adults, children do not like to do whatever they believe they cannot do well. The message that everyone can write in his or her own way declares that spelling and other conventions need not be the first considerations in writing when conveying ideas is the goal.

Second, children need to know that parents will not tell them how to fix all of their mistakes or what to write. Kids can write on their own, without adults changing or correcting what they have done.

Without confidence that it is okay to experiment and write in unconventional ways, youngsters think that they cannot write unless they know how to form letters, spell, and punctuate sentences correctly. Creativity and thought are sacrificed to form. Writing becomes something that others do, but not them.

Finally, as our colleague Byrd L. Jones points out, conventions are amazingly difficult to acquire. It takes a powerful motivation to memorize letter arrangements for 2,000–5,000 words or to know and recognize grammar rules that fill a textbook. How many adults know when to use "affect" or "effect" or "imply" or "infer," or when to place contractions in sentences? Only by discovering the purposes and pleasures of sharing ideas does a writer find it is worthwhile to master conventions. Otherwise rules about usage, like the Latin names of trees or isolated dates in history, remain unconnected to a child's meaningful activities.

Do not wait till your child demonstrates familiarity with standard spelling, correct letter formation, or punctuation to discover what she wants to communicate. Ask your child what she has written when she has made a squiggle or a line or an invented spelling. If she has intended to write something, she will tell you what it says. If she reads it to you, it is an example of her writing. Marks on paper are her early attempts to do what she has seen others do. Avoid dismissing these as merely scribbles or play; they are legitimate writing that represent a child's physical capacity and conceptual understandings. Scribbles are not irrelevant simply because adults cannot understand them.

RESPONDING TO WRITING YOU CANNOT READ

When asked by his grandmother what his writing said, five-year-old Sam replied, "Use your head!" He believed that he could write, and he knew that she could read. He thought that the two together ought to produce understanding.

Like Sam's grandmother, you will be confronted by children's writing that you do not understand. Just as a toddler's babbling and early conversation needs interpretation, a child's scribbles, shapes, and early drawings need explanation. Parents do not worry about immediately understanding children's oral communication. Do not worry about being unable to read written communication, either.

When you encourage children to write any way they can, there will always be written text that the two of you need to figure out. When your child understands that you cannot read the shapes and forms he is making, he will read the message to you when he wants you to know what it says. If the writing is for play or experimentation rather than to convey a message, he may ask what it says and find out that you do not know.

It is perfectly fine to say that you cannot read a child's writing. When your child asks you to read something and you have no idea what it says, authentic and supportive responses are helpful to both of you. Remind her that you want to know what her writing says and request that she read it to you.

- "Look at that writing! Could you read it to me? Then I'd like to have a turn to read it to you."

Sometimes she will read it. But if she cannot remember what it says, expects you to be able to read it without assistance, or is experimenting to find out if the marks or letters say something, she will reply, "No, you read it."

If the text is comprised of letters, you might read them as they sound: "BBFLBVBLS." Of course the message will not make sense, but your child will hear what she has written.

If she asks you to read her writing but you do not know what it says because the marks are not letters—or if they are, it is not easy to read the letter sounds—invent a message on the spot and try this reply:

- "If I read this wrong, tell me how to read it correctly."

Sometimes she may assure you that you have read it exactly. Other times she will correct you by reading it differently. It is impossible to know whether what she then reads is what she originally intended the writing to say. There may not have been a message before you invented one—it might have been purely experimental writing. Occasionally vary your response by joking with your child about what the message does *not* say!

- "I'll bet this doesn't say that the teddy bears are having a party tomorrow."
- "This doesn't say that we're having spaghetti for dinner, does it?"

If you do not want to attribute meaning to a child's symbols and she does not tell you a message, compliment her experimentation. Children experiment all of the time in their quest to learn.

- "I like to see your writing and watch you thinking and trying out ideas."

Thank her for letting you see it and inquire if she wants to put it where others can see it too.

To preserve the meaning of a child's writing to reread at another time, write the text in conventional spelling at the bottom or on the back of the page. Debra Jacobsen, a reading and writing teacher of seven- to ten-year-olds, assists her students in rereading their writing and concentrating on its meaning by including a standard spelling near a puzzling invented spelling. Youngsters do not have to struggle to understand their text because this technique enables them to reread their writing easily.

Some of your child's writing will be for play rather than for posterity. If you are unsure what you want to save—or what will be important to your child in two years when she looks at it and says "What did I write?"—record the message in conventional spelling on as many samples as you wish and decide later which to discard and which to save.

WHEN CHILDREN DO NOT WANT TO WRITE

"I can't write!" five-year-old Vanessa told us when we met her for the first time at a birthday party.

"Can you make wavy lines like this?" asked Sharon.

"I do those for decorations," Vanessa explained. "But mine are like mountains, not like waves." She began making the pointed-topped lines she had described. "That's not writing!" she adamantly asserted.

"When you want to write a message, what do you do?" questioned Sharon.

"I do this," replied Vanessa, and she began writing letters. After making a few she remarked, "I can write my name," saying the names of the letters aloud as she wrote them.

"How would you write 'Happy Birthday'?" we asked. Vanessa wrote more letters underneath her name.

"Read what you wrote," said Sharon, pointing to the writing.

"I can't read!" exclaimed Vanessa.

"Oh, I thought you were writing 'Happy Birthday.' "

"I did," she retorted.

"So this says 'Happy Birthday'?" inquired Sharon, moving her finger underneath Vanessa's letters.

"Now I'm going to write 'Happy Birthday to you,' " explained Vanessa as she wrote more letters next to the others. " 'Happy Birthday to you,' " she said when she had finished.

"Would you like us to come read your message with you?" we asked as she got out of her chair to deliver her birthday card.

"No," replied Vanessa emphatically, "I can read it!"

It is not uncommon for children to say "I can't write!" or "I can't read!" They have seen older children or adults writing words using letters and realize that they don't know how to do the same thing. When an adult defines writing in terms of what children can do—making marks to represent what they want to say—most kids will write without hesitation.

Ask why your youngster feels that she does not want to write. Listen considerately and attentively to the explanation you receive. Children require different responses from adults at various times and at different ages, but encouragement is always appreciated. Criticism never contributes positively. Sometimes youngsters write for their own purposes without anyone suggesting that they do so. At other times they need to be encouraged by someone else's responsive interest in their text. Parents, grandparents and other relatives, friends, siblings, and acquaintances of the family support by complimenting, suggesting writing, and writing themselves.

Some youngsters rarely pick up a pencil or crayon to write or draw. A child's hesitancy might manifest itself in a quiet or clear refusal to participate in writing activities: "No, I don't want to." Inspiring unwilling writers involves understanding the circumstances that surround a child's decision to write or not to write. There are reluctant writers who say, "I can't" or "I don't know what to say." But we have seen no *non*-writers! As soon as they discover new purposes or find compelling topics, they write enthusiastically.

The Ideas in Your Head

Assure children that they already have what they need to write: the ideas in their heads. Remind them: *"Your ideas are your own. They are something that no one else has in quite the same way."* Ideas come from everywhere: home, friends, school, books, television, and all the other things a child does or observes during the day.

Books and oral stories show children that they have ideas just as published authors do. Visiting elementary-school classrooms in Newport News, Virginia, we read David McPhail's *Pig Pig and the Magic Photo Album* to the children. While waiting for his picture to be taken, young Pig Pig lands in many unusual predicaments each time he says the word "cheese." The youngsters loved chiming in with the text, loudly yelling "Cheese!" as Pig Pig moves from one misadventure to the next.

When the story was finished, Sharon explained that the book was written by someone who had used the ideas in his head to create the story. "You can do the same," she told the students. "You could write about something that is interesting or important to you. What ideas do you have to write about?"

The children began eagerly composing their topics and stories. One first-grader chose Bart Simpson, another decided on Ninja Turtles, and a third wrote about the adventures of "Danger Girl." Even children who rarely wrote in school began happily communicating their ideas.

Strategies for Encouraging Writing

Adults inspire children to write by making the process fun and easy: playing writing games, taking the child's dictation, telling stories orally, providing new materials, answering questions, and connecting written communication to ongoing family activities. They also assist by listening and responding to children's feelings. Every situation is different, even with the same child, but sensitive assistance with flexibility and humor are always key ingredients to success.

There are many ways to respond when a child turns down a suggestion to write. Each of the following strategies clearly demonstrates your belief that your child can write and that you value writing. If you do not press a child to follow any particular suggestion, writing is more likely to occur because you are not forcing on her something she does not want to do.

BECOME A SCRIBE AND TAKE DICTATION

Write dictation for your child if she is tired, wants you occasionally to do the writing, or has a story to tell that is too long for her to write all by herself. As you take dictation, your child observes how you record what she says. When you finish, read the writing back to her so that she can confirm its accuracy or make changes. This involves her in an oral revising and editing process with your help.

An adult transcribing a child's words demonstrates the permanence of writing. Words remain to be read and reread at different times. Children enjoy hearing their stories read aloud and they also like to read them. Read your child's communications to friends or relatives, or with your child as part of a read-aloud time.

COMPLIMENT YOUR CHILD'S THOUGHTS AND WRITE THEM YOURSELF

Respond to something memorable that your child says in this way: "That is so interesting. I want to write it down so I don't forget it." Then write it! This invites a youngster to suggest other things for you to write. Before long you may hear your child say, "You don't want to forget this. I'd better write it down for you."

OFFER TIME TO RECONSIDER WRITING

After an initial refusal, give a child some time to reconsider. Don't be confrontational. Say something assuring: "If you change your mind and want to write something, I'd be glad to hear it when you're finished." If it's appropriate to the situation, add, "I'll help you (mail it, publish it, copy it) if you'd like."

INCLUDE YOUR CHILD IN THE WRITING YOU DO

Make it a point to involve your child with your own writing activities. As you get ready to do a letter, suggest: "I'm writing a letter to Aunt Lucy. Shall I tell her you hope that she visits again soon (or sends a picture, likes your poem, catches a fish)? Is there anything else you want to say?"

Or, when creating a list or note, remark: "I'm writing a list. Is there anything you want to put on it?" "I'm writing a note. Is there anything you want Uncle Steve to know?"

SUGGEST MAKING A PICTURE, A DRAWING, OR OTHER ARTWORK
Connect drawing with writing. You could write your child's story if one arises from the art. If not, there may be a title that your child gives to the work that you could write while she signs her name.

- "Do you have a picture you want to send with my letter?"
- "Would you like to decorate this note to Cindy?"
- "Does this picture have a story that you want to write or tell?"

MAKE A TAPE RECORDING TOGETHER
Instead of writing her thoughts, your child might wish to record them. She can orally leave a note, send a letter or greeting card, or compose a story, and the tape can be shared with others.

MAKE WRITING PORTABLE
If you have paper and pencil attached to a clipboard, your child can carry it easily in the car, outside, or anywhere in the house, and the materials for writing are immediately handy. Your motto might be: "In case you think of something you want to remember."

READ BOOKS THAT INCLUDE WRITING IN THE STORY
Read books whose characters are writing different genres and refer to the books in your conversations. For example, after reading *Beans on the Roof*, by Betsy Byars, suggest: "We could write poetry like the Beans did. But we don't have to sit on the roof to do it!"

SPOTLIGHT WRITING IN CONVERSATIONS
Talk about writing with your child. Imagine and describe to each other things you might write. These oral rehearsals help both of you to acquire and exchange ideas and to think about them before writing.

Ask questions of each other:

"Last time you wrote to Sharon you told her about the moutains and the cactus. What would you tell her if you were writing today?"

"Have you seen something that made you laugh today? We could make up a funny song or a poem about it. If you like it, we'll tape it."

WRITING AGAINST THE GRAIN

Children's writing reflects what they know and what they wonder about, sometimes with disquieting results. They are aware of and are curious about social problems in our society: violence, abuse, war, and discrimination based on gender, class, ethnicity, and race.

Youngsters acquire knowledge about these issues from many sources. A dramatic example is how gender identity is learned by boys and girls. Preschool boys play adventure games with action toys and in the process learn to manipulate and control parts of their environment. From their play activities and reinforcing messages they receive from adults, the media, and society, boys gain a sense that they are builders, in charge of making things happen. Young girls, by contrast, because of the very same sources of information and reinforcement, learn to respond more passively to outside circumstances through gender-specific play that does not involve the same action orientation. They learn that girls care for others in families and in many careers. Adults dedicated to changing these stereotypes find themselves confronted by their children's choices: Boys want guns, action figures, and vehicles; girls choose stuffed animals, dolls, and kitchen and houseware items.

The media has made these gender stereotypes a compelling reality for many children. According to *The New York Times*, children's Saturday morning television programming is overwhelmingly dominated by male characters. Not one of the cartoons on the major networks' Fall 1991 schedules had a female character lead. "It is well known that boys will watch a male lead and not a female lead," said one TV executive in the article. "But girls are willing to watch a male lead." Shows are based on the exploits of famous contemporary men such as Hammer, Bo Jackson, and Wayne Gretzky or male cartoon characters like the Teenage Mutant Ninja Turtles. While males create the action and drama on these shows, girls are included as sidekicks, assistants, or individuals in need of help.[6] Youngsters watching prime-time programs and MTV also see and hear male characters in dominant roles.

Children's interactions with other children sustain their learned gender bias. "Kindergarten is a triumph of sexual self-stereotyping," noted Vivian Gussin Paley. Watching children at play, Paley discovered that around the age of five, boys become focused on the superheroes championed in the media of their time, while "the girls turn to dramatic plots that eliminate boys and bring in more sisters and princesses." They respond differently to situations encountered in school or on the playground: "Boys clap out the rhythm of certain songs; girls sing louder. Boys draw furniture inside four-story haunted houses; girls put flowers in the doorways of cottages. Boys get tired of drawing pictures and begin to poke and shove; girls continue to draw."[7]

Sexism is compounded by teachers' responses in classrooms. Research confirms that teachers pay more attention to males, in time and responses, and expect them to be more independent. The effect of this practice is dramatically apparent beginning in the upper grades of elementary school and continuing through college. The number of girls pursuing careers in math and science is far lower than the number of boys.

Children learn other myths from the media and society. Between the ages of three and seventeen, children will see 18,000 acts of violence on TV.[8] They witness incidents of violence perpetrated by youngsters on other youngsters and the apparent police brutality against minority citizens and youth that is regularly reported in daily newspapers. Many children regard force as a way of handling their own problem situations.

Sexist, racist, or violent themes and content may appear in children's writing as a result of all that they see and hear. As parents, you face a difficult dilemma. You want to explain why your family believes what it does and behaves in certain ways without imposing limits on your child's creativity or curiosity. How do you let children think for themselves and still counter negative ideas they might learn and express about gender, race, ethnicity, or religion?

If you are part of a two-parent household and believe that this is the best way to raise children, how will you convey to youngsters that single-parent homes are also an acceptable way to raise children? If you live in a house rather than an apartment, do you ever explain that this is not because some people are more capable or responsible than others? That many factors affect a person's choices, economic status, and resources?

By discussing issues of violence, stereotyping, and racism in age-appropriate ways, and by affirming your own support for equality and justice, you are conveying strong positive messages. Parents cannot make children think or behave in certain ways, but they directly influence how youngsters react to situations when faced with their own decisions. Modeling behavior and values that you think are important to express in your own life is a strong influence on your child's beliefs and behaviors.

Challenge negative messages and assumptions by discussing them in conversations and by reading bias-free and multicultural books to your child. Reading books, biographies, and poetry written by or featuring people of different races and religions imparts information about those races and religions, models your values, and demonstrates your feelings about the importance of inclusion rather than exclusion of differences.

Racial myths lose their power to influence children's thinking when greater understanding about people of color is actively promoted by adults. Information about the historical accomplishments and achievements of African Americans is widely available in children's literature because multicultural children's books are being published in greater numbers today than at any other time. The same ideas apply to enabling white children to understand more about the diverse cultural heritages of Hispanic, Asian, and Native Americans.

Create role reversals to counter sex-role stereotyping. Read books or watch shows with your child in which girls are leaders and problem-solvers. Borrow from the library or subscribe to children's science and nature periodicals that picture girls as well as boys experimenting and gathering information. Look for biographies of women who work in math and science fields and books featuring girls as heroines and main characters behaving as adventurously as boys. Jane Yolen has written a series of adventure stories featuring Commander Toad and his crew, the security officer of which is a female. These stories do not include violence. In *The Paper Bag Princess*, by Robert Munsch, a quick-witted princess saves a prince carried away by a dragon. Beverly Cleary writes true-to-life stories about young girls.

Provide building blocks, trucks and cars, Legos, paints, clay, maps, puzzles, stuffed animals, puppets, and science materials—magnets, magnifying glasses, batteries, and bulbs—for use by girls and boys alike. This challenges the stereotypic playthings advertised for girls and boys on television. Watch television, read books, write, play all kinds of games—computer, cards, strategy, and sports—cook with boys and girls, stay active in sports, and do countless other cooperative activities with children to acquaint them with all the different things they could enjoy doing together.

Talk about anything in your child's writing or conversations that troubles you. Their topics may reflect fears needing to be expressed, ideas from cartoons or prime-time television shows, or active imaginations. You will not know till you discuss these things in a patient, inquiring way.

Clive Barker, a successful suspense novelist, discussed the beginning of his writing career in an interview on National Public Radio. He revealed that as a youngster his writing had reflected his imagination and had made his parents uncomfortable. Not knowing what to do, and thinking that there might be something wrong with their son, more than once they had taken away his materials so he could not draw and write. Removing the materials did not curtail his ideas, or his desire to write them. As a professional writer, Barker has found the scariness of his stories has not driven readers away. Discussing children's sources of ideas and feelings gives you insight and information about their reasoning and will aid your choices of stories to read, television shows to watch, and toys to purchase.

Encourage children to freely express what they are thinking about in their writing. It is sometimes easier for them to write about their feelings than to talk about them. During the 1991 Gulf War, five-year-old Kristina wrote the story "Unicorns Look Down," in which she expresses her feelings about the deaths of thousands of people. Reading her text, with its references to war and nightmares, you see the importance of responding thoughtfully and sensitively to children's written expressions. Writing about the realities of life is a way for children to understand them.

Unicorns Look Down

by Kristina

I dedicate it to all of the children in us.

There was a war.

The unicorns heard about it.

This is how many unicorns were killed, 50,000,100,000.

They found out their boyfriend was in it.

But he didn't get killed.

I was very happy.

I was very happy that the dinosaurs weren't winning.

I liked watching the war.

I had nightmares.

About The Author

I like school. I like baking with my mom. I like making friends.

I was a unicorn in this book.

2

Enjoying Writing

Part 2 presents ideas and activities drawn from the experiences of adults and children, including making writing an integral part of family activities; playing with language through words, pictures, and games; creating fiction and nonfiction stories, journals, diaries, and newspaper articles; using computers and other technologies; and learning about the alphabet, handwriting, spelling, and other conventions of print. "A Note to Teachers" suggests ways that educators might use these ideas in classrooms and in partnership with parents.

There are several years' worth of strategies here—probably more than any one family will use. Do not feel obligated to try them all. We included so many in *the hope that you will keep coming back to this book to find new things to do as your child's interests change. In general, the ideas in each chapter are arranged in a younger-to-older format, but we purposely avoided labeling activities as appropriate for a specific age group. Kids are remarkably inventive and will find ways to adapt ideas to their interests. Look through the chapters, use some of the suggestions, and feel free to create your own versions of the writing activities you find successful. As you try a suggestion, consult our "Young Writers' Bookcase" for books to read with your child or for children to read by themselves. These books may also inspire new writing possibilities.*

CHAPTER
5
Writing Is
All in the Family

One Wednesday afternoon, two-and-a-half-year-old Dory decided to give her teddy bears a ride in the living-room swivel chair. When the bears were arranged, Sharon suggested that she could write a sign identifying the "Bear Chair." Dory promptly went to the kitchen, got paper and a pencil from her mother, scribbled some lines on a page, and taped the sign to the chair. When her father and brother arrived, she read the message to them. Prior to this impromptu sign-making, Dory's writing had consisted solely of adding her name to greeting cards sent by her parents to relatives and friends.

Two days later, Dory said that she wanted to put a dinosaur sticker by everyone's place at the dinner table. Her mother suggested that she use Post-It notes to make place cards and added, "You can write the names, too."

"I write 'Daddy.' I write 'Joshua.' I write 'Grandma,'" replied Dory happily, and on her own, she penciled small scrawls on the papers for each person.

When her seven-year-old brother saw the place cards, he asked, "Did you write these, Dory? Does this say 'Daddy'? 'Joshua'? 'Grandma'? You're a good writer!"

On Saturday evening her grandmother left a note on Dory's pillow. It said: "Dear Dory, Good night, I love you." Dory spontaneously wrote a reply and read it to her mother and grandmother. Then she pointed to her marks, identifying them: "A, D."

On Monday her mother said, "Help me remember to tell Joshua and Daddy that we fed the fish."

"I write!" said Dory. She composed another sign and, with her mother's assistance, hung it on the side of the aquarium. When her father came home, she read her note to him. Each time she read it, the words changed slightly, but the meaning remained intact.

Dory's week of writing demonstrates three important points about young writers in families. First, she wants to write in the way that she can, communicating thoughts and ideas to other people through her scribbles. Second, at an age that many adults consider too young for writing, she had begun to do so on her own and at her parents' suggestion. Third, a foundation of success with written lanugage is being established for Dory through positive experiences with the members of her family.

Her mother, father, grandmother, and older brother continually make materials available, find occasions for writing in daily activities, and respond enthusiastically to her messages. They are creating a home environment conducive to learning and self-expression. Psychologists and educators agree that such experiences are one of the keys to successful writing by youngsters throughout their preschool and elementary-school years.

A FAMILY SELF-STUDY SURVEY

The following self-study survey invites you to examine your family's writing and reading behaviors. There are no right or wrong answers and no score. Use these questions simply to gather information about literacy acitivies in your home at the present time. You can assess and then potentially change how adults and children are responding to the many learning opportunities that arise every day. Many families repeat familiar behaviors without realizing that they are doing so. For instance, one person might always read to the children, even though reading aloud is an idea endorsed by everyone in the home. Recognizing existing patterns lets you consider changes—perhaps rotating who is reading to the children or including children in your letter-writing.

In addition, children often pursue different topics when writing at home than at school. They exhibit interests that teachers never see first-hand. You might use these questions to look more closely at what your children like to do with their free time: music, sports, math, science. Build these interests into family activities. Inform teachers so that connections might be established between home and school for your child.

The survey begins with a series of questions about reading and writing. These are intended to provide a profile of the literacy interests and activities of each member of the family. Questions 9 and 10 ask whether you think of your youngsters as readers and writers already. When parents broaden their definition of these terms, reading and writing become activities that children show interest in at young ages and steadily gain more knowledge about from their access to materials and support from adults. The survey concludes with questions about school and education. Use them to develop an understanding of how your children's teachers are approaching literacy learning. Parents and teachers can become effective partners in promoting children's writing, especially if each realizes how the other views his or her role. If you want to, discuss your answers to these questions with your youngster's teachers. You may find new ways to work together.

A FAMILY SELF-STUDY SURVEY

The following questions ask you to describe your family's reading and writing activities. Please read the entire survey before answering any of the questions.

1. What reading does your child see you do regularly at home: newspapers, recipes, product labels, maps, graphs, instructions, or books?

    How often does your child see you reading?

2. What writing does your child see you do regularly at home: lists, checks, a budget, letters, a journal, crossword puzzles, school assignments, poetry, or notes?

    How often does your child see you writing?

3. Who reads to your child?

   What is read: fiction, nonfiction, poetry, newspapers, science, geography, sports?

   How often is your child read to?

   When does this usually occur?

4. How often does your child read at home?

   What does your child read: favorite books, notes from you, signs, pictures, her/his own writing?

   Does your child read alone, with adult assistance, or both?

5. How often does your child write at home?

   What does she/he write?

   Does your child write alone or with adult assistance?

   Is the writing published in some way: displayed, mailed, or put into a book?

6. Is there a regularly scheduled time when writing occurs at home?

7. Do you and your child engage in writing activities together?

   What do you write?

8. Do you play games, sing, or make up stories or poems when you are with your child?

   Which do you do most often?

   Do you write any of these down or record them on tape?

9. Do you think of your child as a reader: memorizing favorite stories, asking what print says, pointing out words she/he knows, reading her/his own writing, reading books independently?

10. Do you think of your child as a writer: scribbling, dictating text, inventing spellings, writing different genres?

11. In your opinion, what is the daycare or classroom teacher's role in teaching your child to read and write?

    In your opinion, what is the family's role in the development of your child's reading and writing competencies?

12. Do you know how reading and writing are taught in your child's daycare or school?

13. Are you familiar with any of the following teaching methods?

    a. Process approach to writing

    b. Invented spelling

    c. Whole language teaching

    d. Phonics

    e. Homogeneous groups

    f. Cooperative learning

14. Does your child have pencils, crayons, or felt-tip markers, paper, notebooks, and chalkboard accessible for use at home?
15. Does your child regularly use these materials?
    What does she/he do with them?
16. Does your child use a computer or typewriter at home?
    What does she/he do with it?

Having completed the questions, you are probably wondering how to assess the meaning of this self-survey, and where your family fits in the scale of responses. Since there are no right or wrong answers per se, we offer some broad comments to keep in mind as you consider your responses.

First, adults who raise children—whether single individuals, couples, or extended families—are pivotal to a child's intellectual and physical growth and development. Young children incorporate adult assumptions about the world into their personal attitudes, social values, and characteristic behavior patterns. They actively acquire knowledge and understanding through their interactions and relationships with other people. As the late George Dennison observed:[1]

> The infant is surrounded by the life of the home, not by instructors or persons posing as models. Everything he observes, every gesture, every word, is observed not only as action but as a truly instrumental form. And this indeed, this whole life of the form, is what he seeks to master. It is what he learns.

Second, children need materials and support in order to develop their areas of personal interest. For example, professional trumpeter Wynton Marsalis and his talented brothers, saxophonist Branford and trombonist Delfeayo, were raised in a family of six children where music is a primary focus. Their father, a professional jazz pianist and teacher who helped found a jazz program for the New Orleans Center for the Creative Arts in 1974, told *Time* magazine that although he did not push the boys toward music, he did expose them to it, and when they showed interest in learning to play an instrument he found able teachers for them. Think of the thousands of other families in which music (or other activities like writing) might develop if materials and support were present.

Third, developing children's literacy interests is not a time-consuming or burdensome task. In *The New Read-Aloud Handbook*, Jim Trelease explains how parents can create in youngsters an enduring interest for reading by spending fifteen minutes a day enjoying stories together. Personal experiences of sharing stories, feeling the emotions evoked by the text, and being together during that time are keys to developing an ongoing interest in books. Adults who tell how they began their love of reading often describe first a father's voice or a mother's attention before they mention the stories they remember.

The presence of books and adults who read to children in a household matters. In *Children Who Read Early*, Dolores Durkin found similar characteristics among the home environments of children who were independent readers before they entered school. All of the families had books, read to children, and provided ready access to paper and pencils. No one pushed or deliberately taught the youngsters to read. Instead, parents or older siblings followed the lead of the child and supplied information about books, language, and writing when requested. Early readers came from a wide range of socioeconomic backgrounds, one- and two-parent families, diverse racial and ethnic groups, and rural, suburban, and urban communities.

Finally, why do some youngsters become independent writers at home while others do not? The explanation does not reside exclusively with the children. It does not appear that some are more naturally gifted or talented. More frequent writers do not necessarily possess greater literacy knowledge or greater ease in communicating their thoughts on paper than less frequent writers. Instead, what we have found in our research is that differences in home influences affect children's experiences with writing. Independent, self-sustaining writers have participation and guidance from parents and other adults who regularly do some or all of the following activities:

- read aloud and write along with kids;
- make materials readily available and accessible;
- praise a youngster's efforts at oral and written communication;
- suggest writing as an activity;
- display writing in the home or workplace;
- talk about and point out print;
- listen to a child's oral stories;
- answer questions about language;

- take dictation;
- send writing to relatives and friends;
- read to others what a child has written;
- establish regular family writing times during the day or week; and
- brainstorm and discuss possible topics and stories.

LETTERS, GREETING CARDS, AND POSTCARDS

Letters, greeting cards, and *postcards* are ready-made opportunities to initiate and sustain enjoyment of writing. Young children gain confidence with their writing by corresponding with adults and friends, and they get excited about receiving mail. They write letters and cards because they like to receive letters and cards in return. A week after sending his Christmas cards to family members, four-year-old Sam threw his hands in the air and said, "I wrote all those letters and nobody wrote to me!" He was hoping for a quick return set in the mail.

Youngsters of all ages can correspond through *letters* that reflect their age and style of writing: a drawing with a few words or symbols or more detailed information provided to the person receiving them. Correspondence can be long or short, depending on a child's interest and the time available. Letters are often completed in one sitting. The following illustrations show children of different ages communicating their wide-ranging interests through letters.

Three-year-old Dory's letter to her friend at daycare [Dear Austin Bo Boston. I love you. Dory]

Dear Professor Stoffolano,

    Please could you answer me a question? Do you know who flies better, butterfly or moth? Do they ever make mistakes, like falling or bumping into a house? I got your letter. Thank you. From Daniel

Seven-year-old Daniel's letter to a professor

Dear miss Edwards

I liked the stickers you sent me in the letter and I liked the little Kaleidoscope too.

I am sending you a picture of Nati I took through the Kaleidoscope.

I went with my brother Gadi camping.

We shared a tent.

I like school because I have good friends.

I like to study math, English and when we get a topic I like finding materials for it.

I like to watch American programes on TV: Dannis the menace, Whos the Boss and catoons.

Today we are going to watch The film "West Side Story" I know The songs and i am very excited about it.

Love
Yael

Ten-year-old Yael's letter to her former teacher

Children can write letters to:

- relatives and other adults
- friends and neighbors
- pen pals
- Santa Claus
- public officials
- their teacher
- siblings
- authors and other celebrities

Long-distance relationships can be sustained with a letter every few months. One boy sends letters to grandparents in Europe using a computer modem. Sometimes the letters are three short sentences in invented-spelling English. His grandparents reply via the computer.

Enclosing a stamped, self-addressed envelope and blank paper in your letter to a child offers an invitation to the youngster to write back if she desires. This is a way to establish a letter-writing relationship with a youngster who may not have easy access to envelopes and stamps.

A rubber stamp with a child's name and address on it or printed address labels to affix to stationery draw a child's attention to letter-writing.

If your child would welcome the opportunity to communicate with a child in another locale, *pen pals* are a good idea. One teacher told us that a first-grader in his class "hadn't been writing. He didn't know what to write about. Then he wrote the pen pal letter and he's been writing ever since." For information about corresponding with a pen pal, contact:

Creative Kids
P.O. Box 6448
Mobile, AL 36660

Youngsters in grades four through nine interested in being pen pals with scientists can join the Science-By-Mail Program sponsored by the National Science Foundation. There is an annual membership fee, and children receive three science experiments a year that they can perform at home. For information about the program's chapter in your section of the country, contact:

National Office
Science-By-Mail
Museum of Science
Science Park
Boston, MA 02114-1099
800-729-3300

Postcards and *greeting cards* can be store-bought or child-made from a youngster's own drawing and writing. To encourage writing, suggest to relatives and friends that they ask your child to send them a card.

There are two major types of commercial greeting cards: those that must be read to kids and those with short texts that kids can read by themselves after hearing them once. Look for cards that match the reading-development level of the children receiving them. Beginning readers between the ages of two and six appreciate cards that have few words in big, bold print and interesting drawings. Independent readers want more challenge from cards. Riddles, mazes, word puzzles, and jokes appeal to these youngsters. Children of all ages like the added dimension of flaps and pop-ups.

Seven-year-old Alain's summer vacation postcard [Hello, we went to the zoo and we went in the rain forest. We sat on a bench but a big bird went on the bench and wanted to eat our food. Bye-bye. Alain]

Six-year-old Juhwan's tiger-shaped greeting card, which opened to reveal a riddle [What did the elephant do when he hurt his toe? He called a tow truck.]

Children can write cards for invitations and notes of appreciation or personal or family occasions that are important. Cards also provide a way to learn about national holidays or events of historical importance. For example, visiting the Lincoln Memorial could be an opportunity to send a card recalling the Gettysburg Address or Martin Luther King's "I Have a Dream" speech.

Personal postcards made from family photographs and the stick-on backs sold at photo-developing stores are an easy, unique way to sustain regular correspondence. Your child adds writing to photos of family, school, or special events and mails them to family members and friends. Recipients can save the cards in a photo album to have a visual record of a child growing up that includes the child's writing.

Artwork—decorations, cartoons, maps, drawings, puzzles, and doodles—are an integral part of children's letters and cards. You will likely receive letters with artwork from youngsters. Add your own in a reply:

A riddle: What do you call a mummy who eats cookies in bed? Answer below ↓

```
H g t y s l f
a summeri
P g t w m b s
P o s t u m h
y o yo y o y
```

June 13, 1991

Dear Brian,

    I love looking in my mailbox and finding a letter from you. Thanks for writing. It is almost summer and getting so warm that we need a fan in my classroom to keep us cool. The kids are looking forward to their summer vacation. Can you believe that we are in school while you are on vacation? Come and visit me and you can come to school with me. The kids would love that!!

*words
happy
summer
go
fishy
yoyo*

*Who is
this?
Is it a
cool cat?*

    You are wondering about Bob's softball team. They have begun the season with a good record and are winning more than they lose. Bob plays many positions--catcher, pitcher, right field, and designated hitter. These teams play in the rain, too. Even if it is pouring down rain, unless the field is flooding, they finish the game. I'm glad to be just watching. How is your dad's softball team doing? What position does he play?

    What are you and Horace doing each day during your vacation? Have you written any other stories lately? Write soon and let me know what you are doing now that you can get up everyday and have the whole day to do what you want to do.

    I think Big Bear is getting ready to send you another Treasure Hunt. I better tell him that you might have other kids at your house. He will probably send some treasures for them, too. Look in your mailbox soon.

*Billy Bob
is a hot
cat outside
today.*

P.S. I didn't know you got a radio! What does it look like? Can you carry it around or do you keep it somewhere in your room? Did Sam get a radio, too?

P.P.S. Your cursive writing is beautiful. It looks like you really enjoy writing in cursive. It's fun, isn't it?

P.P.P.S. You got a stopwatch? That is so exciting!! I always wanted a stopwatch when I was a kid. They seemed so interesting and very useful. The next time I see you would you show me how to use your stopwatch?

P.P.P.P.S. Why did you get a radio and a stopwatch? Did I miss something-- like a surprise birthday or Christmas in June at your house?

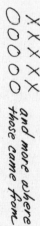

*This is what
I'm doing at
the beach - pretty soon! I'll see hermit crabs, too.*

Reply from Sharon to eight-year-old Brian

Remember that the goal is to enjoy writing. Children learn from seeing and using words. Answer their questions and praise their ideas, but do not make an issue of art, spelling, or penmanship in letters and cards.

NOTES, LISTS, MENUS, AND SIGNS

Children will write notes, lists, menus, and signs whenever appropriate occasions arise. Illustrations or cartoons that often accompany the text are engaging complements to this writing. They can be written on the spur of the moment, in the context of what is happening, or elaborately planned and completed over an extended period of time. A child's enthusiasm to write these communications can be stimulated by your invitations: "Do you want to make a sign with me?" or "Let's write a note." Create them together by dividing the writing: a child writes one part and you write another, or you add on to each other's text.

Let's Leave a Note

Notes can be written by even the youngest child scrawling lines on paper. Record the intended message in small letters on the note so someone can understand it, or include a note to accompany the text.

COD WE SLEP in OR
S LEPINE BAGS ONTEH
WECAND FROM PAT

Six-year-old Pat's note to his mother [Could we sleep in our sleeping bags on the weekend? From Pat]

Display notes written to family members on a bulletin board, pillows, doors and mirrors, or leave them in mailboxes, lunch boxes, pajamas, jacket and sweater pockets, or other special places around the home.

There can be notes for all occasions:

- reminders (The goldfish were fed.)
- announcements (Leaving school early today.)
- messages (Two cookies each.)
- fun (Your birthday is being changed to this month. Let's plan a party.)

Let's Write a List

Lists are easy, usually quick, and a practical part of many family activities. You might write them together, or your child might do one for you:

Five-year-old Kyle's list to take to the store and (at right) *six-year-old David's grocery list* [*cereal, milk, toothpaste, ice cream, bread, juice, tissues, cookies, mustard, ketchup*]

Compose lists of:

- groceries
- errands to do
- things to get on a shopping trip
- the day's activities
- television programs
- favorite books or stories
- things the child knows how to do
- things the child wants to do on the weekend

Let's Create a Menu

Menus can be written for:

- breakfast, dinner, or snack
- eating at a restaurant
- a party with friends or relatives

Menu Detective is a game to play at mealtime. The rule is that anyone can come into the kitchen to smell the scents and to look around for scraps and utensils in order to deduce what the real menu might be. While it is permissible to look in the garbage or the recycling bin for clues, no one can lift pot lids or peer into the oven to see what is actually there. The child then writes a menu based on what she has been able to learn through her investigations. Several family members can play. Display the menus on a chalkboard or bulletin board. Everyone reads their menus before the meal is served.

A variation of Menu Detective is played each day in Sharon's classroom. One child writes the real lunch menu, while two others compose fake menus. When the three are read to the class, everyone elese tries to figure out which one is correct. Your child can do this at home, composing a real and a fake version to read before dinner to the family. Everyone votes on which they think is genuine.

The humor of *make-believe menus* excites a child's sense of fun. If lunch is soup and a sandwich, a child's pretend menu might read "Jello sandwich and ice cream soup." When you take a child to a restaurant, create a make-believe menu together: "Spaghetti with lollipop sauce and chocolate-covered ants for dessert." Establish together the rules for what can and cannot be used as dinner items.

Six-year-old Paul's make-believe menu [*Today's menu is frog rice and lizard legs*]

Children enjoy creating fantasy menus:

- dinner for a dinosaur
- lunch for a snowman
- breakfast for a giant
- a meal for an imaginary friend
- a snack for a fictional character

Let's Make a Sign

Signs fit many occasions. They are fun for a child and parents to make together. Sign-making allows children to express their feelings and assert their wishes.

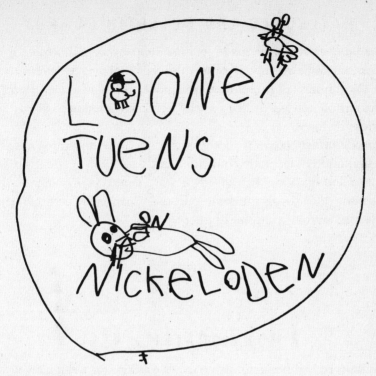

Six-year-old Alain's television sign

There can be signs for many occasions:

- birthdays
- holidays
- regular daily events
- special family activities
- lost-and-found items
- warnings and declarations

Children are surprised and pleased to learn that signs communicate their ideas to large numbers of people. When one youngster lost her ring at school, she decided to make a sign rather than personally go from classroom to classroom to see if it had been found. The lost-ring sign worked: She got the ring back and other children saw first-hand the results of communicating through written messages. The following week another child put up signs about his lost toy.

MAILBOXES AND BULLETIN BOARDS

Family mailboxes can be made from shoeboxes, cereal boxes, or large envelopes. Family members write messages, notes, and letters to each other. Short notes left in children's mailboxes stimulate their writing back to you. An often-used mailbox easily becomes a regular part of family activities.

A *family bulletin board* is another way to incorporate writing into family communications. Decorative bulletin boards are easily made from pieces of cloth hung on doors or walls. Notes are taped on. A chalkboard or a refrigerator door serves the same purpose. Change the communications regularly to sustain your child's interest.

A HOME GRAFFITI WALL

Many adults remember getting into trouble as kids for writing somewhere they were not supposed to: for example, on the walls of their bedroom or on a parent's important papers. Staff members of the Summer Writing Camp for Kids at the University of Massachusetts decided to turn those experiences into an inviting writing opportunity. They designated a section of the room at camp as a *Graffiti Wall*. The campers filled it with writing of all types and sizes: slogans, posters, unusual drawings—whatever they found interesting and creative.

A graffiti wall in your home channels everyone's creative energies to a place on which it is permissible to write. Choose a location where youngsters can write freely on big sheets of paper hung on a wall. One mother painted over the wallpaper in her son's room so he could create his own wall of writing and artwork. Add some of your own graffiti to the wall. Another way to do this is to have a big chalkboard or large bulletin board on which children can tape or tack up what they have written. You may even want to have some sort of ceremony each time a new piece of writing is added to the wall. Rotate the display periodically so that everyone gets to add their latest ideas to this ever-changing collage.

TRIPS, OUTINGS, AND ERRANDS

Trips, outings, and *daily errands* with children are challenging times for adults. Children often become bored and restless while sitting in a car, bus, or plane or waiting in a line. Adult conversations and activities do not hold a child's attention for long. Writing and drawing are engaging ways to spend time while traveling, especially if a child has some ongoing project to do en route.

Writing is also a wonderful way for children to spend time constructively while waiting in restaurants or offices, and it takes only a minimum of preplanning on your part. Look around the next time you go out. Chances are that you will see some children happily engaged with paper, pencils, and other materials. The adults with them may be joining in or just quietly conversing among themselves. The situation is one of calm enjoyment for everyone.

Bringing materials when you go places allows a child (and adult) to write, play word games, create stories, draw, read, or use activity books. Many activity books are sold in grocery and department stores. Dover Publications offers a variety of pocket-sized "Little Activity Books" for children ages four and older that cost a dollar each.

Other Family Writing Ideas to Try While Traveling

TRAVEL DIARY OR TRIP JOURNAL

Going to new places or revisiting familiar locations becomes the basis for a written description of the day's activities in a journal or diary. You and your child might write the entry together, with one of you dictating to the other, or you using one side of a notebook and your child using the other. Report on different experiences or your reactions to the same event. Add to your daily chronicle drawings, cartoons, hand-drawn maps, postcards, ticket stubs, maps, brochures, photos, and names of the newspapers from which you clipped out the weather reports. Save items about your trip for a travelogue the two of you might put together, to show to others when you return home.

A VIDEO ALBUM

Create a video version of a trip diary, and include narration and dramatizations of events by children and adults. The travelogue of daily pictures can be expanded by adding stories, jokes, and observations at the end of each day, so that you'll have a complete diary on tape.

RESTAURANT GUIDE

Compile a guide to eating places. If these are mostly fast-food restaurants, your child can list the towns in which you ate and mark them on the map. Local terms could be explained, and you could note regional specialties or other differences in the menus.

Discussing a restaurant near his home, one five-year-old wrote:

> **michael steepiljac is radid 12. thir is**
> **viry good stac. the fich soop is avrij and**
> **the chaclit rasbiry cak was good.**

Steeplejack is rated 12. There is very good steak. The fish soup is average and the chocolate raspberry cake was good.

FAMILY TRAVEL GUIDE

Using the model of a commercial travel guide, your child can describe favorite sites and experiences on a trip. For example, she can mention things to see: "When you go to Boston you might like to see the Swan Boats"; where she liked the food: "A good place to eat is Quincy Market"; and the highlights of the trip: "We especially enjoyed the aquarium."

TELLING STORIES TOGETHER

Storytelling promotes writing. While traveling or doing short errands, talk with your youngster about what you might write in a diary, story, song, or poem. The conversations may inspire your child to write or dictate something to you.

DAILY AND WEEKLY ROUTINES

With only a little planning and imagination, writing can become a positive and helpful part of your family's *daily* and *weekly routines*.

Before school or at other times while a child is waiting, regularly suggest writing. To change the morning routine in one family, a mother and teacher suggested that a six-year-old stop watching television while waiting for the bus and write instead. At first he wrote the daily weather report to read to his teacher. Then he began composing his own riddles— inspired by the ones he read on his breakfast cereal packages—to read aloud to his classmates. Other students liked his idea and began creating riddles at home to read aloud as well.

Many parents have found that while they are *making dinner*, their child enjoys being close by using paper, pencils, and crayons. It is a social time when a child asks questions and shares ideas about writing or storytelling topics.

After school is another time to establish a regular writing routine, when your child is alone or when friends visit. Writing eases the transition from a school schedule to home activities.

Prior to bedtime is often when children like to read, write, and talk with you. From the time her daughter was a few months old, one mother took a few minutes each evening to sit with her before bedtime and "talk about today." The mother described things they had done during the day, sang some songs, and put her child to bed. When her daughter was old enough to say the words, she would announce, "Talk about today, talk about today, Mommy!" The two of them established a routine with oral language that might easily include "writing and drawing about today."

On Saturdays, instead of watching cartoons all morning long, use some of the time to write together: a list of weekend activities, a chore schedule, cards or letters to family and friends, or articles for a family newspaper.

For birthdays, holidays, New Year's, and other family occasions, everyone can make an event of writing their greetings. Homemade items can be given or sent to friends and relatives.

During the summer, join a vacation reading club for children sponsored by a library or school. After reading or hearing books, youngsters report on them orally, in writing, through art projects, or pictures.

Any other time of the day or the week might be a good time for writing.

One family took a Writing Box to church on Sundays. The children had something they liked to do and the parents could pay attention to the service. Include writing in your daily schedule as a quiet period for children and adults alike.

WRITE HOW YOU FEEL

Writing about personal feelings provides a way to reduce the stress and tension that surface between parents and children. Kids do not always cooperate with adult directions or plans. They do not always follow your rules, complete their chores, and go when you want to go or stay when you want to stay. At a store, youngsters may request a toy or a snack that you do not want them to have. Crying, arguing, or other unhappiness results from your disagreements.

Instead of disagreeing, offer writing as a way to quietly and calmly move the focus of attention from one activity to another. For example, you are ready to go to the store but your youngster wants to keep playing with toy trucks. An alternative to taking away the trucks and dealing with the child's yelling and screaming is to bring them along with paper for making maps. Let writing serve as a bridge between what the child is doing and what you want to be doing.

If you do not want to take the trucks into the store, suggest that your youngster bring the paper and draw a map of the inside of the store to use with the trucks when you return to the car. As a second activity, count all of the trucks that you see on the way home. These suggestions seek ways to diffuse tensions while promoting learning.

Writing is also an excellent way to respond to potential confrontations between child and adult. In one case a young boy was unhappy because he did not have time to show a visiting friend the space truck he had assembled. He angrily threatened to kick the adult who was with him. "Write a note so we'll remember to show it first thing next time," she suggested. His focus changed immediately, and his happy mood returned as the two of them worked on the note together.

Four-year-old Michael's reminder note to himself about his space truck

In this instance, writing gave him an outlet for his frustrations and an alternative to continuing the argument.

In another family, the nightly job of wiping the dishes became a subject of bickering between a mother and her eight-year-old son. Preferring to do other things, the boy avoided his job as long as possible. After attempting many different responses to avoid arguing, his mother decided to try writing instead of scolding. She sent him to his room with instructions to return when he had written three different things he could do rather than argue about doing the dishes. After a while he came back with a list:

"I WON'T YELL AT YOU."

"I WON'T PROCRASTINATE."

"I'LL GET RITE TO MY WORK."

Reading his proposals together, they talked about their feelings and worked out a new solution to the situation. The mother estimates that since then she has used writing to initiate discussions about disagreements with her son "ten or twelve times" during a year.

To express his anger at his mother, a six-year-old drew a series of pictures to illustrate his feelings. As he finished each of the drawings, he delivered them to his mother, which gave her several opportunities to comment positively about how angry he was. Drawing gave him an acceptable way to let his feelings be known without throwing a tantrum, crying, or stubbornly threatening her with running away from home.

In these examples, writing and drawing allowed positive communication to evolve between adults and children. You may find this to be an alternative to arguing with, scolding, or ignoring a child. You might also find that your child wants you to confirm or deny something he is wondering about, as shown in the following message:

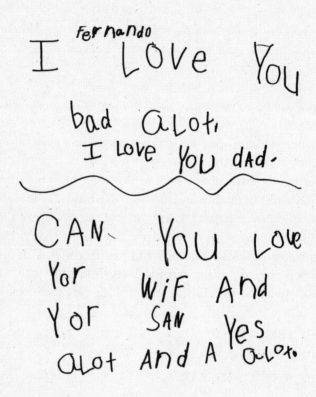

Seven-year-old Fernando's note [I love you, Dad, a lot. I love you, Dad. Can you love your wife and your son? Yes. A lot and a lot.]

A ''SHOW ME'' SHELF

A *"Show Me" shelf* in your home is an easy, inexpensive way to turn your child's interests and accomplishments into occasions for writing and oral storytelling. It is also a way to promote communication between the child and other family members that may not occur otherwise due to busy schedules.

A mother whose toddler was just beginning to speak intelligibly came up with the first version of this idea. She wanted to share with other family members the special things her daughter was doing and learning each day. By putting items on the "Show Me" shelf, the youngster had things to show and talk about when Daddy, Grandma, and her cousins came home.

Once you designate a bookcase, tabletop, or other prominent location that is child-height as your family's "Show Me" shelf, this idea can work in many ways.

Your child puts items she likes on the "Show Me" shelf. They can be anything that interests her: a bug she found, a picture, a toy, a letter from a friend, something she made in school. To designate something she did for the first time or is learning how to do, she uses a representative item or note. Then at supper time, bedtime, or whenever you choose, she can show you, tell you about, or write about what's on the shelf. The shelf becomes a way for you to connect directly with your child's thinking and learning. It also becomes a guarantee of attention later if you are too busy to give your full attention at once. Other members of the family often comment upon and ask about shelf items.

The shelf also serves as a mini learning center for models, posters, drawings, stories, and child-made books that illustrate your youngster's interests. Items that reflect your child's curiosity about a current topic, such as volcanoes, growing seeds, the life of someone famous, or animals from different parts of the world are kept there for any length of time. Some items represent broader areas of study: A growing plant symbolizes a science experiment, a favorite song book that you and your child sing from stands for your enjoyment of music.

Add things to the shelf yourself. "I was thinking about you today when I saw this" is a way to introduce a special surprise you have brought home for a youngster. This is an easy and fun way to explore math, science, history, geography, or any other educational topic. Dice, maps, puzzles, museum tickets, books about famous people, newspaper or magazine stories about different topics are all items you might put on the shelf and then investigate together.

With a bulletin board, chalkboard, or a write-on wipe-off board next to the "Show Me" shelf, *you and your child can correspond through pictures and messages to each other:* "Keep trying your cartwheel. You'll get it!"

However you use a "Show Me" shelf, there are positive outcomes for your child and your family. First, it showcases a child's achievements. Your child demonstrates her mastery of new information by talking or writing about whatever she puts on the shelf. Her learning and accomplishments have a central place in family life because they are on the shelf for everyone to see.

Second, it celebrates your family's interest in learning. Everyone gets to learn new things as information is discovered. "Did you know . . . ." becomes a regular question in family conversations. Placing something on the shelf tells everyone that this is a topic to converse and learn about.

Third, it involves family members and friends in your child's activities. They can hear or read about what is on the shelf when they come to visit. They can respond too on the message board.

SIBLINGS AND FRIENDS

Writing is a fun way for siblings and friends to spend time together—an alternative to rough-housing, playing with Ninja Turtles and Barbie dolls, or arguing about toys and what to do. Supplied with materials, space, and adult interest in what they are doing, youngsters become so involved in their work that time passes without their knowing it. Try the following strategies to promote interest in writing among groups of children.

Writing Siblings

When children draw and write together, they explore their ideas and imaginations by exchanging information and creating new things together cooperatively. Older brothers and sisters influence younger siblings. The younger children observe, imitate, and decide what they want to write and draw. This process of observing and imitating works the other way as well, with younger siblings providing new ideas to older siblings and friends.

One day seven-year-old Pat began paying closer attention to his five-year-old brother Michael's Lego-building activities when an adult made up an oral story about the exploits of pirates and soldiers on an island.

When Michael returned to the Lego set the following day, Pat suggested that they write Chapter 2. "Let's call it 'The Disappearance of the Island Fortress,' " he said to his brother, and he dictated a beginning:

After that great battle and that workman being so mad, you could expect the soldiers would be a little more careful about what they did.

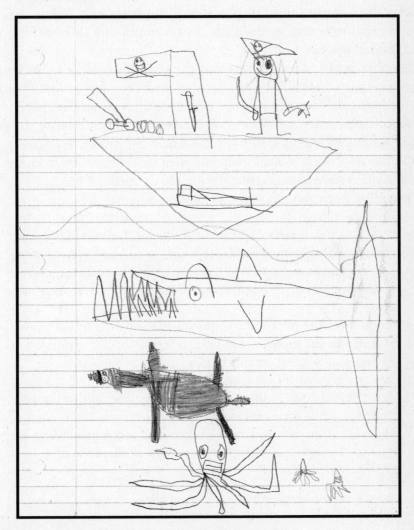

Five-year-old Michael's drawing of the pirate ship

Writing Parties

A writing party is surprise entertainment for small or large groups of kids. Materials and your time are all it takes to start the enterprise. Invite children and suggest they bring some of their own writing with them. Tell them it's a "Come and Try Something New Party" and give them materials when they arrive. This is a great way to spend an afternoon with children. The youngsters teach each other by exchanging ideas and engaging in positive learning activities. Writing parties include lots of opportunities for writing: notes, signs, letters, radio and TV news shows, and book-making.

Supplies might include giant-sized paper, small notebooks, stickers, stars, postcards that children can decorate with drawings or with photos of themselves, and envelopes of different sizes, with colored paper to make cards. Depending on your plans for the party, you might have stamps available so that when the cards or the letters are written, everyone can go to the post office to mail them and then to an ice-cream store for a treat, a video store to rent a film, or the library for story hour.

There are many ways in which to conduct a party:

- Choose a story or two to read aloud in which a character uses writing as part of the plot. When you are finished, discuss the kinds of writing that the children have done or have not yet tried. Youngsters choose to write something, inspired by one of the stories or from their own ideas.
- Set up a treasure hunt at the beginning of the party. Hidden writing materials are gathered as the group proceeds from clue to clue. When the last item is found, writing begins.
- Have a video camera ready: to film the play they act out, the news show they produce, or the puppet show they write, or to record the children reading their own stories, songs, or poems. This is another way to stimulate creative activities because most children love to see and hear themselves on tape. They may work all afternoon on a show that they want recorded.

Writing Boxes for Every Child

In families where materials are always readily available, and children's efforts are encouraged, children do more writing. The appeal of materials is independent of age. Older and younger children want their own things and can safely use many of the same items. When supplies are used exclusively by older children, available only sporadically, or reserved for special occasions, the purpose of encouraging writing is defeated.

Equip each youngster in your family with a Writing Box filled with age-specific items and establish procedures for using the materials. This helps assure youngsters that they can share items and trust that things will not be broken or ruined. Refill or replace items when necessary. Equip a "Guest Writing Box" to have available for visiting children. They will look forward to using these writing supplies. When children have their own materials and a place to work and display what they have done, the writing will be a regular choice for group play.

Group Projects or Writing Pairs

Assist children in a group writing project, such as a family or neighborhood newspaper, a mural, a large card, a sign, or a book of stories and poems. Suggest the ideas and have the necessary materials available to carry them out. In these projects, children choose what they want to do: write, illustrate, design, or deliver them. Roles can be exchanged so kids enjoy different ones as the projects become regularly occurring activities.

Some children write together with siblings or friends. These pairs and groups create playful events, develop stories about the same topics, or use the same characters while composing their own adventures. Three girls (between the ages of ten and twelve) in Sharon's school spent an entire summer creating a mythical town built around a cast of sixty characters. Each girl wrote biographical sketches of twenty characters that they exchanged with each other in order to write about the daily lives of the fictional people. They called their group "The Writers Club."

Members of a writing team might create a combined library of their stories or exchange roles as they work: One illustrates while the other writes, then they switch jobs for the next story. They might make their own cards and stationery, leave each other mail, conduct a survey, or try any of the ideas in this book together.

Two pages from a story by Fernando, age seven, and Pat, age six [The entire story, titled "The Cool Dinosaurs," reads as follows: The dinosaur was walking down the street and he went into the rocks. And another dinosaur bumped into a car and a lady screamed and her car crashed into a rock. And there was a car that everyone thought that it was bigger than the Empire State Building and than a triceratops. And the car was not even past the knee (of the dinosaur).]

Family Histories

Constructing family histories can be a group activity for sisters and brothers, or for friends. A new book by Ira Wolfman, *Do People Grow on Family Trees?: Genealogy for Kids and Other Beginners*, shows children how to become "ancestor detectors" who investigate and formally record their family's past. Pairs or groups of children work together to discover the family tree, interviewing parents and grandparents and assembling their information into a family portrait.

Six-year-old Lea's story [*When my sister was ten months old, she locked my mom out of the house. Our next-door neighbor had to break (the lock).*]

6

Playing with Language Through Words, Pictures, and Games

A paper airplane marked "Air Mail" flies into the living room from the kitchen.

"Hi Brian, Emily, and Sam!" reads the message inside the paper plane. "The first clue is near the oak tree in the back yard. Your friend, Big Bear."

A treasure hunt is about to begin. Clues have been hidden around the yard and in the house for the children to discover. We claim the clues have been written by Big Bear, our own fictional character. As the children locate and read each clue, they will move closer to a surprise that awaits them at the end of the hunt.

The children run quickly out of the house to search for Big Bear's clues, laughing and yelling as they go. They locate the first clue after a moment of searching, read it together, and race off in pursuit of others

—to the clothesline, the piano, the old chair on the front porch. They are oblivious to everything but the game and the fun.

As they run from clue to clue, the children loudly contend that one of us is Big Bear. "No way!" answers Bob. "Big Bear gave me these clues and your special surprise at my softball tournament the other night. He hopes you have lots of fun playing this game."

The children do not believe his denials. "You're Big Bear!" states four-year-old Sam, repeating what his seven-year-old brother has already said.

Emily, age eight, is next to speak. "Bob is Big Bear!" she declares wisely, holding up one of the clues in her hand. "The handwriting is the same."

We continue jovially denying any role in the treasure hunt other than delivering the clues from Big Bear. The three children are fully engaged in reading, searching, and arguing who Big Bear might be. Sam, who does not read words yet but wishes he could, enthusiastically joins his brother and cousin in the pursuit.

While Brian and Emily are searching for a clue, Sam accidentally finds one out of sequence. He asks what it says. Sharon reads it aloud, and he repeats the words after her. "You can read that clue!" she exclaims. He runs into the house to read it to his mother and grandparents and returns to wait for Brian and Emily to arrive so he can read the clue to them instead of listening to them read it to him. Imagine their surprise as they round the corner and see Sam with a smile on his face and the clue already in his hand! Then, to their astonishment, he reads it! Correctly! They are momentarily confounded. But in their haste to get to the next clue, they do not stop to determine how he knows what his clue says. They all race away together. The game continues till the surprise is found: ice cream cones for everyone.

Later that day everyone plays the game again, but the roles are reversed. This time the children want to write the clues and hide them. Bob, still claiming that he is not Big Bear, joins the adults in searching for the surprise. Eagerly anticipating this new treasure hunt, Emily and Sam begin writing. Brian, asserting he does not want to write clues, listens to the discussion about potential hiding places. "I'll write a clue for the living room," Emily announces. Meanwhile Sam begins printing letters on paper and reading the messages aloud. As he finishes writing each one, Sharon prints his message on the back of the paper in small script to assure that the adults finding the clues will be able to understand what he wrote.

"My toe hurts," Brian announces to the group.

"Write and you'll forget it," suggests Emily.

"No, it really hurts," he replies.

Everyone else continues writing. Sharon holds up one of Sam's clues and reads it aloud. Brian and Emily look at it solemnly, realizing that he has not used actual words to write the clues, but neither of them comment. Sharon holds up another of Sam's clues and reads it aloud. Again, the other two listen and observe without comment. Then, Brian abruptly grabs paper and pencil and writes two clues.

Before hiding any of them, Sharon and the children discuss each clue to make sure the adults will understand where to go. She questions one: "Go to the old tree." Does it mean the tree in the front yard or the back? Deciding that some clues are confusing, the children add more information. Brian, fully involved in this editing process, is more critical of the messages than the others and suggests further clarifications for some of them.

The adults' treasure hunt is as enjoyable as the children's, who help at every turn. "Warmer! Warmer!" they shout when someone gets close to a hiding spot.

"You're getting colder! Colder!" they yell when someone moves in the wrong direction. The treasure at the end turns out to be a large collection of acorns the children have gathered for everyone to guess the number and then count.

These treasure hunts have become fun-filled literacy events for the children. All of them participate, regardless of whether or not they can read and write conventionally. The game has a continuing allure. Emily and her brothers eagerly await the treasure hunts and request them whenever we visit. We send them in the mail to Brian and Sam, whose mother and father hide the clues and then stand back when the boys discover a treasure hunt waiting for them.

Moreover, the children have included our fictional character, Big Bear, in their own writing, drawing, and conversations. Discussing the letters she was writing to friends and relatives, Emily stated: "I wrote to Bob, too. Big Bear, I mean." Sam wrote a thank-you letter to Big Bear after a treasure hunt arrived by mail and sent it to Sharon's address. A few weeks later Brian spontaneously wrote a Big Bear letter to Sam one evening while his brother was taking a bath. He told Sharon that he thought Sam "wasn't feeling great" and hoped the letter would make him feel better.

"I'm going to tell him I wrote it when he's nineteen," Brian added.

We never would have predicted that the children's affection for Big Bear's treasure hunts would make his name synonymous with the idea of comfort, fun, and good cheer, as implied by Brian's letter to his brother. And we also did not expect that the treasure hunts would inspire the children's writing. We invented the game to help them enjoy reading. It became a writing activity when the children themselves used it. One child enjoyed a treasure hunt so much that he rehung the clues in different places around the house when it was over.

Play is one of a child's self-created contexts for learning. Big Bear's Treasure Hunt is but one example of how children and adults create playful contexts using words and pictures. Writing is integral to their enjoyment. The players have an authentic reason to read and write: to create the good times that the play provides. Yet connecting writing with fun and enjoyment may be a new idea to many families. Remembering their own writing experiences as uninspiring and constantly having to correct conventions, adults associate writing with work and formality rather than with entertainment, amusement, or playful self-expression. As they learn together through language play, adults and children find many ways to include words, pictures, and games as part of daily family life.

WORDPLAY

In telephone conversations when he was four and five years old, Kyle provided remarkable demonstrations of a child learning how language can communicate ideas and feelings. He would begin by telling us about something he had done that day, such as riding his bike up and down the hill next to his house. Then without pausing he would say, "You know what?" and launch into a description of some other activity: going swimming with his sister and brother, burying his dump truck in the front yard, or how happy he was after finding the broken toys his mother had hidden when she cleaned his room. He talked on and on. The phrase "You know what?" acted as a bridge to each new topic. It was hard to get a word in edgewise, even when we tried to do so. Kyle needed those opportunities to express himself orally to adults who would listen attentively to his remarks.

All kinds of wordplay support and stimulate children's learning and contribute to a young child's overall writing development in the following ways.

THROUGH BANTER AND CONVERSATION, CHILDREN EXERCISE THEIR ABILITY TO CREATE AND COMMUNICATE IDEAS

As they talk, children experiment with words and develop confidence in communicating using speech. Reading and telling stories to each other, reciting rhymes and chants, enjoying riddles or jokes, singing songs, and making up lyrics or verses all give children knowledge about words that they need to create written language. They discover that they can entertain, inform, amuse, or even offend others by how they use language. They inquire about the meanings of words and learn that the same word can convey different ideas in different contexts. Familiarity with rhymes, jokes, songs, and other forms of spoken language assists children in creating their own versions of each. As they personalize verses or lyrics by inserting their own names or phrases, they are experimenting with words and developing confidence in their ability to speak and write.

CHILDREN CREATE THEIR OWN HUMOR BY THEMSELVES AND WITH SIBLINGS AND FRIENDS

As anthropologists Iona and Peter Opie found in Great Britain during the 1950s, many children's rhymes, riddles, jokes, chants, nicknames, slang words, and songs are distinctive forms of language play used primarily within peer groups. Five thousand children from all sorts of backgrounds and communities—rural and urban, low income and affluent—contributed to the Opies' collection of school and playground language, which, they discovered, "circulates from child to child, usually outside the home, and beyond the influence of the family circle." These "verses are not intended for adult ears. In fact part of their fun is the thought, usually correct, that adults know nothing about them." The Opies concluded that rhymes, jokes, songs, and other language play are an integral part of children's "culture."[1]

ORAL LANGUAGE PLAY ACQUAINTS CHILDREN WITH DIFFERENT WRITING GENRES

Parents who talk about language with children invite youngsters to express themselves using many different combinations of words and phrases. They let kids construct child's-eye accounts of daily events. They learn from a child's conversations, even as youngsters struggle to formulate their ideas. Encourage talk about personal interests. Reply to her statements and keep the conversation going. Using language is the way to learn language. School-age children who have heard and told stories and engaged in many forms of language play know that fiction, nonfiction, poetry, songs, and rhymes are different. They are familiar with these genres and their characteristics and will try them in their writing.

STORYTELLING

Linda Ellerbee, former national television reporter and network anchor-woman, now an author and independent producer, was asked why so many TV news anchors—herself, Dan Rather, and Jim Lehrer, to name three—come from the state of Texas. She replied, "I think it's the tradition of oral storytelling. One of the first things I learned in my family was that a story has a beginning, a middle, and an end."[2]

Storytelling is neither a trivial nor an idle pastime. It is an activity that enables children and adults to explore their creativity, problem-solving, humor, and persuasive communication. Adults may not realize how important storytelling is to nurturing a child's intellectual development, but it is certainly a vivid form of learning for children because of their interest in and ability to remember stories. Stories engage children's full attention, utilize their imagination and memory, and familiarize them with vocabulary, sentence structure, ideas, and concepts. Furthermore, storytelling gives children the power to create from their imaginations as well as from daily experiences. As Gordon Wells observed: "What is so important about listening to stories, then, is that, through this experience, the child is beginning to discover the symbolic potential of language."[3]

At an early age, children begin telling stories as a way of expressing their thoughts and creating pretend play. In *The Boy Who Would Be a Helicopter*, Vivian Gussin Paley estimates that three- to five-year-olds spend three-quarters of their time engaged in some sort of fantasy play that involves creating and telling stories. This play contributes to their understanding of ideas and concepts and to their social growth and development. She notes:

There is a tendency to look upon the noisy, repetitious fantasies of children as *non-educational*, but helicopters and kittens and superhero capes and Barbie dolls are storytelling aids and conversational tools. Without them, the range of what we listen to and talk about is arbitrarily circumscribed by the adult point of view.[4]

While exploring writing, children formulate oral stories that many of them cannot or choose not to write because of their length and detail. But their imaginations and capacities for storytelling seem limitless. Much of Ryan's fantasy play between the ages of three and six involved his imaginary dog, "Shelfie," his best friend and loyal companion. Few conversations with him went on very long before he talked about his dog.

"How is your dog?" Sharon asked him during a telephone conversation.

"He's sick," Ryan replied.

"That's too bad. What's wrong with him?" she inquired with concern.

"I don't know" was his exasperated reply. "I'm not a doctor!"

A few months later Ryan was again discussing his dog, during another phone call. "My dog jumps up on people. His claws will scratch you," he explained.

"What do you do when Shelfie jumps up on people?" asked Sharon.

Without hesitation, he responded, "I say, 'Halt!'"

Ryan also told us a story about his imaginary frog:

"My frog is bigger than the house. That's why I keep him outside. He's as big as the sky.

"He says, 'I want to come in,' in a little voice.

"I say, 'You're too big, okay?'

"He's just a little baby but he's big."

Sharon asked if she could see the frog the next time she visited.

"Yeah, yeah. He's going to be in his bedroom in the hall closet. The hall closet with the toys and the bureau. He has toys and medicine. It's froggy medicine. It has bugs. The medicine has bugs in it and one cookie."

Familiarity with stories is not a luxury for a child but a prerequisite to understanding written language and to becoming a proficient independent reader and writer. Children who have heard oral stories or have been read to regularly develop a greater understanding of print and are better prepared to be successful learners of reading instruction in school. It is easy and enjoyable to tell or read a story to a child and then to discuss it together. Children request stories repeatedly, never tiring of their favorites, some of which might be made-up or accounts of things that happened to you when you were young. Ask children to tell you stories that you like to hear them narrate as well.

You may also record a child's stories on paper or on tape in order to reread or hear them again. Hearing their own stories prompts youngsters to create new ones or alternate versions of the same one. Ryan tells Sharon stories over the telephone, which she types, copies, and sends to him in the mail. When he talks with her, he is always ready to recount the further adventures of his frog and dog. By writing down a child's stories and reading them aloud, you demonstrte the importance of the ideas. Here is seven-year-old Thijs's oral story, with a drawing added:

Some people are inside here and some people went in the cellar. And there was a shark under the water. It was a great day. But it was summer and it was time for dinner. And in summer it's light when you go to bed. They had a warning whistle for bedtime and when it was bedtime, they blew the whistle.

RHYMES

Rhymes have been part of children's play for decades. While writing *The Lore and Language of Schoolchildren*, the Opies found versions of rhymes in circulation today that were sung by children 150 to 200 years ago and have been passed orally from generation to generation.

Song lyrics often pair rhyme with rhythm. This language seems to ring and repeat in children's memories, providing an effective way to teach facts or concepts. The late Joe Raposo composed rhyming lyrics and put them into melodic rhythms for "Sesame Street," producing some of the finest examples of communicating feelings and information through songs. Perhaps as a child you learned multiplication tables or other information through a rhythmic or musical form. Many adults still put information they want to recall quickly into a rhyme or song.

One way to delight a child is to occasionally include a rhyme in your conversation: "Mom is away today so you and I will stay here and play." This produces a surprising message that children usually respond to with interest and amusement. The unexpected context of the rhyme—in parent-child conversation—transforms your words into more than information. You are producing a form of language play that captures a child's attention.

Singing is a natural way to demonstrate rhymes. Insert your child's name into the lyrics of Shirley Elliston's catchy rock and roll song "The Name Game." Drop the first letter of a name and replace it with "B," "F," or "M" to produce the lyrics:

> "Shirley, Shirley, Bo-birley,
> banana bana Fo-firley,
> Fe Fi Mo-mirley, Shirley!"

> "Rob, Rob, Bo-bob,
> banana bana Fo-fob,
> Fe Fi Mo-mob, Rob!"

Use any consonant as a replacement in the lyrics: "L," "T," or "P."

> "Shirley, Shirley, Lo-lirley,
> banana bana To-tirley,
> Te Ti Po-pirley, Shirley!"

"Rob, Rob, To-tob,
banana bana, lo-lob,
Le Li Po-pob, Rob!"

If you are creating your own rhymes as part of language play, your child may also. There are many books of children's rhymes, jump-rope jingles, poems, and chants to read with your youngster. Write rhymes for your child to see and read with you and write the lyrics to favorite songs. Taking the time to read these together, however briefly, can be a literacy event in a young child's day.

Play a *Rhyme-a-Word* game, orally or write the words. Choose a word to make rhymes with and begin. Nonsense words delight children:

submarine
hubmarine
lubmarine
chubmarine

They also enjoy creating rhymes from their name, your name, a friend's name, or a pet's name:

Michael
Sicheal
Picheal
Wichael

Letter sounds and rhymes are two language concepts children learn from this game, and observing words inspires questions about spelling.

RIDDLES AND JOKES

Riddles and *jokes* have great appeal for kids. They entertain with something that children are curious about: words. Riddles and jokes use familiar words in unexpected or unusual ways to create humor, as in this oft-told children's riddle:

"What do you get when you cross a stick of dynamite with a sheep?" "Ba! Ba! Ba! Boom!"

The incongruity produced by pairing the sound of a sheep with dynamite exploding is what makes kids laugh. Like adults, they see humor when they understand how the context creates it. For example: "What is black and white and red all over?" has more than one possible answer: "a newspaper" or "a zebra with a sunburn." The answer that occurs to adults—the newspaper—may be difficult for children to understand or to find funny unless they know that newspapers are *read* by adults everywhere. A zebra with a sunburn pairs an implausible situation with an experience many kids know about to create the humor.

Telling riddles and jokes is a way for parents and children to have fun exploring language together. Children like to laugh and to make someone else laugh.

Six-year-old Errol's joke sign [*Joke: No Come in. Sharon, I Like You.*]

Q: What time is it when the clock strikes the White House?
A: Time to throw the White House away.

Q: Why did the puppy watch the news broadcast?
A: Because he wanted to see himself on TV.

Q: Why did the car blow up its motor?
A: Because the gas man fed the car laser instead of gas.

Selections from Juhwan's Joke and Riddle Book

Creating jokes, riddles, and funny statements stimulate children's imaginations and use of language, even when their attempts do not make sense by adult standards. Children know that riddles and jokes derive their humor from changes of meaning in wordplay, but they do not know how to create this effect themselves. Thinking that jokes and riddles are supposed to make people laugh, they assume that if something is funny to them, it will be to others. They do not realize that if the joke only makes sense to them, it will not be funny to someone else. Over time, with practice and feedback from others, their humor becomes more obvious and more easily understood.

SONGS

Children compose their own *songs* by substituting their words for those in a familiar tune or making up their own. One preschooler sang the conversations between the small stuffed animals he was playing with, creating a short operetta in his pretend play. Sharon recalls making up the lyrics and melody to a song that was part of a neighborhood show she organized when she was seven:

> "My hat and my cane go together like shoes and socks,
> "My hat and my cane go together like shoes and socks."

Create alternate versions of old standards by adding new lyrics to the borrowed melody. To the tune of "Have You Ever Seen a Lassie" substitute the word "monster":

"Have you ever seen a monster, a monster, a monster?
Have you ever seen a monster go this way and that?
Go this way and that way, and this way and that way?
Have you ever seen a monster go this way and that?"

There are endless variations that you can do with your child: sailboat, dizzy duck, flying kite, jumping frog. As you make up alternate versions, you will notice things to put in the songs that you had never thought of before.

Use your own, a friend's, or the child's name to create rhymes with a message appropriate to your youngster. To the tune of "Mary Had a Little Lamb," sing:

"Emma has a little train, little train, little train.
Emma has a little train. Its wheels go clackity clack."

"Sammy had a little duck, little duck, little duck,
Sammy had a little duck, its feathers soft as silk."

Write down the lyrics so you do not forget them, or record the songs on tape. Listen to them together. Singing with children requires no musical instruments or special musical training—just enthusiasm and a lack of self-consciousness. No matter how awful you think your voice may be, you and your child are singing for your own pleasure. Favorite songs can be printed on paper and hung where your child can see them—the bedroom, kitchen, or playroom—or they can be written in book form with your child's illustrations.

Playing music from different countries and cultural traditions is an easy way to celebrate the rich diversity of our country and world. Play tapes of different types of music or listen to foreign-language broadcasts on the radio. Popular performers are writing and recording songs that include musical influences and musicians from outside the United States. Paul Simon's *Graceland* album features the South African men's choral group Ladysmith Black Mambazo. Linda Ronstadt's mariachi songs in Spanish and Bobby McFerrin's use of his body as an instrument are two other examples that illustrate the diversity of sound that children can hear.

POETRY

Coming in after recess on a day when the sun had been alternately brightly shining and blocked by clouds, a six-year-old remarked, "It's like the lights are turning off and on outside." He was not deliberately speaking in poetic terms but expressing his thoughts naturally.

One way to introduce poetry is to write what children say. A teacher of first- and second-graders hangs clipboards around the classroom in order to record poetic statements when she hears them. After children have heard many poems, their familiarity with the genre helps them recognize when something they say sounds like poetry.

In *Wishes, Lies and Dreams: Teaching Children to Write Poetry*, poet Kenneth Koch describes how he taught youngsters in a Manhattan elementary school to write verse. Visiting the school, he had been inspired by "how playful and inventive children's talk sometimes was. They said things in fresh and surprising ways. . . . They enjoyed making works of art—drawings, paintings and collages." Wondering if they would write poems in a similarly joyful and spontaneous manner, he set out to investigate. The story of how Koch and the children wrote poetry together is a classic in the field of education and offers many ideas for parents who want to encourage poetry within home writing fun.

Many of the youngsters did not think of themselves as writers, and to most, poetry "seemed something difficult and remote." Koch asked each student to contribute one line for a poem. Shuffling the lines, he read the phrases together as one text, some of which made sense and some of which was nonsensical. The children enjoyed this immensely: "It made them feel like poets and it made them want to write more."

With another group, Koch suggested the children write a composition in which every line began with the statement "I wish." He recalled:[5]

The poems were beautiful, imaginative, lyrical, funny, touching. They brought in feelings I hadn't seen in the children's poetry before. They reminded me of my own childhood and how much I had forgotten about it. They were all innocence, elation, and intelligence. They were unified poems: it made sense where they started and where they stopped. And they had a lovely music.

When children hear poetry regularly and select their favorites, they develop a fondness for this form of expression and will write poetry just as they do journals, stories, and comics. Poetry has long been taught in ways that make it remote from casual reading, but this does not have to be. There are many books of poetry for youngsters, some of which are very funny.

Today's children's poets are as well known to some youngsters as book authors. Jack Prelutsky, Shel Silverstein, Miriam Cohen, Arnold Adoff, Gwendolyn Brooks, Lucille Clifton, David McCord, Aileen Fisher, Karla Kuskin, Myra Cohn Livingston, Eve Merriam, John Ciardi, and Lilian Moore are a few in a long line of poets that children like to hear. To learn more about them and about poetry with children, look at Lee Bennett Hopkins's *Pass the Poetry, Please!*

Children who hear poetry also write it themselves or construct versions of poems they have read. Here a six-year-old girl expresses her sadness at her father's absence in her version of a poem she had heard.

A poem by Kristin [*Dear Dad, / Squirrels belong in trees, / Dogs belong free, / Coconuts belong in coconut trees, / Birds belong in the sky, / And I belong with you.*]

Children who have not heard poetry or who must wait till they leave elementary school to read poetry in English class will be the poorer for the experience. Your child need not wait. He will enjoy poetry if he shares it with you, and the two of you together can certainly compose your own poems.

DRAWING

A *child's drawing*

Drawing, an activity that most children feel they can do without help, invites written and oral communication. Treat drawing as if it were integral to the process of thinking and writing so as not to miss its importance as a vehicle for expressing ideas and telling stories.

"The drawings of young schoolchildren are often their most striking creations: vibrant, expressive, exhibiting a strong command of form and considerable beauty," notes developmental psychologist Howard Gardner.[6] In his book *Artful Scribbles*, he describes how children move through stages of artistic development marked by new issues and discoveries. Infants begin artistic expression when they make marks on paper. Preschoolers develop "a vocabulary of lines and forms" that culminates when they first create "a recognizable depiction of *some thing* in the world." Youngsters produce compelling artistic expressions into their early school years, when their free-flowing creativity is replaced by play, social relationships, and a desire to create more adult-like drawings.

Gardner points out that even preschoolers can be considered artists because they think about and use certain key dimensions of artistic expression. When a youngster shows that he knows how to vary the use of line, that he attends to such aspects as color, expressiveness, and shading, that he intends to produce a certain effect, and that he (and others) are gaining pleasure from the results of his activity, then we might properly view that child as a young artist.

It may be astonishing how much self-satisfying learning and fun your child will accomplish through pictorial language activities. Drawing, painting, and picture-making enable children to express themselves artistically and are integrally connected with youngsters' story creation and thinking about their experiences. Comics use pictures and text to portray meaning. Maps, graphs, and charts are understandable to a child because of their illustrations.

Drawing helps children develop self-confidence in their capabilities and their ability to sustain an activity of their own creation. Support youngsters' interests, supply materials, ask what they are doing, and help them to display and feel satisfaction in what they have done. The following responses to a child's efforts will influence continued play, experimentation, and discovery through art.

LET CHILDREN EXPRESS THEIR IDEAS FREELY

Through drawing, children express personal views of people, situations, and objects that are not governed by adult notions and concepts. Houses, flowers, and persons may be all the same size. Two suns might appear together in the same picture. Subject matter that appears disconnected or imaginary—a dish and a flying horse—are perfectly sensible to the child creating the scene. Looking at children's art, adults may not understand that for youngsters, disparate details, whether fantastic or real, can fit together without contradiction. A picture does not need to be a congruent whole in adult terms to be interesting and complete to a child.

What role can you play in your child's artistic expressions? Not art critic or drawing teacher, for a child's expressions are personal and not meant to be judged. A suggestion about how a child might improve something or a statement of mild disapproval can reverse a child's feelings from enjoyment to discomfort. Instead, consider how you might guide a child to heightened awareness of her position in the environment and her relationship to other things in it, thereby assisting her growth in concepts and ideas without imposing your judgments.

FOCUS ON ARTISTIC CONCEPTS

During walks outside, on trips, while doing errands or visiting new places, discuss relationships of sizes, colors, shapes, or patterns of things and concepts such as how objects overlap each other, the different textures of things, and where shadows fall. Opportunities to see and discuss these ideas surround us in our daily routines: in illustrations in books and magazines, in photographs, nature, and architecture. Identifying relationships and concepts develops mutual awareness and shared vocabulary between adult and child. This makes it easier to recognize elements from your conversations and observations as they appear in your child's art. As you notice them, you can comment about them.

Point out different shapes of flowers, leaves, shadows, trees, the shapes of buildings, windows, doors, and decorations. Relate the sizes of objects to each other: a house to a tree, a doorway to a building, a skyscraper to lower buildings, the insects to the plants, the leaves to a tree, the clouds to the sky. Children see things from their own perspective, and these conversations assist them in enlarging their awareness.

Look at the different colors of objects, remembering that you may not know whether colors appear to your child as they do to you. Discuss the fact that each of you might be seeing the same things in different ways.

CRITIQUE RATHER THAN CRITICIZE

Young children want to evaluate the quality of artwork, whether their own or someone else's. They know when something looks good or not so good, even though they may not have the vocabulary to say why they think so. You can help them describe what it is that they see that makes one thing look better than or different from another. Model how to express in words what both of you see. This is critique rather than criticism. Ask questions, such as "Does something look as if it will off the page? Are all the bright colors down at the bottom? Does it look as if there is not enough in it? Is there blank space you want to fill?" These questions focus on ideas that help youngsters consider their own and others' work without implying that they've done something wrong.[7]

COMPLIMENT INVITINGLY

Children's self-doubt and self-consciousness about their drawings is heightened when someone criticizes their work or comments upon something that could be improved. A child feels compelled to defend what he is doing, even if it's simply for exploration or play, rather than for a specific purpose. Children become increasingly more conscious of their art as they grow and watch what others do. They see comics or adult renditions of action figures and sometimes become less willing to draw from their own inspiration.

How you compliment your child's work has important implications. Saying "That's very interesting! Why did you draw it that way?" opens an opportunity for your child to tell you about her thinking and reasoning. It gives you an opportunity to learn something. Exclaiming "Oh, I love that!" or "We'll put it on the refrigerator!" offers no invitation to your child to explain anything. It simply expresses that you are pleased by what she has done, even if she had no such intention. It also suggests that something else she does might not please you as much. The question then arises whether her work is supposed to satisfy herself or you.

COMICS

Do you remember as a child what part of the newspaper you went to first or what books you wanted to buy when you had some money to spend at the store? For many people, the answer is the funnies.

Children today still love *comics*. Some of the characters have changed: Ninja Turtles have replaced Superman; "Peanuts" and "Garfield" are regulars instead of Mickey and Minnie Mouse. Bart Simpson has become a television star. But the basic purposes remain the same: fun and entertainment for the reader or viewer.

Comics provide opportunities to enter worlds of adventure and dreams. Youngsters battle evil villains or ferocious monsters and "boldly go where no one has gone before." They delight in the antics of wonderfully funny characters in ordinary or improbable situations. They see other children and adults dealing with issues that they too face in their own lives.

Comics do not restrict children's intellectual development. A 1988 study found that children who read comic books are also children who read well.[8] They are a source of enjoyment and ideas. Some comics in particular are wonderful vocabulary-builders for young writers. "Calvin and Hobbes" uses many unusual words, particularly when Calvin is transformed to Spaceman Spiff or is discussing the meaning of life with Hobbes.

Comics are "distinctively American art forms." The first comic strip character, "The Yellow Kid," appeared in a newspaper in 1895; the first comic book, "Funnies on Parade," came out in 1933; Superman arrived on the scene in 1938. Today more than 200 million comic books are published every year. Professor M. Thomas Inge, who wrote about comics for the Smithsonian Institute's exhibition on American cartoon art, believes that children who read and write their own comics learn about value systems, humor, drama, narration, dialogue, artistic styles, political satire, racial and ethnic stereotyping, language, and how to arrange ideas in sequence. He asks: "Why not use the power the comics have for children as a means for furthering their education?"[9]

There are numerous ways to promote the writing of comic strips and comic books by children:

READ BOOKS WRITTEN IN A COMIC FORMAT

The comic-book format is appearing more frequently in children's literature. James Stevenson, a cartoonist and children's author, uses the features of multiple frames on a page, dialogue in balloons, and words illustrating noises in many of his books.

Bumble Cat: How She Came to Be, by Phyllis F. Kerr, is another story written in the style of comic-book frames. It describes the adventures of a shy young cat who becomes fearless when she changes into a bee outfit and is able to fly. Using the format of large and small boxes with dialogue bubbles on some pages, the story is an example of a classic comic scenario: a character overcoming a problem through use of a disguise that leads to heroic action.

The translated Belgian comic series describing the adventures of Tintin is action-packed, beautifully drawn, and very well written. Vocabulary, plots, and characters are carefully thought out, and they have proven enduringly interesting to generations of children since their appearance in 1929.

Comic books themselves, although regarded by many parents as the last thing they want their children to read, are the very thing that many youngsters most enjoy. Pairing the drawings with little text makes it appear that there is not too much to read on each page. Choose comic books that appeal to your youngster to enjoy together. Many parents have told us how much their children enjoy reading the book anthologies of popular comic strips.

READ COMIC STRIPS IN DAILY AND SUNDAY NEWSPAPERS

One or two characters may be of great appeal and interest to both of you. "Tiger," by Bud Blake, and "The Family Circus," by Bil Keane, ring true for young children.

DESIGN A BLANK COMIC STRIP

Make boxes on paper for your child to create a personal comic strip, as in the following example:

Six-year-old Neda's Writing Cat [The Writing Cat / This is a writing cat. / The writing cat is going to write about his mother. / And his other brother, / And his sister, / And his dad, / And his uncle, / And his aunt.]

MAKE OR BUY SPEECH BUBBLE STICKERS

Hallmark Company makes peel-off stickers of empty speech bubbles to write in and affix to other things. If you cannot find theirs, buy stick-on address labels to cut into homemade versions of your own. These are fun to add to pictures, drawings, photos, magazine covers, cards, and home-made books or comics that you and your child write and draw yourselves.

GIVE A COMIC-MAKING GIFT KIT TO A CHILD

Blank paper, comic books, and blank speech bubble stickers or address labels, with colored pencils or markers, make great additions to a Writing Box and are a gift that many children would like to receive. They suggest that the child write his own comics and give him all the materials he needs to get started. If you want, you could also give some sheets of paper with boxes already drawn in place.

Another version of this idea is to give a package of people stickers. There are many different kinds of these. People stickers can be used as comic characters for which the child draws speech bubbles and writes dialogue.

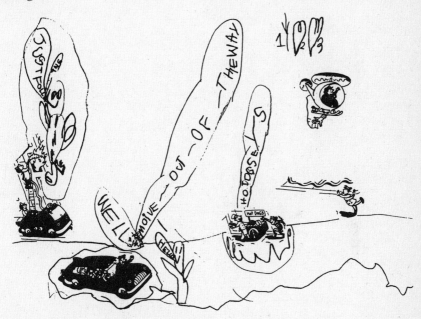

Seven-year-old Samuel's comics

CREATE POSTCARDS AND GREETING CARDS
FROM THE COMIC-MAKING MATERIALS

Give your child some thin cardboard in various colors (called oaktag in art stores) cut to regular or large postcard sizes. A drawing or a photograph of your child with speech-bubble dialogue becomes a postcard or a greeting card to send to someone. Speech bubbles and drawings are also entertaining additions to child-made stationery.

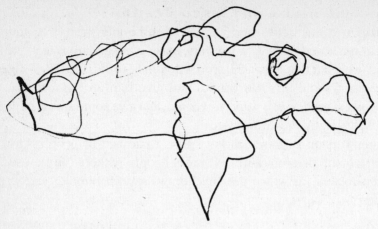

Four-year-old Ryan's map

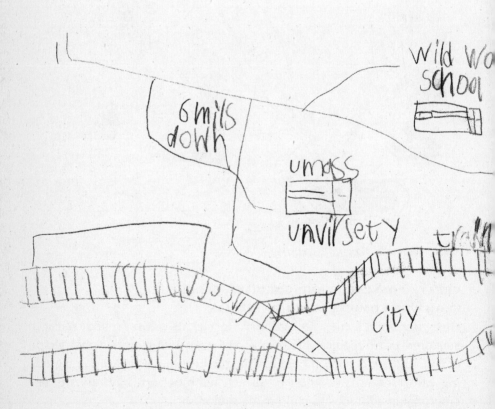

Six-year-old Juhwan's map of Amherst

MAPS

Maps, usually precisely rendered by cartographers, are uniquely made by children. Some young authors explore maps as a new way to connect drawing with writing. On this and the preceding page, the map drawn by one four-year-old is far from recognizable, while the map by a six-year-old of the town of Amherst, Massachusetts, with references to the university, the downtown area, and a nearby mall, is clearly understandable and an interesting attempt at representing distance.

Children clamor to see maps and globes and identify faraway places in the world. Their fascination provokes an urge to experiment with constructing their own.

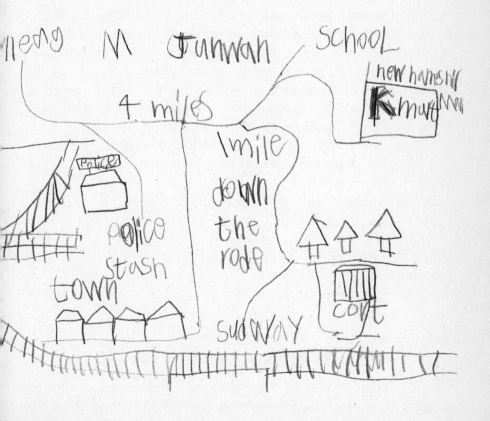

While at Bank Street School in New York City in the first half of this century, Lucy Sprague Mitchell helped children to build floor maps big enough for them to sit in and maneuver toy boats, trains, and cars through. The children learned about maps from first making their own. We often wait till children can read before we introduce them to maps, but building floor models, drawing their own, looking at maps of the world, and reading some of the newest books written for four- and five-year-olds is a wonderful way to introduce maps to youngsters.

Maps of real or fictional places are fun to make with children. They need not be confined to paper, either. Three-dimensional maps, constructed of blocks or household junk (empty boxes, cans, tubes, or other containers and cardboard that are usually thrown away) give a wide choice of ideas for play.

Treasure maps are exciting and, with their accompanying pictures, are usually not complicated to read. The pictures help children remember the names of places and teach an important reading skill: using pictures as a way of getting information about the text. Some youngsters try making maps as a way of linking drawing with writing. Before creating a treasure map with your child, you could read a pirate story like *One-Eyed Jake*, by Pat Hutchins, for five-, six-, and seven-year-old youngsters, or the "Tin-tin" comics for older children.

Include a map as part of notes you make with or leave for your child. If you are going to the store, the library, the playground, the bus, or the subway, draw a map showing the route to your destination. The illustrations need not be elaborate. Watch your youngster begin to do the same in her notes to you.

Children might create *fictional maps* for:

- a treasure
- a dinosaur's trip
- a monster's town
- a fictional character's vacation

GRAPHS AND CHARTS

Young children have endless questions they want answered. Creating *graphs* and *charts* to visually represent information is an excellent way to connect their questions with mathematics in exciting ways. You might graph family members' and friends' birthdays to display on a wall. Add information to the graph about new friends and relatives to:

- assess which months have the most birthdays
- remind you and your child to send cards
- introduce the ideas of quantity, size, and scale
- show how mathematics is part of your daily lives

Chart information about dinosaurs, fish, lizards, frogs, dogs, trucks, or any other topic that your child wants to learn about. Add data as you find out new things. The chart on display becomes a central item to refer to, something to read together, and an ongoing writing project.

Graphs help children develop their understanding of spatial relationships and how information can be represented visually. This is an important ability for all youngsters, and particularly so for girls, who must overcome gender stereotyping that discourages their development of mathematical skills. As the authors of *How to Encourage Girls in Math & Science* noted, spatial thinking forms "the very framework of geometry, a subject in which many bright, high-achieving girls begin to develop the difficulty that eventually deters them from mathematics."[10] Encouraging play with and daily use of mathematical thinking and problem-solving when children are young is an effective way to establish a foundation for successful experiences that will influence future math and science endeavors.

The success of constructing graphs and charts for young children depends on the concreteness or abstractness of the information being collected and the pictures, photographs, and drawings that accompany the text. At four, five, and six years old, kids can graph things they are familiar with: the daily weather; birthdays of friends and relatives; favorite foods; how many times they hear or read favorite books. At seven, eight, and nine years old, youngsters can graph and chart more abstract information. For example, a child can record the results of a dice-rolling experiment to determine whether it is true that some numbers appear more often than others, as described in *Teach Your Child Science*, by Michael Shermer. This can be an ongoing activity that a child can do alone, with friends, or with you. The following pages illustrate how two children chose to represent the information they'd compiled:

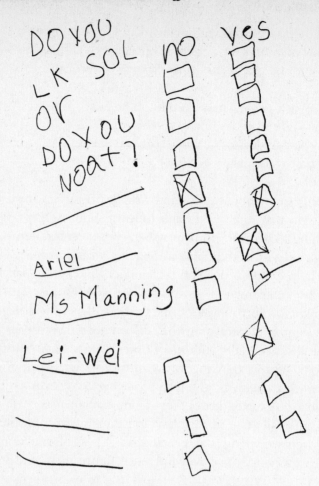

Six-year-old Valencia's "Do-You-Like-School" survey

Conduct surveys among family members, visitors, friends, or neighbors to accumulate data for your graphs and charts. For example, you could ask people which is their favorite apple food: apple pie, apple juice, a baked apple, or applesauce. The results of their survey may be recorded on a simple bar graph. Older children might ask others what television shows they watch regularly or movies they have seen in the past month. Once the data is accumulated and displayed on the graph or chart, introduce and reinforce various counting and computational skills as well as the math concepts of mean, median, mode, and range.

Name PAt

1 ✳ S = 6 sIDes

⊂✳ = 21 sIDes

⊂✳ = 18 sI Des

4✳ = S4 sIDes

Six-year-old Pat's chart of snowflake sides

Many of the preceding ideas build on activities already taking place in your home: newspaper-, magazine-, and book-reading; looking up information in the dictionary, encyclopedia, or almanac; watching television; talking with other people about something you have seen or heard. Naturally occurring everyday situations can be fun graphing and charting occasions.

Ongoing graphs match a child's interests. If trucks and buses attract a child's attention, keep a tally sheet to take on walks or rides to record the numbers of trucks and buses seen. Two columns ruled on a piece of paper, one with a picture of a truck at the top, the other with a picture of a bus, make a tally sheet. Every time one or the other is seen, a child makes a check mark for it. When you arrive home, your youngster can color in squares on a graph to record the information collected that day. The next day the tally sheet goes with you again and so on until the graph is filled. Then you may add more spaces or start another graph.

Keep a chart in your home of mail that your child receives and sends. Record the information on a picture chart. Draw or hang photos of the people who regularly correspond with your youngster. Next to their pictures, place blank papers with two sections ruled on them: one for letters received and one for letters sent. Use a date stamp to record this information or write in the date. This helps keep track of who gets a letter next.

CHILD-CREATED WRITING GAMES

Children create their own *writing games*. They are fun for kids and adults and provide additional ways to promote language play. Some games can be organized and played by children without an adult or small group audience or assistance. Some are clever forms of communication within families. It's important to note that while writing is integral to these child-created games, it is not the exclusive focus of activity. Following are two examples:

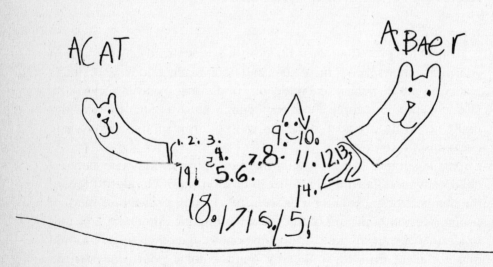

Seven-year-old Andy's dot-to-dot

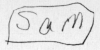

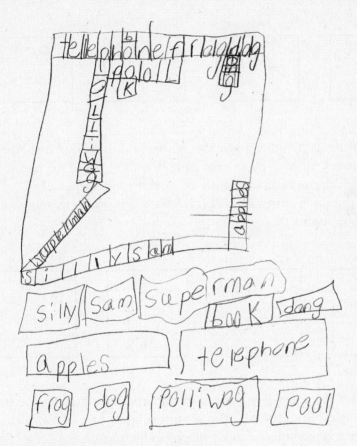

Eight-year-old Sam's crossword puzzle

 Line-Design Games are an alternate way to invite children to use their imaginations while combining drawing and writing. A line, a hole, or a shape made by you or your child on the paper becomes part of a drawing. If a story evolves with the drawing, your child might tell it aloud for you to record on tape or write down. If your child likes to do line designs, they can be displayed in the house, sent as gifts, or collected into book form. A tape of the oral stories could be made so that the stories can be listened to. Here are three variations to try:

A *line on the paper* begins with a line of any size, shape, or color on a piece of paper. The line's shape and size give ideas to the child of what the drawing might be.

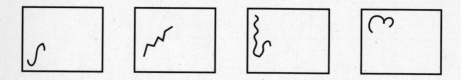

A *hole in the paper*, like a line on the paper, is a hole of any size or shape cut into a piece of paper. The hole becomes part of the picture. A different picture can be made on the other side of the paper as well. The child drawing the pictures can choose which drawing to write about— or write about both.

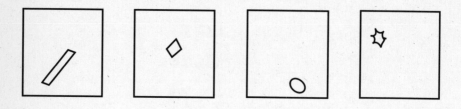

A *shape on the paper* is a colored or patterned paper scrap glued or taped to a background sheet. The scrap becomes part of the picture. Another version uses two or three shapes in the picture.

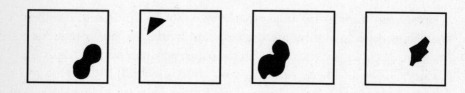

7

Expressing Imagination

THE PIRATES

A story by Brian, 6 years old

This book is about pirates on an island and there is an X. (X means treasure)

1. Story Begins

This pirate is on an island and found a X and is lucky because he found the X. He is rich. He is calling the ship. The ship is not coming. He got caught by the bad guys. He will get out of the bad guys so he will be able to get back on his ship with his monkey and his crew and beer and they are safe on his ship with his cannon and his gun on the ship and his friends.

2. The Escape

He got away and got back on his ship but the bad guys got on the ship. The good guys won.

3. The Gold

The good guys found the gold and was rich. The bad guys found the fake treasure and the bad guys is never coming back.

4. The Fight

The bad guys came and went on the ship and wanted to fight. But the good guys said, "No." But the bad guys said, "Sorry, good guys, you don't have any choice!" and the fight began. One of the good guys punched the bad guy. The good guys win again.

5. The Deserted Island

When the pirate went onto the island, he saw the underwear store. He went to buy a pair of underwear. His wife, she is going to use the underwear for shorts.

6. The Killer Whales

When the good guys got on the boat, they sailed out into the ocean. They got out 36 inches deep. They saw Moby Dick, the white whale. They were scared. Moby Dick crashed into their ship. The pirates jumped into the water and swam to shore. One sat on a X! He said, "X X X X!" They dug it up and was rich. After they were rich they put a fake treasure for the bad guys to find. Moby Dick was nice to the good guys.

7. The Forbidden Island

It has coconut and banana trees. They had a ship. The ship was tied to a coconut tree. There was a fire. They were cold. The fire was hot. They were tired. The bad guys were back. They wanted the real gold.

8. The Big Plan

On the forbidden island, the bad guys had captured them in a trap. A pirate named Long John Silver had looked into the hole and said, "Such a pity!"

The good guys had fallen for the old trick and they said, "You'll pay for this!"

Long John Silver laughed, "Never, never, never! You will come with us!"

And the pirates said, "Yay, yay, yay!! Let's go into the hideout!"

"You won't get away with this!" said one of the good guys.

"And lock them up in jail!" and they all started to laugh.

Brian began writing *The Pirates* after buying two long-awaited items at the store: a small Lego set with a pirate, parrot, treasure chest, and cannon, and a Trapper Keeper notebook. As soon as he got to the car with his shopping bag, he assembled the Lego pieces. Then he opened the Trapper Keeper and began to write the story, completing the first four chapters in two days. He wrote the rest during the following three weeks, one chapter at a time.

The Pirates is a vivid example of how children construct stories: by blending what they know with what they imagine. The sources of Brian's story were his experiences, imagination, and creativity. He had learned about pirates from cartoons, movies, comics, and books. While writing the story, he watched television videos of *Moby Dick* and *Treasure Island*.

Some of what he absorbed from viewing them—vocabulary, scenes, and characters—were fashioned into a story uniquely his own. Like Brian, other youngsters draw from what they know and what they imagine to create writing ideas and topics. They express their thoughts through different variations of plot, perspective, dialogue, and detail.

As they get older, however, youngsters encounter one of the most unfortunate myths or misconceptions that adults convey to children about writing. Novels, poetry, drama, and short stories are regarded as creative forms of written expression—the province of real writers. Other writing is for use in school or in jobs. This is writing that one has to do—as homework, for a test, or as part of work and career requirements. These communications are thought of as functional, task-oriented, and less significant as a creative or imaginative accomplishment. Children are quick to detect these distinctions in adult minds. Many abandon the free-flowing creativity shown in Brian's pirate story to express themselves in a more "facts only" manner. Others decide that since they are really not interested in writing imaginative stories or poems, they do not possess the talent to be a writer.

Peter Elbow thinks this widely held distinction between creative and functional writing is not only false but harmful to the self-confidence and intellectual development of a writer. He states "that a good essay or biography requires just as much creativity as a good poem; and that a good poem requires just as much truth as a good essay."

Creative, imaginative writing can be done by anyone for many different purposes, claims Elbow. But to communicate effectively what you are thinking to a reader, "*you* must experience your thoughts fully as you write." See your thoughts in your mind's eye or pretend you have just come up with a revolutionary new idea that you are expressing for the first time. Let the ideas flow from your mind and from your body to the page. Writing what you are thinking is a powerful way to generate more thinking and more writing. Perhaps, he reasons, this is why "children who are never asked in school to write about their own thinking often get worse and worse at experiencing thought."[1]

Expressing one's imagination through writing does not just keep happening on its own. It must be nurtured and rewarded. Whatever their ages, children do not simply make things up out of thin air, as adults sometimes assume that they do. Instead, their stories reveal a complex interplay between their creative thinking and their daily experiences. What children experience in their lives is what they know, and what they know forms a basis for what they think, say, and write. Using imagination and creativity, they mix fact and fiction into stories, poems, essays, reports, and many other descriptive communications.

"IS THIS FICTION OR NONFICTION?"

"Are these books real?" a five-year-old asked one morning as he looked at the materials about dinosaurs on display in his classroom.

Sharon explained: "Some of these books tell what scientists believe is true about dinosaurs, and some are make-believe stories that have dinosaurs in them." Then she briefly explained fiction and nonfiction to him. Later, during the afternoon class meeting, the boy told everyone else the difference between the fiction and nonfiction books and showed examples of each.

Sharon was surprised by his interest, because the distinction between the two categories was not one that she usually talked about with children of this age. The next day there were more questions. Soon the children regularly inquired, "Is this fiction or nonfiction?" Following their lead, the adults in the room answered the questions, and the categories of fiction and nonfiction became a part of general conversations about books.

After one girl read aloud a story that she had written at home, a classmate asked, "Is that fiction or nonfiction?"

"It's mostly nonfiction with a little fiction," she replied knowingly.

Young children sometimes signal their interest in fiction and nonfiction by asking "Is this real?" regarding things they have heard or read. They want to know what fiction and nonfiction mean and how these are used in writing. This is not an easy question to answer.

Adult distinctions about what is true and what is imaginary are not always clear to children. Parents purposefully portray some make-believe things in a family or societal culture as real: for example, Santa Claus or the Tooth Fairy. Other things—monsters under the bed or children's imaginary playmates—that seem real to a child are dismissed as made-up fantasies. Children are fascinated by these issues precisely because they are not sure whether ghosts, Bigfoot, the Loch Ness Monster, or space creatures from UFOs are real or not. These characters are never seen, but they may exist. By the same logic, dragons, witches, or an invisible dog may be real as well, even when adults say they are not.

Accepting the interweaving of fiction and nonfiction in children's writing allows young writers to begin understanding both concepts. They express the awe and wonder that come with imaginary or fantastic creations in stories, letters, poems, songs, and drawings. They learn relevant facts and information about a topic and use them in journals, newspapers, or biographies. They mix the two together and create fictional facts and factual fictions. By contrast, when children assume that rigid distinctions exist between fiction and nonfiction, they may be reluctant to express themselves fully or even to try certain kinds of writing.

Encourage your youngster to explore, invent, and enjoy stories that combine fiction and nonfiction. Fiction and nonfiction are part of all writing, even if the material seems straightforwardly factual. An author always chooses the information to include or leave out of a text. Writing is a version of events as the author views them. In children's pretend play, oral tales, and writing, mixing facts and make-believe provides young writers with a way to express their thoughts and ideas in creative and self-fulfilling ways.

Ask your child occasionally about the decisions she is making as she writes. Inquire if a story is based on personal experience, a real person she knows, or facts read in a book. Point out that an author's purpose determines whether to write fiction, nonfiction, or a combination.

Be aware as you talk with children that their thinking about these issues may influence their writing. If they believe that rigid distinctions exist between fiction and nonfiction, they may not want to write certain things, as shown by the experiences of the following two youngsters.

Six-year-old Adam loved to tell elaborate stories about his own experiences: the day he jumped from a high ladder into a packing box full of styrofoam peanuts and the time he went flying through the air on his sled and fell through the ice at the bottom of the hill. The children and adults he told the stories to were enthralled by the details and the humor in them. However, he never wrote the stories. He was not comfortable writing stories that were largely embellished by fictional elements because he feared that would be viewed as not telling the truth.

Twelve-year-old Charles, the editor of a neighborhood newspaper that he started on his own when he was seven, also feels strongly about fiction and nonfiction. "I would hate to have to write just nonfiction," he explained. "I want my writing to be interesting and fun for someone to read. I start with something that really happened and then add things to make it more exciting."

Both of these youngsters assume that fiction is made up and nonfiction is completely factual. Adam is reluctant to write his oral stories because he mixes the truth and fantasy, and Charles thinks that nonfiction is too confining a form of personal expression. Once children realize that all writing combines imagination and perceived experiences, the issue is not solely focused on what is true and not true, but how to most effectively use fiction and nonfiction elements in factual accounts or make-believe stories. This realization enables youngsters to use imagination, creativity, and facts to produce self-satisfying communications for many different purposes.

STORIES

Young children are natural story creators. Their ideas emerge from many sources—play, new materials, the urge to try different styles, personal experiences and interests, fascination with fictional or familiar characters, and interest in producing their own versions of stories—and they naturally blend together elements of fiction and nonfiction.

Sometimes children write about the same topic repeatedly. One parent said that her son holds the world's record for stories written about Bigfoot trucks, which, for a time, were of immense interest to him. He left that topic to write about others when he was ready. Writing might vary greatly, shifting from one topic to another. Sometimes children write for themselves; other times they seek an adult's response to their work.

When children begin their stories, they usually do not know how long each one will be. Their story writing can vary in length from one page to many, and might be expressed in a chapter book or single-story format. Children choose their own length, and they write till they are done. A supply of different size and shape papers and preassembled blank books encourage different styles and formats.

Stories from Play

Between the ages of two and nine, children's stories are integrally involved with fantasy play with invisible playmates, physical play with friends and siblings, and stories that they hear and read. Events in play often become oral stories and written text.

As part of a pretend play game at school, Evelyn and her friend created and acted out a story about a mother dog and her pup, titled *Rough Dogs*. Evelyn then went home and wrote the stories in a chapter book. Here is an excerpt:

Two pages from five-year-old Evelyn's "Rough Dogs" [. . . another house. So they looked and looked. But there was no house that was bigger than the first one. Chapter 2: Baby and Momma Make a House So they went to the woodshed . . .]

The possibilities for generating stories from play are virtually endless. Take dictation or tape record a child's narrative to remember the oral story. A written or taped version allows a child to add to the story or make up others involving the same characters in new situations. These might be written partially by you and partially by your child. Combine oral and written material to develop new characters and plots. Transcribe a story for your youngster to illustrate.

Personal Experience Stories

Personal experience stories chronicle things children have done or events that have happened in their own lives or families. These can be developed orally with friends or family members, then written by a child or an adult taking the child's dictation. Kids retell these stories all the time. Here are accounts by two youngsters:

My Cat

written and illustrated by
Clayton
made in Amherst, Massachusetts
1989

My Papa and me caught a cat for my sister.
The cat was standing on my sister's head.
My sister named her Katy.
The cat always jumps on my sister's bed.
The cat always has her tail up.
The cat always drives Mom crazy.

The End.
About the Author
I love to write books.

Easter Egg
dictated by
Eugenie
made in Amherst, Massachusetts
1989

I got a big, huge Easter egg in front of my mom's door and there were chocolate kisses inside. Outside in the yard we had an Easter Egg hunt and a chocolate kiss hunt. Me and my cousin had a huge Easter Bunny but we didn't like the taste of it. It was chocolate. And we found chocolate kisses in the mud mountain in back of my yard and we added them to our baskets. We both got 22.

"All About" Books

"All About" books come from children's intense interest in the world around them, reflected in their reading and information seeking and their collecting of models, pictures, and games. Suggest to your child that she create a book "All About" a favorite topic.

Some that we have seen cover such subjects as:

- butterflies
- ghosts
- worms
- vehicles
- dinosaurs
- sharks
- lizards
- rocks
- my family
- my ping pong table
- how to build a house
- cats
- the solar system
- snakes

"All About Me" Books

Children can also write autobiographical descriptions in *"All About Me" books.*

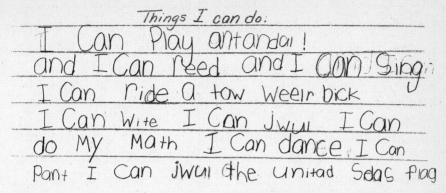

Things I can do:

*I Can Play antandai!
and I Can reed and I Can Sing
I Can ride a tow weeir bick
I Can Wite I Can jwui I Can
do My Math I Can dance I Can
Pant I Can jwui (the Unitad Sdas flag*

A six-year-old's "Things I Can Do" book [I can play Nintendo. And I can read and I can sing. I can ride a two-wheeler bike. I can write. I can draw. I can do my math. I can dance. I can paint. I can draw the United States flag.]

"All About Me" topics might include:

- weekend or vacation fun
- favorite foods or hobbies
- jokes, riddles, or rhymes
- activities with family and friends
- things to do after school

Fictional Characters

Children invent fictional characters—inspired by television, the movies, children's books, or their own imaginations—and feature them in stories. After reading Smurf comic books, six-year-old Alain created a fictional character called a Mila that had three legs, no fingers, and no toes. He and his classmates wrote a series of fantasy books about them, including one by Christian titled "The Milas Go to the City."

The Milas go to The City

The Milas went to The City

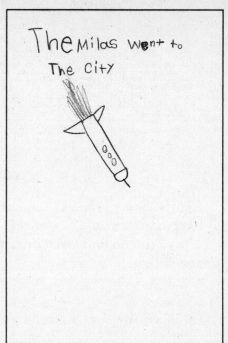

The Milas were scAred

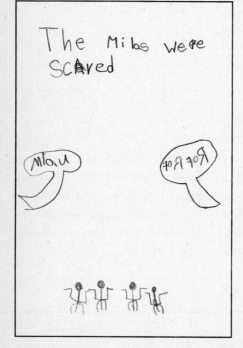

But The Milas Wantd to go home. But Tuy didt knoe WaV is the spcShp Was.

Opposite page *"The Milas Go to the City"*
[*The Milas went to the city.*]
[*The Milas were scared. "Meow." "RufRuf."*]
[*But the Milas wanted to go home.*
But they didn't know where is the space ship was.]

Inspired by the Milas, other children created their own fictional characters called Wilas and Weirdos. During one summer vacation, seven-year-old Christian used Milas as the central characters in twenty fictional adventure stories that he wrote and illustrated. He and his parents also composed Mila stories together. His titles included:

- "Milas Go to the Secret Castle"
- "Milas Go to the Car Store"
- "Milas Go to the Beach"
- "Milas Go in the Time Machine"
- "Milas Go to the Lake"

More than a year later Alain, the originator of the Milas, created a Mila Language Alphabet and used it in his letter to Sharon.

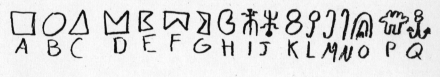

Alain's Mila Alphabet

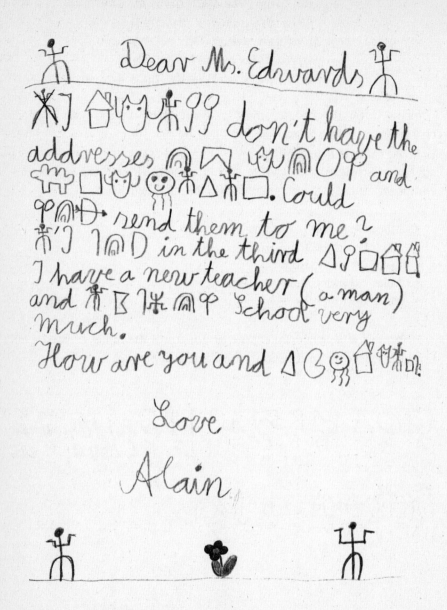

Alain's letter to Sharon [Dear Ms. Edwards, I still don't have the addresses of Toby and Patricia. Could you send them to me? I'm now in the third grade. I have a new teacher (a man) and I enjoy school very much. How are you and Christian? Love, Alain]

In addition to being part of stories, fictional characters often take on lives of their own that a child interacts with on a regular basis. Parents may use fictional characters with writing in many ways. Notes from a character can appear in lunch boxes, on pillows, on the bathroom sink, to say hello, to predict a treasure hunt later, or to hint that a family adventure may be coming up. If your child is not doing some expected task, such as putting shoes away, a fictional character might leave a note advising:

If you put your shoes in the closet you will always know where they are! If you don't, only I will know where they are!

    Signed,

The Shoe-Collector

Of course, you might create a series of made-up creatures, instead of just one. As soon as you admit that you are the first character, any notes you write after that will be suspect. "I know who wrote this!" your child will exclaim. Realizing that this is a game, she may reply to you through her own made-up characters.

Some adults feel that children have too many fictional characters in their lives already—Santa Claus, the Tooth Fairy, the Easter Bunny, cartoon characters they see on television—and certainly do not need more. Our experience is that children are interested in creating or helping to create a fictional character of their own and are eager to correspond with those you might create. Children who identify the familiar handwriting they see that supposedly belongs to the character develop a tongue-in-cheek attitude. They enjoy notes, letters, cards, and treasure hunts, but they know that the adults around them are doing this in the name of a fictional character (though we may insist otherwise!). Younger siblings hear their comments and hypothesize about who might really be doing the writing, but they are more excited by the sense of mystery involved. They like the element of surprise created by not knowing what the character might say or do next.

Child-Created Versions

Children retell or sometimes create their own versions of familiar characters or oft-told tales. Inspired by the children's classic *Heidi*, one girl wrote her own story called "Heidi." While she was writing other fiction stories completely from her own ideas, constructing a version of Heidi was important to her. The same child wrote seven versions of *Cinderella*.

A popular activity with many youngsters is creating their own version of a book after hearing it aloud. This provides a framework for organizing their thoughts and gives them a way to think about how language is used. This idea has worked successfully for children's authors and cartoonists for a long time. In the "Rocky and Bullwinkle" TV show, Edward Everett Horton's narration of the hilarious segment called "Fractured Fairy Tales" presents old stories with funny twists.

Children's authors produce their own versions of well-known stories. David A. Carter's easy-to-read version of *In a Dark, Dark Wood* concludes with a surprise pop-up at the end. Alvin Schwartz included a rendition of it in his chapter book, *In a Dark, Dark Room and Other Scary Stories*. Ruth Brown wrote a slightly different text with another ending for her beautifully illustrated *A Dark, Dark Tale*. Harriet Zeifert and Mavis Smith set the story in a flap-book titled *In a Scary Old House*. Which ones do children like? All of them. With so many versions to read and compare, it is easy to suggest that your child might create her own.

Numerous versions of old tales, fairy tales, songs, and stories are available today. Read or tell the original story of Jack and the Beanstalk and then introduce your child to Raymond Briggs's *Jim and the Beanstalk*. Mordicai Gerstein's flap-opening rendition of *Roll Over!* can be contrasted with Merle Peek's two-color version of the same story. After singing "The Wheels on the Bus" with your child, read a few of the versions in print: *A Pudgy Board Book*, illustrated by Jerry Smath; Harriet Ziefert's predictable reader format; Maryann Kovalski's slightly changed and very funny story; and Paul O. Zelinsky's pull-the-tabs, lift-the-flaps, turn-the-wheels interactive version that is great fun and full of humorous detail. Seeing and enjoying some of these choices assures children that their ideas and drawings will create yet another version to add to the shelf next to the published ones. And theirs can be as different as they want it to be!

Many authors also use a general story line more than once but with different illustrations and text. Laura Joffe Numeroff followed her enormously popular story *If You Give a Mouse a Cookie* with a second, *If You Give a Moose a Muffin*. The story structure is similar, so children who know one can predict what might happen in the other, but the words and characters in the books are different.

Bill Martin Jr.'s and Eric Carle's much-loved predictable book *Brown Bear, Brown Bear, What Do You See?* now has a companion volume, *Polar Bear, Polar Bear, What Do You Hear?* Another author, Susan Williams, uses a similar format in *I Went Walking*. Children who hear all three will recognize the similarities and be able to contrast the differences. Suggest that your child write and illustrate a version of a favorite song, rhyme, old tale, or story.

Different cultures have different versions of well-known fairy tales. The Cinderella story is beautifully written and illustrated in John Steptoe's African setting for *Mufaro's Beautiful Daughters*. In an ancient Chinese version retold by Ai-Ling Louie, *Yeh-Shen, a Cinderella Story from China*, children see again the moral of the story that binds all three tales and can appreciate the differences in the words and illustrations. Check a library or bookstore to see who else has published a version.

JOURNALS

Journals are unique forms of communication within families. Their structure of daily or regular entries written by adult and child enhances the probability of their frequent use. The benefits of writing in journals are different from those of composing a grocery list, a letter, or a story. Journals are vehicles for communicating information that might not otherwise be exchanged. They provide an opportunity to share ideas and a time to write. Keep a journal together about ever-changing nature, sports items, interesting activities, or places visited.

Journal-writing depends on continually adding to the text. There are special joys for young writers with this kind of writing. Because the journal constantly grows and changes as new entries are added, children get to see the writing take on new forms and meanings over time. Journals can be joint projects between parents and child or with siblings or friends, or by the child alone.

Interestingly, journals (or diaries) serve two quite different purposes for any writer. First, when by yourself, you can save thoughts for later examination and promote an inner dialogue about important issues. Alternately, when life seems too hectic, a journal facilitates moments of reflection and perspective and brings a sense of order out of multiple, pressing experiences. Journals encourage after-the-fact understanding of events. For instance, jotting down notes about books read helps recall main points and remarks on authors' different writing styles; keeping a log of what is happening on favorite television shows develops skill in summarizing details and understanding of the idea of plot; recording thoughts about an experiment for school describes what is happening and celebrates what one has learned about complex scientific principles.

Children six and older might want to begin their journal-writing in an attractive bound, lined notebook like *My Own Journal: An Illustrated Notebook*, published by Running Press (Philadelphia, PA). *Me and My Stepfamily: A Kid's Journal*, by Ann Banks, lets children interview and describe relatives from all sides of the family. Dover Publications makes small, inviting, inexpensive, lined paperbound books that youngsters can use for their journal-writing. Many children will want one like the ones they see parents and older siblings use.

Dialogue Journals

With a *dialogue journal*, you and your child can communicate messages to each other about the day's activities, topics you may not have had time to discuss, or feelings that you want to express to each other. What you write can be—but does not have to be—in response to what the other person has written. Read and discuss the journal with your child. Time shared with journals creates an intimacy similar to that developed when family members read together.

Observe how your child's writing progresses over time. Journals are good vehicles for learning about writing conventions. Your child sees adult script and gains information about standard spelling, spacing between words, punctuation, and other print conventions. Whatever your child writes in invented spelling, you can incorporate into your response so that the standard spelling is available for her to see. For example, if "shping" is one of a child's words, "shopping" might be in your entry.

Following are two selections from a journal kept by a mother and her six-year-old daughter.

JANUARY 1990 27
MOM KAN OWAGO
TO the PJSTAT
IS OEN PJS IT is
BD AND SK GAS
TAR IS A RSt DRNt
LOVe J

January 27, 1990
Dear J

         I did not know
that Bread and Circus had
a restaurant. The next time
we go to that place   or
near Bread and Circus, you
can remind me about the
restaurant and we can buy
something there.

Journal entries [January, 1990, 27 Mom, can we go to the place that is one place? It is Bread and Circus. There is a restaurant. Love, Jerusha / January 27, 1990 Dear Jerusha, I did not know that Bread and Circus had a restaurant. The next time we go to that place or near Bread and Circus, you can remind me about the restaurant and we can buy something there. Love, Mommy]

Family participation in journal-writing directly and positively affects the reading and writing development of young children. Two hundred and four first-graders and their parents from three schools in central Florida participated in a five-month study in 1988. One-third of the children wrote in home dialogue journals with parents three times a week. Another third wrote at school in dialogue journals with their teacher three times a week. The remaining children did not participate in dialogue journal-writing. On tests, the child-parent dialogue journal-writers were the highest scorers. Researchers concluded "that dialogue journal-writing is an essential approach to beginning literacy whether it is administered by parent, teacher, or older student singly or in combination with each other."[2]

Topic Journals

A *topic journal* records events, activities, or information that both parent and child find interesting. The journal can have as many topics for writing as a family has areas of interest, or you may even want to have several journals, each with its own topic. For instance, a family who likes to do number games and puzzles together might record mathematical concepts and rules. Another family interested in nature might keep track of animals that appear in the yard: deer, skunk, opossums, or groundhogs. A new pet, a bird feeder, or a recording of the weather are topics you could chronicle daily. A mother and daughter who follow baseball or football through the sports pages or on television might keep records and clip articles throughout the season.

Sharon's students had great success in the classroom with journals about sprouting bean seeds. The growth of the plants was surprisingly quick, so keeping a journal of the daily changes was a way to experience the awe of watching a plant develop.

"I Wonder" Journals

"I Wonder" journals are interactive, child-specific, and a great way to make reading and writing integral parts of children's learning activities. These journals record what children are wondering about: the questions that they often do not ask or those that they rarely receive answers to because a parent may not know or may be too busy at that moment to explain. Some questions from Sharon's students included whether emeralds are real; why people dream; how a hermit crab gets inside a shell; how many stars are in the sky; how people get last names; how electricity gets in the sky; what makes your body move.

Each "I Wonder" statement becomes a topic for investigation. For example, Andy asked how river water becomes salty when it goes to the ocean. He and a classroom aide researched this in the library together. Andy returned to explain to his classmates about estuaries, and he brought the library books home to share with his mother.

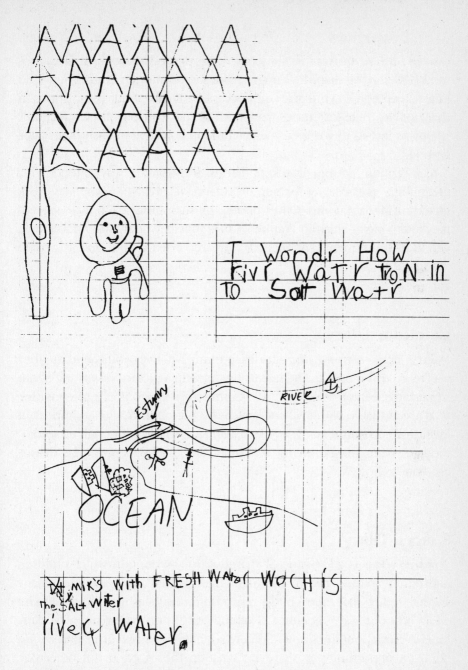

Selection from Andy's "I Wonder" journal [Question: I wonder how river water turns into salt water?]
[Answer: The salt water mixes with fresh water which is river water.]

DIARIES

Diaries save memories that someone wants to recall. Like journals, diaries can be solitary or shared writing activities in a family. You and your child might keep your own diaries and occasionally talk about your entries. A shared diary includes entries from both of you. You may discuss together what you intend to write or you might read your text to each other after writing.

Many famous people have kept diaries. Some were always intended for the public, as those by former president Richard Nixon or New York governor Mario Cuomo. Other diaries, by such historical figures as Leonardo da Vinci, Benjamin Franklin, Laura Ingalls Wilder, and Anne Frank, although subsequently published, were recorded at the time as private thoughts.

Calendar Diary

Make a large *calendar diary* for each month. It gives your child another way to record thoughts and events by drawing a picture or writing about something seen or done each day. Commercial versions of a calender for kids are available with stickers, which are put on to designate important events or appointments. They are usually not spacious enough to accommodate writing and drawing, so homemade, wall-sized calendar diaries are better choices.

Shared Diary

A *shared diary* is a variation of shared journal-writing in which children and adults share some of the highlights of their day's activities. Many parents tell us that their child's response to the question "What did you do in school today?" is either "Nothing" or "I don't remember." A daily time to chat about the day and record a sentence or two gives parent and child an opportunity to share information that is often not otherwise communicated.

Shared diaries also allow parents and children to describe orally their day's activities, which may be preparation for writing, as we found out one day with Emily. Riding home at the end of a day full of different events, Sharon suggested to Emily that she write about all the things we had done together. Emily said she did not want to do that. Sharon did not reply to the comment. Instead, she mentioned one activity they had done that day. Bob named another, and Emily added a third. The three of us spontaneously took turns describing all the things we remembered.

Later, on her own, Emily sat at the computer and began to compose a diary of the day's activities. When Sharon saw this, she waited till Emily said "That's all I'm going to write" and asked if Emily wanted to dictate anything else while she typed it. They spent the next few minutes together at the computer, Emily talking, Sharon typing, till her entry was completed.

Instead of trying to coax Emily to change her mind, Sharon suggested an alternative approach to diary writing. Emily was free to choose how to proceed. The oral rehearsal, the novelty of the computer, and an adult's participation inspired her to write. What follows is a selection that she called "A Full Day at Sharon's":

in the morning i got up and lerned a little spanish. then we went to breakfast. boght bread and i had a chocolate umbrella. Then we went to Peg's house. Then we went around with the magnifying glass and looked at old stuff. Then we went to lunch and had something to eat. Sharon had a peanut butter and jelly sandwich and so did Bob but I had a roast beef sandwich. After that we went over the Bridge of Flowers and took some pictures. And then we went to get some postcards. Then I went to stick my feet into the pothole water and then I spotted some snails and some baby fish.

Then we went to Magical Child and did some looking around. After that we went to an antique store and bought a doll house for me. Then we went to Wilson's and bought some clothes. They are going to be for when I go back to school. Then we went out for pizza and we watched two Star Treks. . . . Bye now! See you tomorrow! Emily

EXTRA! EXTRA!
YOUNG CHILDREN CREATE NEWSPAPERS

"Your daily newspaper is a source of wonderful writing ideas and reading possibilities for young children," we told the members and guests of the local Reading Councils at their annual dinner meeting in Newport News, Virginia, in February 1991. We had been invited to speak about young children's writing development and our Writing Box by the Councils and Melanie Reuter, "Newspapers in Education" Coordinator for *The Daily Press Times-Herald*.

A question about publishing children's writing from Patricia Gordon, a kindergarten teacher in the audience, inspired us to try a new way of having kids create a newspaper, one featuring children's phrases and invented spelling. Instead of editing and correcting the children's writing, we decided to print it as written, accompanied by the standard spelling to help everyone read the material. A first-grader's weather report was published this way:

WAWR REPT

TO MAROY IS SAE.

[*Weather Report: Tomorrow is sunny.*]

The experience of creating and publishing their own child-written newspaper demonstrated to us what an enjoyable and inviting writing and reading activity this can be for school-aged youngsters.

To introduce the idea of writing their own newspaper, Sharon brought copies of *The Boston Globe* and *USA Today* to school several days in a row for the class to examine. The children looked through the sections and discussed the variety of pictures and stories they found in the newspapers. Then, to practice news-writing, everyone including Sharon wrote about what they had done during their February school vacation. After the stories were finished and read aloud, Sharon and a group of seven children began assembling the first edition of the newspaper for distribution to classmates and their families. Brainstorming what they would like to write for the paper, the children chose comics, jokes, a fake school lunch menu, lost-and-found announcements, and a survey for readers to answer.

Just as commercial newspapers have deadlines, so did this one: the end of school on Thursday. Sharon assumed the role of managing editor: reading the pieces with the writers, asking questions if the articles were unclear, helping young authors add punctuation to their text, complimenting the children's efforts. The parts of the newspaper were photocopied and reduced in size for placement on the front and back of a master page. The children joined in the process, pushing the buttons on the copy machine and questioning how it worked: "How did it make things smaller?" "Where did the light come from?" "Why were the copies warm?" Hot-off-the-press lives on at this newspaper! On Friday afternoon the first edition of the newspaper rolled off the copy machine and went home with the children.

Once the other students saw this first edition, they all wanted to contribute to the next edition. A second group of seven wrote jokes, mazes, comic strips, stories, and the weather forecast. Several of these youngsters had not demonstrated regular self-initiated writing in school, but they were eager to contribute to the paper. Perhaps their enthusiasm stemmed from having classmates and family members read their material; perhaps it came from choosing among the many different playful and serious writing styles found in their newspaper.

Newspapers Appeal to Children

Several factors contribute to children's interest in newspapers.

First, the photographs are visually enticing. They stir a child's curiosity and invite questions about what was happening before, during, and after the picture was taken. Pictures can initiate discussion, storytelling, and fiction and nonfiction writing. Children comment about things the pictures remind them of and tell stories about events or adventures in their lives, or they might recognize people and objects that are familiar to them. A picture of Michael Jordan or the space shuttle may make them want to know what the accompanying news story is all about. Color adds to the attraction of visual images in the photographs, headlines, ads, charts, maps, and graphs now featured in many daily papers. *USA Today*'s national weather map, with its warm reds and oranges and cool greens and blues, attracts the eyes of young readers who learn to read it through daily viewing.

Second, because children's individual interests vary, they are drawn to different parts of the paper. Parents can use these interests as the basis for interaction with the newspaper.

Some youngsters relish the comics, especially the colorful, larger-sized Sunday funnies, where they can follow the adventures of their favorite characters. "Comics whose drawings convey much of the message with few words are wonderful beginning-reading materials. This is frequently the case in comic strips such as "Tiger," "Garfield," and "The Family Circus."

Other children enjoy the kids' pages, where they can see drawings by young children, read an article or interview written for youngsters, play a word game, or solve a puzzle. In our state, as in many others, elementary-school children contribute articles and activities to the kids' sections of local newspapers.

Some youngsters look through the sports pages, recognizing athletes and following the exploits of a favorite team.

Some kids are interested in the ads. One day Sharon observed two boys happily looking through the car ads and asking an adult about the prices of vehicles. On another occasion a five-year-old was examining the circulars and recognized the pictures of video games on sale for 20 percent off. He read the figures as the price of the game and asked Sharon if twenty dollars was too much money for the game he wanted.

Third, children want to know what is occurring in the world. They hear bits and pieces of information about current events and they become concerned about what war in the Middle East, acid rain, or the election of a president may mean to them. Reading about and discussing issues reported in the daily newspaper is a way of answering childen's questions and examining fears and anxieties they might be feeling. Conversations can also stimulate a child's curiosity and promote further research about topics of personal interest.

Newspapers in Families

Newspapers are a versatile medium for literacy learning in families, as shown in the following activities which you might wish to try.

READ THE NEWSPAPER TOGETHER WITH CHILDREN

The newspaper is never dull. It is always changing, offering many interesting topics to talk and write about. Reading the newspaper demonstrates authentic adult literacy habits in front of children.

GATHER INFORMATION FROM NEWSPAPERS

Integrate features of a newspaper into daily home life: in reading, writing, math, science, social studies, and geography. Articles and questions about science, the world and national map, features about animals and people—all are sources of current information about many areas of children's interests. Children enjoy humor, which is one of the reasons the comics are so inviting to them. Look for jokes about sounds of letters, puns, numbers, science, and maps in the comics. The child-directed format of the "Mark Trail" comic strip informs everyone about nature.

DISCUSS DIFFERENT KINDS OF NEWSPAPER-WRITING

Use the newspaper to stimulate discussion about different kinds of writing. Newspapers provide many writing models for children: headlines, weather forecasts, television listings, menus and recipes, comics, articles, and editorials.

Orally play with the written format of the newspaper by telling stories about things that you or your child did during the weekend. Make up jokes, riddles, word puzzles, and pretend headlines about what is happening in school or at home; review movies and television programs; add advertisements and announcements.

SUPPORT PUBLICATION IN INVENTED SPELLINGS

The purpose of a family newspaper is to make writing exciting and inviting. An important reason for encouraging children to write their own way is that otherwise they quickly lose interest when the process involves too many steps. To complete a first draft, edit and copy it over, and then proofread the final draft a second time is tiring for young children. Writing becomes a task, and the newspaper does not go out as often or with a sense of easy accomplishment on the part of its young authors. To make reading the newspaper easier for others, write the text in conventional spelling underneath the child's version.

CREATE A "HOME NEWS" BULLETIN BOARD

A "Home News" bulletin board gives everyone a chance to:

- tell about themselves or something that happened to them;
- comment about an issue they are thinking about;
- write or draw something for everyone to see; and
- share a joke, a maze, a puzzle, or a mystery clue.

The bulletin board might be divided into sections—comics, headlines, news, weather, menus, maps, opinions—and children's writing can be placed in the appropriate section. If a date stamp is available, each writer can stamp the date on the writing before it is posted so readers will know when it was written.

Rotate the stories regularly, just as daily newspapers or weekly news magazines must do for their readers. Save the old news stories in a clip file or seasonal scrapbook, or assemble the material into a special monthly edition of your newspaper and send it to family members and friends.

DISPLAY "READ ALL ABOUT IT!" HEADLINES

An "Extra! Extra! Read All About It!" section of the "Home News" bulletin board can be reserved for announcements of children's accomplishments written in newspaper headline form: "Ryan Finds Frog in His Backyard" or "Emily Can Count by TWOs." Children can decide on their own headlines, read them aloud, and then compose news stories about the event, if they choose.

SUPPORT A CHILD'S PERSONAL NEWSPAPER

Some youngsters will write their own family newspaper with adult support. When he was seven years old and living in Glasgow, Scotland, Charles began his own newspaper titled *Weekly World*, in which he wrote about school activities and school life. Initially, he wrote the paper at home by hand, adding pictures and drawings to each page. His father made multiple copies on a photocopying machine at work, so Charles could pass them out at school. Soon Charles had a staff of young reporters, columnists, and editors who voluntarily contributed news stories, music and movie reviews, word games, visual puzzles, a horoscope and fortune page, opinion polls and surveys, advertisements, a serial comic strip, jokes, and point-of-view essays. After moving to Massachusetts, he continued writing his newspaper for friends and neighbors. His parents bought him a typewriter, and he has become an accomplished self-taught typist.

LET CHILDREN CHOOSE THEIR OWN DESIGNS AND LAYOUTS

If you assemble an assortment of shapes and sizes of precut papers and blank comic-strip formats for writing, children can create their own designs and layouts for their newspaper. The shapes and sizes can simulate the columns, boxes, comic strips, and spaces found in a newspaper. After determining their choice of paper, youngsters write in pencil so changes can be made easily, then trace over their finished text using a rolling ink pen to make it dark enough for the copy machine to print.

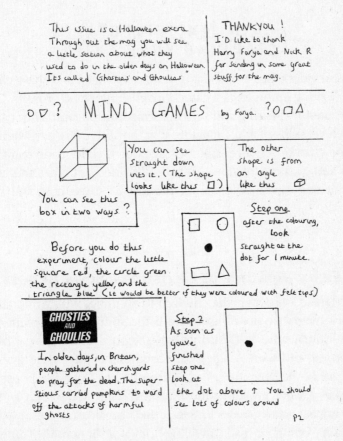

A page from Charles's newspaper, Weekly World

OPEN A HOME POST OFFICE

Children may want to send copies of the newspaper to friends and relatives. You and your child can operate a home post office, complete with stamps, envelopes, postcards, and mail-pick-up times. This is a wonderful way to teach geography. Display a map of the United States or the world (depending upon where the mail is going), with notations of where the newspaper is being sent. Parents can help their child to copy addresses of grandparents or others into a booklet that can be kept in the post office with envelopes and stamps. A model envelope on display assists a child to see how to address correspondence correctly whenever he wants to do so by himself.

AUDIO- AND VIDEOTAPES STARRING YOUR CHILD

Audio- and videotapes are versatile ways to facilitate and share children's writing. Writing emerges as a natural extension of tape projects. Children are fascinated by hearing and seeing themselves on tape. They can create their own versions of adult activities that they see every day. Family news or comedy shows, story-reading, songs, poetry, child-made commercials, or jokes and gags can be taped on audio or video or both. Other activities might suit one or the other better because of space, cost, and available time.

"The Fishy Weather at Christmas News Report"

Portable tape recorders invite children to do things with writing that they might not otherwise do. An example is the spur-of-the-moment creation of "The Fishy Weather at Christmas News Report" by seven-year-old Brian and four-year-old Sam. Visiting her brother's family while attending a seminar at the nearby university, Sharon had to leave the house before her nephews were awake in the morning. To stay in touch with them, she put notes and Hershey's Kisses at their breakfast places.

"Hi, Sam!" one note read. "I will be home for dinner. After dinner we'll play the dreidel game and see who wins the most Hanukkah candy tonight. Do you think it will be me? See you later! Have fun. Love, Sharon."

Both Brian and Sam had thanked her for the chocolate, but neither mentioned her notes or wrote replies during the weekdays when she was writing to them. On Sunday morning, Sam appeared at the breakfast table with a note. Accepting it with a smile, Sharon said, "Thank you, Sam. What a nice surprise! I love to get notes. Why did you write to me?"

"Because you wrote me all those notes!" he said, in a voice that implied she should have known this.

"Would you like to read your note into the tape recorder?" Sharon asked.

"Yes," he replied eagerly, "I would!"

Brian had entered the room to hear their conversation and wanted to stay for the taping. After Sam had read his note and listened to himself on tape a couple of times, Brian suggested they use the tape recorder to create a news show. "Want to do that?" he asked his brother.

"Yes!" the younger boy replied.

Sharon mentioned that news reports are usually written and then read aloud. Brian demurred, saying that he didn't want to write. Sharon didn't reply, but she left the room for a minute to put something away before beginning the taping. When she returned, both brothers were busily writing. She joined them to write a news story too.

When their stories were finished, Sharon and Sam accepted Brian's suggestion of a name for the show and agreed that he would be the director. Then they started taping. "Hi, this is our new show, 'The Fishy Weather at Christmas News Report,'" announced Brian into the tape recorder. "I have something very important to tell to Emily, Kyle, and Ryan. And now for our latest report from Brian."

Over the next three days, they continued adding news stories to the tape. Some were spontaneously reported and some were written first and then read. All the news reflected their activities: visiting an art museum, locking the keys in the car and then coincidentally meeting the boys' parents at the grocery store, awaiting the arrival of Santa Claus. The recording is filled: Brian ad-libbing his conversations with the imaginary audience and Sam sometimes singing instead of reading his script.

The "Fishy Weather News" tape displays remarkable creativity, thanks to technology in the form of a small portable tape recorder. It allowed Brian and Sam to tell oral stories and to write in ways they had not done before. The desire to hear themselves inspired the boys to mix scripts with oral language, and the enjoyment of hearing their first production sustained the boys' desire to compose additional material. Playing them back for others to hear also proved to be a more compelling reason for writing than had Sharon's daily notes. They listened to their shows and requested blank tapes so they could continue the project after she had returned home.

Advantages of Audiotapes

A portable tape recorder is an inexpensive and easy tool that you and your children can use to promote fun and writing.

CHILDREN CAN USE AUDIO RECORDERS INDEPENDENTLY

With audiotapes, youngsters can record and produce a show, sing, or talk by themselves, without the assistance of an adult. A fine battery-operated portable cassette recorder is available in the My First Sony line of products for children. Large-sized push-button controls make it easy to operate. It includes a microphone for recording or for singing and reading along with tapes.

EASY USE MEANS GREATER USE

A tape recorder provides flexibility because it is easier to use than a camcorder. If you are unable to see your child before bedtime, record a message or a story. Your child can record a message for you too. If either of you wants to sing or read a story to each other, the audio recorder accommodates this. Taping may bring unexpected results—as happened with "The Fishy Weather News Report." When your child is beginning to say recognizable words, the excitement of these moments can be captured on tape.

AUDIOTAPES CAN BE USED WHERE VIDEOTAPES CANNOT

Tapes of you reading your child's stories or your child reading his own stories can be played on a car stereo, a portable tape recorder, or a Walkman. Tapes of children's books can be made quickly and inexpensively. As you turn book pages, ring a bell, make a sound, or say, "Turn the page now." This way your child can keep his place in the book as he listens to the tape. Write a list of what you tape and note the number on the tape counter where each story starts.

Videotapes

Making Fun Family Videos, by Carole Chouinard and Randall Baer, is an excellent book that gives many ideas and directions for videotaping shows, skits, movies, and anything else your family may want to try. It is written by a husband-and-wife team who have experience in television production.

A CHILD'S VIDEO HISTORY

Children and adults like to see tapes of special events or milestone accomplishments: your child as she begins to sit up, walk, talk, goes to school for the first time, visits grandparents, or appears in a school play. A video record of a child's development is one way of retaining information for family archives and repeated viewing enjoyment.

Taping a child's oral or written stories and drawings enlarges the scope of her developmental record on tape. It is similar to collecting writing samples over time but has the added advantage of your youngster reading her own work aloud. It not only assures your child that her writing, reading, and drawing are important to you, but it is a fun way to see the changes in her writing and drawing as she grows. Grandparents, other family members, and friends will enjoy hearing and seeing your youngster on tape.

GIVE TAPES TO FRIENDS AS GIFTS

Make a gift for a child's friends of a video- (or audio-) tape with you and your child reading a book or two, singing a favorite song, and your child reading or telling one of his own stories. A tape, the books, and a copy of your child's story all become the present. In the space left on the tape, the child receiving it can add other books, songs, poems, and stories of her own.

CREATE A FAMILY TV SHOW ON VIDEOTAPE

A family TV show written and produced by children and adults includes writing, teaches kids about media, and results in lots of fun with your camcorder and VCR. Decide together what type of show or television segment you would like to create. Invite your child's friends to be part of the production team of performers, camera persons, directors, and writers. After everyone prepares their stories or scripts, these young on-air performers rehearse and watch the rehearsal tape to see if they like their material. A final version of the show is taped for showing to family and friends.

Brian's mother videotaped him giving a tour through a desert park near their home when he was six years old. His dialogue, all spontaneously created, reflected his interpretation of the role of tour guide: "And now ladies and gentlemen, as you can see here . . ." Copies of this tape were sent to family members. You and your child could make signs, a map of places visited, or an explanatory program to accompany your videotape.

It is not necessary to mandate that children write their lines for a video show or have a finished story for recording on tape. At first the taping can be relatively simple: For example, a story or a play might have just a written "Cast of Characters" at the beginning and a "The End" sign to close the performance. More writing will follow as the children gain confidence and decide to make more tapes.

Neither the length of the show nor the quality of the on-camera performances is the object of this event, as Andy Hamilton, one of our graduate students, has demonstrated in his work with children and media. The goal is to let children enjoy expressing themselves on tape—which they do well! Whether building with blocks, pantomiming, or creating a regular show of their own—such as "Earth Rescuer," about a team of heroes and heroines who fight pollution on earth—children and cameras are a dynamic force for improvisation and creativity.

Writing and recording a television show also offers the chance to talk about television commercials. A typical youngster views over 400 commercials a week. Point out to your child how advertisers make claims about products that may not be true or that are designed to sell their products by linking them with cartoon characters. As children write their own commercials, thinking of claims that will sell their products, they gain greater understanding of their roles as consumers.

FILM YOUR CHILDREN'S FAVORITE STORIES

Young children virtually never tire of hearing their favorite books or poems over and over again. A video presentation enables a parent to read to a child as many times as the child wants to listen. Although you are not physically present, your child can hear the stories and experience a feeling of companionship by watching you in the video.

When recording favorite stories on tape, invite some of your child's friends to participate. The children can join you reading the parts that they know by heart, especially if a chorus of voices adds drama and fun. In the predictable story *Jump, Frog, Jump*, by Robert Kalan, children who have heard it know exactly where to join in the refrain, saying, "Jump, Frog, Jump!"

Whoever is videotaping films each page of the book as you are reading and films the children too. Experiment to fine-tune the distance and establish the angles you want. Include children in reading aloud, discussing the story after it is read, or performing some or all of the plot. You can tape two or three stories in a single sitting, or do just one at a time, gradually filling a tape with selections of stories, poems, and songs. You and your child can create a program listing of the titles and the number at which they appear on the tape counter.

8

Using Writing Machines

"It wasn't too difficult," said ten-year-old Annette, recalling how she learned to use a microcomputer for home writing two years before. "The machine tells you, 'If you need help, press Q' or whatever. I just figured it out." According to Annette, writing with a keyboard and lights is "quicker; it's neater . . . just easier."

Annette began using a computer at home during the summer between second and third grade. Her mother had just purchased a second-hand Apple IIC and the Appleworks software package. Computers were not new for Annette; she had played games on one at school. Because there were few instructions with the machine, Annette started exploring the software, figuring out things for herself with "a little help from my mom." By the fall, Annette was writing her own fiction stories and reports for school on the machine and saving them on a disk so she could look them up again later. Typing was not a problem: "I just practiced," she replied when asked about using the keyboard. Most important, she found that writing with a computer was enjoyable. Once, Annette said laughingly, she and her friend decided to write "seventy-five, maybe a hundred sentences" just for the fun of it.

Although five-year-old Kyle does not have access to a personal computer, he is captivated by the technology he encounters every day in his home: a remote-control television channel changer, a VCR, Nintendo games, radio-controlled toy cars, wind-up and battery-powered trucks and vehicles. Three months into kindergarten, he remarked that he intended to go to a "remote-control school for kids" after the school year was finished. When asked why, he replied, "Because I don't know much about my remote-control things." A few months later he explained that he was making a movie based on a drawing of one of his video games that he had done on an Etch-A-Sketch. He asked his grandmother to send a "movie camera, a regular camera, and a printer"—the tools he needed to "make it real."

The experiences of Annette and Kyle suggest why we could hardly write this book without discussing the powerful and enjoyable ways that personal computers can promote young children's desire to think, learn, and write. Such technologies have become a regular part of everyday life for many youngsters, either in their homes or their schools.

According to the Census Bureau, 46 percent of all children between the ages of three and seventeen use a computer at home or in school. The number of households with a home computer doubled between 1984 and 1989 and today totals almost 14 million.[1]

In a recent study of children in Southern California, "94 percent said they had played video games either at home or in an arcade (and many in both places)." Through the end of 1988, almost 14 million Nintendo game sets had been sold in the United States.[2]

Almost all schools use microcomputers for classroom instruction. By 1990, the ratio was one computer for every twenty-two students. In addition, over 90 percent of all public schools use video technology, including VCRs, in teaching.[3]

We asked families with Writing Boxes if children were using machines for writing at home and found that two-thirds utilized computers or typewriters at least some of the time. Most often kids played games—video and educational—but they also wrote letters, stories, notes, the alphabet, pages of random letters and symbols, their names and the names of family and friends, and experimented with spelling and making words.

In one family, a nine-year-old and his friend spent part of their winter vacation writing new episodes of "Star Trek" on a word processor. In another family, a father created computerized word-find puzzles that included words from the stories his sons were reading at home. He told us that all three of his youngsters—five, seven, and ten years old—were very interested in these puzzles. In a third family, an eight-year-old girl wrote both by hand and on a computer. Her first story, in collaboration with her older sister, on the word processor took several weeks to complete.

It is not surprising that children find microcomputers, video games, and other interactive technologies to be challenging yet inviting environments in which to play and learn. These machines let youngsters explore and discover just as they have in many other areas of their early learning through choice, self-challenge, constant repetitions, and minimal criticism from adults for making mistakes.

It is also not surprising that parents have many questions about technology. What are the intellectual and educational consequences of children's ongoing interactions with writing machines and computer games? Are computers and other machines exerting too great an influence over children's thoughts and time? Can children's strong interests in electronic media be used to generate exciting writing possibilities? How might parents go about using computers and other technologies in their homes?

LEARNING FROM TECHNOLOGY

Parents' experiences with computers are often different from their children's playful encounters with the machines. They are not nearly as relaxed around technology as kids are. The differences in use and feelings of ease have established a technological generation gap between parents and youngsters in many families.

Alan November, a technology educator at Glenbrook High School in Glenbrook, Illinois, thinks he knows why so many adults are distrustful of computers' potential to promote children's learning. Adults are "paper trained": They have learned without such technologies to think in linear patterns and to express ideas logically and sequentially. They are more familiar with consulting books, periodicals, newspapers, and other forms of print than with accessing computerized data banks for information. By contrast, today's children have grown up "learning from lights": the rapidly moving electronic visual images provided by television, movies, arcade games, and computers.

How do psychologists and educators explain children's interactions with computers? A computer is a medium fundamentally different from paper. In a computer program, the user

> cannot move to all locations from any given location. You have to know the pathway that links point X with point Y, and this requires a mental model of the program. In a book, in contrast, you do not need a map, but can move freely from one page to any other page.[4]

In using these new learning formats, children are not tied to a logical and sequential pattern of acquiring and using information. Most children use the experience of playing a new video game to figure out the successful strategies for obtaining a high score and defeating less skilled players.

In her enlightening book *The Second Self: Computers and the Human Spirit*, Sherry Turkle describes a four-year-old girl at a computer console playing a learning game. Turkle wonders what is happening intellectually and emotionally for the child while she uses the machine:

> But Robin is not "watching" anything on the computer. She is manipulating—perhaps more problematic, *interacting with*—a complex technological medium. And the degree and intensity of her involvement suggests that (like the children at the video games) it is the medium itself and not the content of a particular program that produces the more powerful effect.

When playing PAC-Man and other electronic games, a young child engages in important strategizing and thinking:

> Working out your game strategy involves a process of deciphering the logic of the game, of understanding the intent of the game's designer, of achieving a "meeting of the minds" with the program. The video games reflect the computer within—in their animated graphics, in the rhythm they impose, in the kind of strategic thinking that they require.

Computer games, concluded Turkle, "are not a reminder of a feeling of control over challenge. They are a primary source for developing it."[5]

It is the inherent interactiveness of computers that promotes children's learning. Unlike television, which requires a viewer to sit passively and absorb a pattern of repeating images, computers physically and mentally engage youngsters who use them for word processing, drawing, experimenting, or playing games. Even what we think of now as simple computer toys are interactive. Children take charge of the process by issuing commands and instructions and figuring things out for themselves. They take risks, make mistakes, and correct errors as they use the machine. Because children can create and solve problems for themselves, they focus on what they want to do and learn large amounts of information in short periods of time.

Computers also stimulate children's mathematical and spatial thinking. Seymour Papert, a professor of mathematics at the Massachusetts Institute of Technology and a pioneer in the field of computer learning, observed how children used a computer language called LOGO to program on-screen movements of a computer-generated turtle. In his book *Mindstorms*, he described:

> A first encounter often begins by showing the child how a Turtle can be made to move by typing commands at a keyboard. FORWARD 100 makes the Turtle move in a straight line a distance of 100 turtle steps of about a millimeter each. Typing RIGHT 90 causes the Turtle to pivot in place through 90 degrees. Typing PENDOWN causes the Turtle to lower a pen so as to leave a visible trace of its path while PENUP instructs it to raise the pen.

Before long, children as young as four years old "could control the mechanical turtles." As children gained proficiency with the machine, they created increasingly complex drawings and figures, as well as programmed the turtles to "seek out or avoid objects." Some even used a music software program to get the turtles to dance electronically.[6]

Given their natural interest in and engagement with computers, children's learning is being transformed in homes and schools by use of some of the following options of this technology:

- *Word processing* eases typing and revising, thereby encouraging interest and creativity in writing.
- *Logo* and the *Geometric Supposer* invite students to create and solve their own mathematical problems.

- *Electronic bulletin boards* expand geographic boundaries as children become computer pen pals with youngsters and adults in other parts of the country or the world.
- *Microworlds* enable the computer to graphically illuminate historical sites such as Boston's Freedom Trail or scientific principles like how gravity affects a baseball on the moon or on Jupiter.
- *Hypermedia* allows users to link ideas and graphics across passages in a text file or data base so a child studying the civil rights movement can read key documents, see a timeline of events, answer questions posed by the computer, or hear speeches by historical figures.

COMPUTERS, KIDS, AND WRITING

A personal computer at home offers young children many opportunities to begin experimenting with writing at a much younger age than most parents ever assumed they could.

WRITING WITH A COMPUTER IS FUN

Children like to pound away on a computer keyboard and watch the results on the screen. Words, letters, and symbols move about in front of them. Images appear and disappear at the child's command after touching a key or a button.

The fun of playing at a keyboard can be true even for children younger than two. Five-month-old Sarah sat on her father's lap and randomly began hitting the keys on his Macintosh computer. This is the writing she "created":

`XXXXXXXXXXXXXXXXXXXXXXXXXXXXXXXXXXXXXXXZ
SAAz

Her father remarked that she eagerly played with the family's word processor whenever they sat together at the machine.

CHILDREN EXPERIENCE FEELINGS OF PERSONAL CREATION AND SATISFACTION WITH WRITING MACHINES

Writing notes, letters, or stories at a keyboard enables children to enter into the mysterious and inviting realm of communicating through print.

In addition, using an "adult" tool further enhances children's interest in exerting control over what they see as an adult activity. Computerized writing gives them a sense of having accomplished something important.

Children maintain their interest in computers as they get older and can read what they write on the screen. It is an interesting change from paper and pencil. One high-school teacher noted that she "never had a student who preferred writing by hand to hunting-and-pecking" on a keyboard.[7] A seven-year-old who did not have a computer at home wrote the following story one morning on a university Macintosh while his mother attended a seminar.

THE LITL TRTL AND THE SEE

WONS THERE WOOSTO BE A LITL TRTOL HIS NAM WAS CWIC SWIM HE LOVED THE SEE COS THE SEE WOS NIES TOO HIM AND ALL THE ATHR TRTALS IN THE SEE CAS THE SEE WAS NIEES TO HIM AND ALL THE OTHR TRTLS IN THE SEE INCLOOTING HIS MATHRAND HIS FOTHR AND THAYE ALL WOR NOIEES TO THE SEE TO CAS THE SEE WAS NIYES TOTHEM.

BIYE BRYN JOHNSON.

Bryn's story [*The Little Turtle and the Sea: Once there used to be a little turtle. His name was Quick Swim. He loved the sea 'cause the sea was nice to him and all the other turtles in the sea including his mother and his father. And they all were nice to the sea, too, 'cause the sea was nice to them.*]

WRITING ON THE COMPUTER IS SOMETIMES EASIER THAN WRITING BY HAND

Youngsters who might not write easily, quickly, or confidently on paper may prefer to use the keyboard and compose on the screen. *Power On!*, a report by the Congressional Office of Technology Assessment, has concluded: "Although word processing by itself does not create better writers, it has helped ease the physical burden of writing and revising." The report also found that access to a computer can be particularly important to youngsters who, lacking enough fine motor control to use pencils and crayons with dexterity, tend to avoid writing.[8]

With computers, older children can follow a technique used by many authors who write for a living: "overwriting," editing, then deleting. It is easy to record ideas as they occur and, in so doing, generate more information than is needed for a school assignment or writing project. From that material, the writer may then choose the phrasing and structure that works best and eliminate the rest. Or a project can be done again by using the material in new ways. There is also the added advantage that "professional looking" products can be achieved without tiresome copying and recopying or leaving mistakes scratched out on the paper.

Here is an excerpt from a long adventure story about a young heroine, named Thenchie, written on a computer by eight-year-old Jerusha in collaboration with her older sister:

She got hungry. Then thenchie looked at the plate. She grabed the plate. She had no fork. What should she do? She ran to the kitchen. Then she was gone. When she got under her bed, she saw the robber.Thenchie was so' scared that she just had to stay there.The robber said whats your name? then she said my name is Thenchie. Then the robber said my name is Tom. The mother came in and said, who is that. Thenchie said this is a robber. His name is Tom. Then her mother screamed and called the cops. Then the cops came and said, this is no robber. Then her mother said oh. Then Thenchie said, oh I did not now that. How come he was stealing my clothes. Huh. "Stealing your clothes!" said the mother. You didn't tell me he stole your clothers. Then the cops said this is a robber. Then they arrested him. No! I want him to stay with us. Said Thenchie. Her mother refused! thank goodness. But the cops agread with Thenchie. But Thenchie's mother said. He can live in jail. But he can't live here. "He's not going to live in jail." Thenchie said. "Oh yes he is, you shut up. "Said her mother." I was just trying to help. "Said Thenchie. In a crying voice." This is a very serious situation." Said the mother. "I know."Said Thenchie. "It's my decision." Said the mother. "I say he goes out of my house into jail." So the police arrested Tom. And that was that!

KIDS ENJOY EXPLORING IDEAS WITHIN A COMFORTABLE ELECTRONIC ENVIRONMENT

Children's involvement with computer technologies is inherently inter-active. Rather than predetermining the outcome of their efforts, the computer insists that youngsters make their own decisions and choices. Complex computer games and interactive stories are a wonderful preparation for writing, contends William V. Costanzo: "Instead of acquiescing to the images on the screen, viewers could make decisions that affected the outcome of the story. They could create and alter characters, explore various landscapes, take actions that might lead to unexpected situations." For children, "the television tube was no longer just a one-way street."9

Six-year-old Kristina worked on the following story for several days in a row, even staying in at recess to write at the computer:

WOTTS PON A TIM THEIR WAS A INDIN SHEE WOTID A BABY SO SHEE HAD WAN SOON THE HAL TRIB WAS DED BAT THE BABY WAS SAF IN A CAMAFOSHD GRAS KRATL THE TRIB DID BEEKAS AV KLABIS THE BABY GROOWU UP THEIR WAS A BABY WIT PRSIN SHEE WAS DTRMND TO HELP THE BABY TO GROE UP THEAE CCHIT CHADID AND PLADE BAC WRD STIKS AND GIINT SNAKS AND LATRS THEAE HAD EEVIN MAR FON MAKINE BOLS AND BASKIS AND BIG BOLS AND SMOL BOLS THEA MAD A TPE AND HOS THE HOS WAS MAD OWT OV HAE THE INDEEIN TOLD HR THEAT IT LOKT LIK A WIG WOM THE WIT KID MAD WEPINS TO PTEKT THEM THE IN-DEIN DIDIT THEEK THEAE WAD NEED IT BAT THE ATHER I THOT THEAE KAD USITE THE INDEIN GROO FRAM 1 TO 2 TO 3 TO 4 TO 5 TO 6 TO 7 TO 8 TO 9 TO 10 THEN THE BABY WAS FAWD IT GROO FRA 1TO 2 TO3 TO 4 TO 5 TO 6 THEIR MENUE WOS MASHT PTATOS AND KOORN THEAT WAS THE MENUE ON SADA THEIR MENUE FRO MODAE WOS BAFLO AND BENS

Opposite: *Kristina's story* [*Once upon a time there was an Indian. She wanted a baby so she had one. Soon the whole tribe was dead but the baby was safe in a camouflaged grass cradle. The tribe died because of Columbus. The baby grew up. There was a baby white person. She was determined to help the baby grow up. They chitchatted and played Backwards Sticks and Giant Snakes and Ladders. They had even more fun making bowls and baskets and big bowls and small bowls. They made a tepee and house. The house was made out of hay. The Indian told her that it looked like a wigwam. The white kid made weapons to protect them. The Indian didn't think they would need it, but the other one thought they could use it. The Indian grew from 1 to 2 to 3 to 4 to 5 to 6 to 7 to 8 to 9 to 10. Then the baby was found. It grew from 1 to 2 to 3 to 4 to 5 to 6. The menu was mashed potatoes and corn. That was the menu on Sunday. Their menu for Monday was buffalo and beans.*]

AN ELECTRONIC WRITING BOX

Software, the applications and programs that run on your computer, will enable you to create an Electronic Writing Box for your family. There are computer versions of most writing materials. Using a computer, your child can:

- write (word processing)
- publish (desktop publishing)
- draw and paint (graphics)
- store and retrieve information (databases)
- design (LOGO)
- compose (music)
- share writing with others (telecommunications)
- have fun with language (learning games)

You will not have to teach the computer to your child. Children learn about technology rapidly and easily when there are opportunities to play and explore with machines. Children get involved with activities that are real or important to them. For instance, a child who is writing stories or poems may want to see how the computer lets him publish them in a "big book" format. Similarly, a youngster working on a science or math project may want to use a computer-generated graph to record the results of her experiments.

Unfortunately, much commercially advertised children's software consists mainly of drill activities: memorizing words, letters, or numbers. Despite some colorful graphics and intriguing sound effects, these programs may be of limited value to children. While such programs provide ready-made exercises for kids, they seldom encourage creativity or extended use. They quickly become obsolete and uninspiring.

Rather than relying on prepackaged material, equip your computer with basic application programs that allow you and your child to perform multiple functions in open-ended, creative ways. Expensive software is not a prerequisite for using a computer at home. Invent your own uses. Get your child involved in doing something real with the machine. Perhaps she wants to publish her stories or create a journal of summer activities. Show her how computers can help her draw and write something she wants to do in a special, exciting way.

Most of the ideas and activities described in earlier chapters can be adapted to the information-processing features of a computer. Create electronic journals, diaries, stories, notes, signs, maps, games, and many other paper and pencil activities. Your child can bring back material for rereading, revising and editing, or printing in a different format. Some material can become part of another project by using the cut-and-paste editing function. You might even conduct a group project on the computer instead of on paper, if you choose to; all it requires is a word-processing program. Other programs let you draw, graph, compose music, or play writing-reading games. Explore these uses together and design your own writing projects. For instance, drawings, charts, or graphs can be part of a story or child-made game.

Such an open-ended approach to the computer uses the machine as an information-processing source. This will generate a tremendous amount of language learning. Your child will be inspired to search out knowledge for her own communication purposes. Plus she will learn valuable keyboarding skills and practice hand-eye coordination when using the mouse or paint programs.

Your software choices will determine the kind of learning experiences your child has with a home computer. Programs that are interactive and less tightly structured let children put together their ideas in many different ways. Then writing and drawing is not just a matter of getting the right answer or a high score. To guide you in designing your own Electronic Writing Box, we offer examples of software for each of the basic applications available for your system. There are versions of many of these programs for the major computer platforms: Apple 2s, Macintosh, IBMs, and IBM-compatible (or MS-DOS) machines. Reviews and ratings of 447 software programs for three- to seven-year-olds are available in a *Survey of Early Childhood Software*, from High/Scope Press.

Word Processing

Word processing lets a child write on the computer, store it on a disk, and print the writing. It also allows a child to edit text on the screen and write different versions of the same piece. In this sense the computer serves as a powerful typewriter and electronic filing cabinet. Many word-processing programs include a built-in spell check, dictionary, and thesaurus.

- *Muppet Slate* (Sunburst): A large-letter word processor with pictures. Ages five to seven.
- *Bank Street Writer*: A popular word-processing program that is also used in many schools. Versions available for Apple 2s and MS-DOS machines (Scholastic, Broderbund, or Spinnaker). Age seven and older.
- *ESL Writer* (Scholastic): Word processor for school-aged children who speak Spanish or Asian languages. Age six and older.

Talking word processors with synthesized voice systems link spoken and written language in exciting ways for young children. *Dr. Peet's Talk/ Writer* and *My Words* (Hartley Courseware) let children hear the letters and words they are writing. Using language software, children can edit the speech, create a bank of familiar words, and play back entire stories for friends and parents. Computerized speech is still being developed. Improved technology will soon enable machines to reproduce human language even more realistically and in so doing will open up many more possibilities for connecting listening, reading, and writing.[10]

Integrated software programs combine several applications in one package: word processing, databases, spreadsheets, graphics, and telecommunications. Widely available integrated programs include *Microsoft Works* for the Macintosh (Microsoft); *Appleworks 3.0* and *Appleworks GS* for the Apple 2s (Claris); and *Word Perfect* (Word Perfect) or *PFS First Choice* (Software Publishing) for IBM and IBM-compatible machines.

Desktop Publishing

Desktop publishing gives children the capacity to share their writing in many different and interesting ways.[11]

- *The New Print Shop* (Broderbund): A versatile tool for a range of printing options including signs, posters, cards, book covers, announcements, and calendars. Age five and older.
- *Cotton Tales* (MindPlay): Word lists and picture lists that help children to write rebus books. Age four to eight.
- *Kidwriter* (Queue): Create computerized storybooks with captioned pictures to go with the child's storyline. More options and electronic images can be found in *Kidwriter Golden Edition*, by the same company. Ages six to ten.
- *The Newsroom* and *The Newsroom Pro* (Queue): Two columns for headlines, text, and pictures on the same page to use with family newspapers and other publications. Age six and older.
- *The Children's Writing & Publishing Center* (The Learning Company): Word processing, pictures, and page design for children to use in editing, illustrating, and publishing their writing. Age seven to twelve.

Graphics

Graphics software will extend your child's interest by using the computer for drawing and art. With a computer it is possible to draw on the screen virtually anything a child can draw with paper and pencil. Graphics include draw and paint programs; desktop publishing software that lets you create banners, signs, and posters; and graphing and mapmaking applications. Clip art, which allows you to cut and paste computer-generated pictures, is also part of graphics.[12]

- *Color Me* (Mindscape): Drawing and painting for children as young as three years old.
- *Color 'n' Canvas* (Wings for Learning): Introductory drawing program with colors and an artist's toolbox that includes mathematical figures. Age four and older.
- *Kid Pix* (Broderbund): A drawing program for the Macintosh that features sound, talking English and Spanish alphabets, a Wacky Brush with twenty-eight different effects, and other creative, enticing features. Ages three to nine.
- *DazzleDraw* (Broderbund): An excellent drawing program for elementary-grade youngsters. Ages six to nine.
- *MacDraw* and *MacDraw II* (Claris): Create and manipulate pictures on the Macintosh. Age seven and older.

LOGO

LOGO is a computer language that lets children tell the computer to do different activities by using a combination of printed instructions and graphics. Problem-solving strategies are a key part of this activity. Children must devise their own sequence of commands to make a computer-generated turtle draw squares, triangles, and circles on the screen. With LOGO, children are computer programmers: They decide what the machine will do rather than react to whatever comes next in a computer game or electronic storybook. Many educators believe this kind of open-ended use of computers greatly enhances children's discovery learning and conceptual thinking.

EZ LOGO (MECC) is a good program for youngsters four and older. Also see *PC LOGO* (Harvard Associates) and *LOGO Writer* (Logo Computer Systems) for older children.

Databases

A *database* is a computerized way to store, retrieve, and manipulate information. Using a database, a young writer can assemble information for just about any writing project, from science and social studies to music and math.

- *Easy Calc* (Grolier): Spreadsheet program specifically designed for young children starting school.
- *Timeliner* (Tom Snyder Productions): Create your own timelines to see personal and historical connections. Great for writing about time travel, family history, and alternative futures. Timelines of science-technology, dinosaurs, and children's literature are also available. *MacTimeliner* allows you to include graphics and merge timelines on a Macintosh. Age seven and older.
- *Instant Survey* (MECC): Children can do their own surveys and generate frequency counts, bar graphs, and other information from the data. *Instant Survey Sampler* provides already designed surveys for youngsters to adapt. Age seven and older.
- *PFS: Graph* (Scholastic): Display information pictorially on graphs. Age eight and older.

Music

You can purchase a *music-processing program* that does for musical notes what word-processing programs do for letters and words. Children write music on the computer and hear what they have written. Most computers "are capable of playing full chords and multiple melodies. Some music applications turn the PC [personal computer] into a jukebox that plays a selection of tunes. . . . Other applications let you write your own music, in some cases by drawing notes on a musical staff on the screen."[13] An MIDI interface is necessary to connect the computer to a keyboard.

- *Sticky Bear Music* and *Sticky Bear Music Library* (Weekly Reader Software): The Sticky Bears music program for young children. Age five and older.
- *The Music Studio* (Mediagenic) and *Jam Session* (Broderbund): Use the computer to play notes and riffs in various musical styles. Age seven and older.

Telecommunications

A *modem* connects one computer to another through regular telephone lines. Once on-line a child can send electronic messages to friends' machines, access electronic "bulletin boards" to read and respond to questions and messages from other computer modem users, or search for books in a library. *Kids Network*, set up by the National Geographic Society, provides a way to share results of home science experiments using electronic mail. The phone number is 1-800-342-4460.

Learning Games

No home computer system is complete without a *library of learning games* for children to play. Most children know about video and computer games like Nintendo, which allows them to manipulate the action on the screen through a series of commands and countercommands. In addition, there are educational games of just about every type and description, from action and adventure programs to software that focuses on building specific skills like problem-solving of analytical thinking. And as children play games, they have a basis for oral storytelling and potential topics for writing.

Some adults assume that children spend too much time with computers or electronic video games while learning little that is useful. Sherry Turkle refers to this as the "myth of mindless addiction." Computers are stimulating and exciting learning environments that, when used sensibly and appropriately, can promote children's creativity and imagination. The games used most often by kids are those that are playful, interesting, and open-ended. Because they allow many possible outcomes, they are not usually played the same way twice. Children learn from the variety of puzzles and challenges they get to solve each time.

Some stimulating learning games for young children, arranged from younger to older, follow:

- *The Playroom* (Broderbund): Explore a room full of objects with activities for counting, clocks, letters, and the alphabet. Ages three to six.
- *Reading Magic Library* (Tom Snyder Productions): Interactive computer storybooks that let a reader choose what happens next. Age five and older.
- *Windham Classics* (Queue): Adventure games that let a child play the part of a lead character from *Wizard of Oz*, *Treasure Island*, *Swiss*

Family Robinson, Alice in Wonderland, or *Below the Root.* Age five and older.

- *Stone Soup* (William K. Bradford): Create original versions of the Stone Soup stories, plus a treasure hunt and a puppet kit. Age five and older.
- *The Oregon Trail* (MECC): Problems and issues faced by settlers on a wagon train in the 1840s. Age eight and older.
- *Where in the World Is Carmen Sandiego?* (Broderbund): Traveling around the world on the computer, the child uses accompanying almanacs and encyclopedias along with logical thinking to find the clues needed to capture members of Carmen Sandiego's gang of criminals. Other games in the series include *Where in the USA Is Carmen Sandiego?*, *Where in Time Is Carmen Sandiego?*, and *Where in Europe Is Carmen Sandiego?* Carmen Sandiego's adventures are featured on public-television stations and available in book form. Age eight and older.

Challenging Children's Stereotypes

Obviously, computer games can become too much of a good thing for some children. Parents should establish an appropriate framework for a child's use of computer games. As you introduce computer technology into your family be aware that:

- Many computer games portray violence and present stereotypes.
- Gender differences persist with regard to children's computer use in schools.

VIOLENCE AND STEREOTYPES

Violence and racial and gender stereotypes are inherent features of many computer programs. Some depict a simplistic good-versus-evil game of searching out and destroying aliens, monsters, or other enemies. The message children can receive from these games is that violence is an acceptable response to situations they do not like. Researchers have suggested that sustained exposure to violent media dulls a viewer's sense of reality and compassion. Many of the same games also perpetuate the racial and gender stereotypes found in other media: minorities and women are rarely seen as heroes or problem-solvers whose actions should be emulated in real life.

Research about the impact of television viewing on young audiences tells us that the best way to minimize potentially harmful messages to children is not to try to ban the programs but to watch and discuss them with your youngster. The goal is to develop your child's critical viewing skills. Simply saying "no" provides a child with little information with which to assess what is on the screen.

Play computer games with your child to acquire information from which to explain your point of view about the content of the material and to help your child analyze what is on the screen. This way children learn to recognize the hidden messages in the material and develop criteria from which to make choices about personal values and ideas.

GENDER DIFFERENCES

Pervasive and powerful gender differences in how children use technology will persist unless adults recognize and counter those underlying patterns. From an early age girls spend less time than boys using computers for play and learning. When children enter school, girls lag behind boys in math and science and their use of technology if teachers fail to actively support and expect participation by both genders. "Two out of every three students currently learning about computers are boys," estimates educator Michael W. Apple.[14]

An early reluctance to play with and learn about technology can dramatically influence life choices for men and women. The implication, as Apple suggests, is that young women will learn about word processing and other clerical uses of machines in business courses, while young men will acquire math and programming skills as a foundation for higher-paying careers in technological occupations.

As a parent you face what one expert has called a "computers-are-for-males syndrome" in male-oriented games, advertisements, television programs, and many school activities.[15] In your interactions with children,

* provide access to computers and opportunities for open-ended play on the machine for girls;
* counter widely held assumptions about gender roles or the pre-

sumptions that certain careers or opportunities are appropriate mainly for women or men;

- promote use of the computer for writing, reading, math, history, and science activities by girls; and
- ensure that girls have many opportunities to see how machines work and to think electronically.

Adult attitudes are often products of long-held beliefs that attribute technological skills to males (and then to only a small number of them). Men are not inherently more technologically gifted than women or better able to perform math, science, or mechanically related activities. Home computers may generate occasions for adults to overcome their own assumptions and fears about technical things while exploring the use of technology in creativity and communication for all ages. Using computers for many different purposes—along with playing Nintendo and watching TV programs together with children—may open new ways to incorporate the power of media to generate positive learning without perpetuating negative messages.

CHAPTER

9

Introducing Conventions of Print

One day Kyle, then five and a half, decided he would rather stay home than accompany his mother on a trip to the store. He asked if she would get him batteries for his toy car and a special surprise he had earned. "I'll write you a list," he volunteered happily.

After getting paper and a pencil, Kyle told her what he wanted to write and asked her how to spell the words. "Write it the way you want to," his mother replied—her standard answer to his questions about spelling.

For the first time in two years of writing he balked at her suggestion, declaring "You won't be able to read it then!"

What a compelling statement about his knowledge Kyle had made! Creating a list for his mother to take to the store without him was clearly very important. Understanding that particular arrangements of letters form words, he wanted to get them spelled correctly. Otherwise, he reasoned, she would not find the exact items that he wanted.

These were new ideas about written language for Kyle. In kindergarten he was writing books in invented spelling. His mother showed him one of his stories in invented spelling and said she could read his list for the store just as she had read his other writing.

"That was for play," he protested. "This is for real. Now are you going to help me?"

Kyle's request illustrates opportunities for parents to assist children with spelling or other writing conventions. He knew that standard spelling was important to his writing in order to make his wishes clear to his mom. To insist that he do it by himself would have been counterproductive to his desire to write. At the same time, providing correct spelling every time stands in the way of a youngster freely expressing ideas about many different topics. When children feel that every word must be correct, then they will use only the words they know.

How, then, do parents assist children in learning about the alphabet, spelling, handwriting, and punctuation marks within a writing process framework? Frustration or a constant pressure to "get it right" will block a child's enthusiasm. A writing process fit for a child continually opens up new avenues of expression and learning that parents and children enjoy together. *Play does the teaching.* Keep activities joyful and supportive, and connect them with children's interests. As one mother told us, "Make something fun to do and children will come to it naturally."

USING THE ALPHABET

The alphabet is an appropriate place to begin introducing children to the conventions of writing. Letters surround them: in the environment, books and magazines, television ads, toys and gifts, and in the oft-sung alphabet song. Combine what children see with what they hear by displaying alphabets in your home and in your child's Writing Box and talking about letters regularly in conversations with your child.

Alphabet activities can last from a moment to minutes. Whenever the child evidences interest, play with letter names and sounds. Games and activities are not meant to be memory contests. Their point is to make it possible for children to become aware of these meaningful symbols. Parents who make a child's learning of sounds, words, or spelling into a contest of "how much can you learn and how fast can you do it" will achieve the opposite results. Children may back away from such learning situations if they are afraid of being wrong. Fear of making mistakes will limit what learning occurs at home.

Alphabet Charts

Many different alphabet charts are available: from the very large to the very small, colorful or black and white, with letters only or with pictures. Displaying different charts throughout the home stimulates a child's comparison of their features and provides a springboard for conversations about letters and words.

Place alphabets where children spend time: preferably at their eye level next to a changing table, a bed, a crib or playpen, a bathtub, or on a placemat for meals and snacks. Laminating the charts or covering them with clear contact paper keeps them clean and tear-proof.

Create your own alphabet chart or book with your child by drawing, painting, or cutting pictures from magazines. Make it long enough to go around the walls of a room or small enough to hang on the refrigerator. Change it every six months to add variety and have fun playing with letters. Mary Kitagawa told us that her mother had made each grandchild a personalized alphabet book using family photos for as many letters as possible and the names of children's pets and stuffed toys.

You might enjoy making a paper alphabet quilt with pockets. Each of the twenty-six pockets has a letter on it and an object inside it whose name begins with that letter. Magazine pictures or drawings can be taped onto popsicle sticks or backed with cardboard to slip into the pockets. A commercial version of an alphabet quilt made of cloth is available from Pockets of Learning.

Alphabet Activities

The following alphabet activities are easy and invite your child to ask and talk about letters. Each one introduces letter names, letter sounds, and concepts about words.

- Sing the alphabet song
- Read alphabet books.
- Use a chart or an alphabet book to point to the letters as you sing songs.
- Post your child's name underneath the alphabet chart or on labels

of other objects: Kirsten's chair, Kirsten's bookcase, Kirsten's mailbox, Kirsten's toys.

- Put magnetic letters on the refrigerator or other appliances.
- Display mail at child-height so a child can examine it often.
- Carry a small alphabet book in the car or in a bag. Your child can look through it by herself or with you, at the grocery store, or doctor's office, or any place you go.
- Keep an alphabet chart in the car where your child can see it: on the back of the front seat or on the door near her.

Letter Identification

Display your child's name on a paper or card on the refrigerator and put the magnetic letters that spell her name in random order underneath it. At some point she will arrange the magnetic letters in the order that spells her name. To assist the process, place one or two letters underneath the same letters on her name card. She will arrange other letters underneath the corresponding letters on the card.

When she is familiar with putting the letters in the order of her name, add your name, siblings' names, or other words to the refrigerator. For instance, "Kirsten" and "kitty" could be displayed with their magnetic letters. After putting them in order, you and your child can sing the letter names while pointing to the letters: *K-I-R-S-T-E-N* spells "Kirsten"; *K-I-T-T-Y* spells "kitty." To vary the game, continually change the words. Don't comment till she asks, "What is that word?"

By keeping a chalkboard close by, you or your child can copy the words from the refrigerator and, as a supplementary activity, name the letters or sing the spelling as you write. To help your child in forming the letters, let her trace over yours or let her play with writing by herself. She can also paint the letters on the chalkboard with a paintbrush and water for a different treat.

The following games also introduce letters:

- Keep a set of alphabet cookie cutters, to use with Play Doh or to bake real cookies.
- Buy or make alphabet puzzles for upper and lower case letters.

- Try to locate all twenty-six letters in the alphabet on signs or in environmental print while traveling. Write a list of those you find.
- While traveling, look around and try to identify objects that start like each of your names. *K* for "Kirsten," *M* for "Mommy," *J* for "Jeannie" (Mommy's real name), *D* for "Daddy," *S* for "Steve" (Daddy's real name).
- Make an alphabet version of Go Fish by printing four cards for each capital and lower-case letter. Play with the cards for just three or four letters. Use all capitals, all lower case, or both.

Letter Sounds

An alphabet quilt with movable objects offers playful ways to introduce letter sounds. Take the objects out of their pockets two or three at a time and sing, "*D, D* for the doggie, doggie. *M, M* for the moon, moon." Putting the phrases into a melody helps your child recall the animals or objects that correspond with each letter and its sound. Sing the phrases when you are riding or doing errands and the quilt is not in front of you.

Play a "Where's Your Home?" game by switching pockets for one, two, or several of the objects. Then say, "No, no, moon. You go to *m*." Your child will begin playing the game by herself, asking you to find what she has switched to put them back where they should be.

A version of the refrigerator game with magnetic letters is useful. Write two words on cards that begin or end with the same letter. Display the cards and place the magnetic letters underneath them. With your child's assistance, arrange the letters in the correct order. Point out what you see and hear in the pairs: Peter and piano, mommy and milk, or hat and coat:

- "Look, they both begin with *M*, *mmm*, 'Mommy,' 'milk,' *mmm*."
- "They both end in *T*, *ttt*, 'coat,' 'hat,' *ttt*."

Play a "Hunt for Sounds" game throughout your house or outside. Look for things that begin or end with a particular sound. Jot down a list of things that you find on your hunt. Show your child the list of all the words.

Adapt an idea from Montessori that kids really like. Collect small objects to organize into plastic cups or the small drawers of a nut and bolt sorter case sold in hardware and department stores. Put a letter on each cup or drawer and, as you find objects that begin with the letter sound, add them to the appropriate container for sorting and play.

SPELL THE WAY YOU CAN

Spelling is an emotional and divisive issue in American education today. Employers lament the misspellings they find on job applications and work reports. College teachers wonder why students' papers contain so many errors. Hearing these complaints, parents expect children to achieve error-free performance in school. Teachers, feeling pressure to ensure that students succeed on tests, spend considerable amounts of class time having their students practice correctness. Many adults assume that performance would be worse if homes and schools allowed children to use their own inventions. In order to make sense of these concerns, and the central role of invented spelling in children's writing development, it is necessary to debunk some widely held myths.

MYTH NUMBER ONE: THE BEST SPELLERS ARE THOSE WHO CAN COMMIT WORDS TO MEMORY FOR A WEEKLY TEST
Not all children who succeed on tests in school will spell the same words correctly in their daily writing. Parents and teachers see this repeatedly. Considering the small number of children who regularly receive 100 percent grades, and realizing that not all of them will remember the spellings consistently, one must ask if adults are accomplishing enough in the quest to teach standard spelling through rote memorization. Children who are successful spellers remember words accurately in many situations.

MYTH NUMBER TWO: SPELLING IS A SPECIAL TALENT
Most of us cannot spell every word conventionally, no matter how quickly or well we learn other things. This is why homes and offices have dictionaries and computers and typewriters have spell checkers. These devices are designed to allow writers to concentrate on communicating their ideas first and fixing their spelling afterward. Spelling proficiency develops as children have authentic writing that they want to do, use their own

versions of language, and receive support, not criticism, from adults. Successful spellers have an incentive to remember correct arrangements of letters just as other youngsters recall batting averages, countries of the world, or names of birds and animals. Children want to spell correctly, and they learn that misspellings can be corrected through their own use of strategies or with assistance.

MYTH NUMBER THREE: EDUCATIONAL ACCOMPLISHMENT IS MEASURED BY HOW WELL A PERSON SPELLS

The notion that the measure of how well schooled people are can be assessed by the accuracy of their spelling is not true. Neither private school education, prominence in the public forum, nor socioeconomic status guarantees spelling facility. In 1991 President George Bush gave his wife an electronic hand-held thesaurus and speller for her birthday. An inveterate campaigner for literacy education, Barbara Bush admitted that she does not spell accurately and added that neither does her husband. Some very successful people are not accurate spellers, and that includes those who write for a living: The author F. Scott Fitzgerald once submitted a manuscript to his editor with hundreds of spelling errors in the text.

Franklin Learning Resources produces the Speaking Ace, a small handheld dictionary and spell-checker with a voice mechanism. Children can type in phonetic spellings or strings of letters that the machine reads back to them. Then the spell-checker suggests a list of words that may be correct and reads each one so that a child can find the word he or she is writing.

Youngsters' ways of spelling reflect their knowledge at a given moment. In order to write, young children need the assurance that they can convey their own ideas in their own ways without having to spell the way grownups or older siblings do. Expressing their curiosity, receiving answers to their questions, and enjoying print are the experiences that teach youngsters about words and written language. Knowledge of spelling evolves from these experiences.

Cues are Clues to Spelling

Although people of all ages use a dictionary or thesaurus, many parents and teachers assume that children's spelling mistakes must be quickly corrected in order to avert permanent habits of incorrect spelling. This notion does not consider how children learn, their capabilities with invented spelling, and the findings of researchers who have studied children's spelling development.

Spelling conventionally—writing words with accuracy and knowing by looking whether an arrangement of letters is correct or not—is attained through a combination of knowing the sounds of letters, how arrangements of letters create patterns, remembering how words look when spelled correctly, and which spelling of a word fits a context, "sea" or "see." These are the cues we all use to spell.

Like other parts of a child's writing process, spelling follows a progression from invention to convention. It is part of the experimentation and learning that youngsters do naturally. As they create their own texts and observe print, they wonder about how to make sense of the ways in which words are spelled. A kindergartner who invented a spelling of the word "lunch" early one morning stood in the cafeteria line at noon and exclaimed aloud, "So that's how it's spelled!" as he stared at the word on the wall menu board. His curiosity initiated a search for the word where he thought it might be.

Researchers of spelling development explain that young children's inventions reflect their knowledge of written language.[1] They produce rule-governed spelling—although their rules are not necessarily the same as adults'. For example, in her story titled "The Skunk Eating My Dolly," a six-year-old wrote the following line [And when we got dressed, we went to the mall.]:

And wan we gat gasa we wat to the mall.

Seeing "gasa" for "dressed," one might assume that she could not hear most of the sounds in the word or that she did not know which letters usually represent them. This, however, is not the case.

To begin to understand how youngsters decide on invented spellings, try this experiment. Say "gym" and then "dress," slowly two or three times. Feel where you place your tongue to produce the beginning sound of each word. You place it in the same spot at the front of your mouth to pronounce both. The difference between the two words is the amount of pressure exerted.[2] This young writer heard the beginning *d* sound.

Either *d* or *g* seemed appropriate choices according to where she placed her tongue to produce the beginning of the word.

What happened in the rest of the word? She heard the *s* sound and wrote *s*, rather than the soft *c* to represent it. Her pronunciation, influenced by missing front teeth, might account for not using *t* or *d* to make the last sound in "dressed." It is also possible that she may have been trying to make the word look like an English spelling—another common strategy. Not knowing the correct letters, she may have used *a* in the spot where other letters would most likely appear in the standard spelling.

In the rest of the sentence, she uses standard spellings of most words. *W* and *t* are the accurate beginning and ending letters of "went." *A* appears to be a "placeholder," which fills the space where she knows other letters should be. Her invention reflects her knowledge of sounds and English spelling patterns. Her reasoning is typical of youngsters who associate sounds with letters, have visual memory of words seen elsewhere, and are willing to take risks in creating a spelling. Children see standard spelling as they read and observe print, and their own spelling reflects their growing understanding of English rules. This youngster's writing evolved over a seven-month period, from wavy lines that loosely resembled adult script, to strings of letters without sound associations, to a combination of invented and conventional spelling.

Spelling in English is not accomplished simply by knowing letter sounds. Many letters in words are silent, and many sounds require combinations of two or more letters. Children see discrepancies between their own spelling and book spelling and are sometimes stymied by it. Figuring out spelling using letter sounds is challenging enough, but trying to figure out where and when to add silent letters is positively perplexing. A child's use of silent letters produces surprising results. A youngster who learned about the silent *k* in front of words such as "knee" spelled his friend's name "DAKNE" (Danny).

Because the evolution of spelling knowledge is ongoing, children's rules for inventing their spellings expand with their use of language in writing and reading. Older children usually do not use the tongue-placement strategy for spelling. They sometimes relate words by context and function: "clothit" is an invention of "closet," explained by the fact that clothes are put in closets. "Cloughs" for "clothes" is derived from knowing that "close" would not be correct, but perhaps a version of the

"-ough" spelling might be. Using conventionally spelled words to create unknown spellings is another strategy, as in "knowtes'd" for "noticed."

Our experience, as well as that of many others, has shown that invented spelling assists rather than confuses children's acquisition of conventional spelling. When kids create and talk about their spellings, they know that they are inventing. This realization increases their propensity to want to know how to spell conventionally. As they begin to read and recognize words in print, they compare their inventions with conventional spellings. They ask "How close am I?" meaning how similar is theirs to standard spelling? Children's interest has a greater chance of remaining strong when spelling is not equated solely with memorizing a list of words for a test each week.

HOW CHILDREN INVENT SPELLING

Given access to writing materials and consistent adult encouragement and support, young writers will try some or all of the following invented spelling experiences. As you examine them, bear in mind, as Marie Clay has observed: "Children of very different ages can be seen doing similar things in preschool writing. There do not seem to be set sequences through which each child must pass."[3] And this is true of school-aged children as well.

Strings of Letters

A youngster brought his story, composed of a ten-letter string, to read aloud to Sharon. She wrote what he said quickly in script, so she would not forget it. When he saw how much she was writing, he took his paper back to his table with the comment "Not enough letters," and he added some more.

As youngsters are able to form letters, their first spellings are represented by short or long strings of letters. Their choices may represent one word or several. They may use the characters they know how to make most easily, which are often those in their name, as in this letter by Kyle to Bob:

Kyle's letter at five years old [Big Bob's Birthday Blow-up. Open the door and you will have a party.]

Standard Spellings of Some Words

A child's name or a known word—"Mom," "Dad," "dog"—may be the first standard spelling to appear in writing. As youngsters recognize and remember standard spellings of names or words, they include these with their inventions, as in Kayla's note to Sharon:

DEAR M2.EDN

I-AM- NAT-GOING-TO-BE-HAR
TOMIRD BELAR I AM GOING
TO MI DAD IFZ 2₀ I
HOPE YOU ARE HA V
FUN

LOVE KAYLA

Six-year-old Kayla's note [Dear Ms. Edwards, I am not going to be here tomorrow because I am going to my Dad's office. So I hope you are having fun. Love, Kayla]

Spellings Are Invented

Debra Jacobsen told us how her four-year-old niece was experiencing great enjoyment from telling aunts, uncles, and older cousins that she knew how to spell "school." Proudly, she would announce the letters. Listening intently, her aunt asked how she thought "Debra" would be spelled. "Q-R-P-M-V," replied the youngster with a giggle. They laughed, and Debra inquired, "If you were writing me a letter, how would you write my name?" "Oh, D-B," said her niece.

Children use consonants and vowels to represent words. How they decide which letters to write is influenced by one or more of these criteria: sounds they hear in words; the position of their tongue when saying the word; making their invention look like an English spelling; using spellings they know to construct others. Letters represent one or more sounds or words. For instance, "DT" might mean "don't" or "do not touch."

One letter of a word may correspond to a sound in that word and be followed or surrounded by other letters that have no correspondence to other sounds in the word.

Jessenia's spelling of "tiger" [*TEIKGFYA*]

Most or all of the letters may correspond to sounds in the words, as they do in this sign [Errol and Sandy's house. Do not touch.]:

Errols ad Sandys hs dntch

and in these words:

"DABL" is **"double"**
"ALOGATR" is **"alligator"**
"SUPR KERYR" is **"supercarrier"**

Some letters represent sounds that children add as they say words aloud and stretch the sounds as they spell them. Youngsters are unaware that they are doing this. In his story "The Milas Go Soayming" ["The Milas Go Swimming"], Tobin stretched the words "swimming" and "swam" as he said them and added extra sounds as he wrote [Once upon a time, the Milas found a pool. So the Milas swam and jumped off the diving board.]:

Waos apoon a time the Milas foaad a paool So the Milas saoaom and jumpt off the daiving baord

Tongue placement to make initial sounds affects spelling. A few letters are produced in such a way that the position of the tongue is virtually the same for both. These letters are used interchangeably in invented spellings: *T, D, CH, J*. One youngster wrote [Why do you call a tree trunk a trunk? Because it's related to an elephant.]:

Way do you cal a tchree tchak a tchak be kas it's reeladid to a elafit

Missing teeth affect spelling also [Fernando is going to search for his shoes today.]:

Fernando is going to srch for heth shoth today

Trying to create plausible spellings in English influences children's inventions. As they begin to read words and recognize spelling patterns, they develop a sense of what looks right in English. Although their approximations of these patterns are not exact, incorrect letters are used as placeholders to make spellings look appropriate:

"OAN" is "one"
"FANY" is "funny"
"RADASHS" is "radishes"
"SYCRAT" is "secret"

Children use conventional spellings of words they know to make spellings of other words:

"THUNDER MRS. YOU" is "Thunder [the family dog] misses you" [uses MRS.]
"TRTALL" is "turtle" [uses ALL]
"ORDOR" is "order" [uses OR]

Some inventions are easier to read than others. Adults recognize approximations of the words with the help of the context and a child's spelling that matches sounds with expected letters. The following message shows separation of words with lines and the inclusion of some standard spelling. This youngster understands that the same words are spelled the same way whenever he sees them, so however he invents a spelling is the way he writes the same word again in his text [A little frog on a log and a turtle on a log. Their log was their house.]:

A-LIT-TALL-FROG

ON-A-LOG-AN

A-TRTALL

ON-A-LOG

DAR-LOG

WAS-DAR

HOWS

Invented Spellings in Other Languages

We have seen children writing in invented spelling in one language compose this way in their other languages as well. Children in Sharon's classes have written in invented spelling in Polish, German, French, Spanish, Portuguese, Korean, Farsi, and Japanese. Many write to relatives and friends. One boy initiated invented spelling writing in Polish to send letters to his grandmothers. His mother told us that "he has written a lot of letters to Poland. We don't ask him to write the letters. He does it himself." Here are two other examples:

LIBE KATHI

DANKA FÜR DAS BUCH ICH GABRAU CH ES VIEL

MIT LIBE,

VON EVELYN

[*Dear Kathi, Thanks for the book. I use it a lot. With love, from Evelyn*]

MAMI,

GO CIERO CE ME DES SNAK

PATRICIA

Patricia's note to her mother in Spanish [Mami, yo quiero que deme de snack. / I want you to give me a snack. Patricia]

Another youngster used his knowledge of sounds in English to help him learn the sounds of symbols in Korean, his first language.

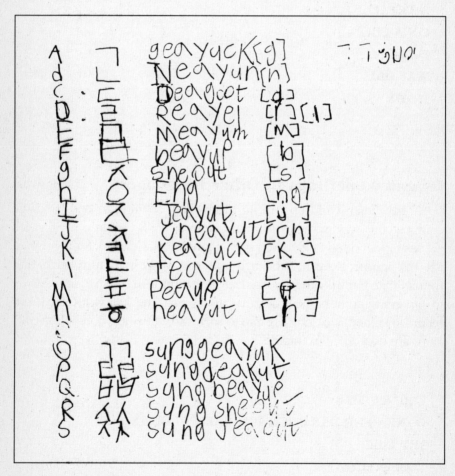

Six-year-old Juhwan's Korean sounds dictionary

ASSISTING YOUR CHILD WITH SPELLING

"What do I do when my child requests help with spelling?"

This question has no single correct answer. Many different responses are useful when a child asks for assistance. If parents have a choice of strategies and are willing to switch quickly from one to another, then spelling does not become an argument but a pleasant learning opportunity for both of you.

Why is this so?

Assisting children with spelling involves a balancing act between encouraging a youngster to take risks and providing information to her about letters and words. Sensing both independence and support, children will write by themselves and ask for spelling when they want to know it. Without a sense of being able to write for themselves, kids will have little reason to experiment and become confident about what they can do. Their writing will include only words they know how to spell. For adults, the issue is focusing on the process of supporting children's discoveries and helping them answer their questions. Kids want to know conventional spelling, but they need to learn according to their own timetable in order not to be overwhelmed and confused.

To give your child a feeling of independence with print and answer questions about spelling, we suggest a variety of strategies.

Encourage Children's Invented Spellings

Encouraging children to use their own spelling inventions enables them to develop a system for spelling, notes researcher Sandra Wilde.[4] The thinking that children do when creating their own rationales for spelling is important. Considering, comparing, and deciding are all involved in creating a spelling system. These same skills help them figure out that there are rules of standard spelling in any language and help them to identify what these are.

There are many choices for encouraging your youngster to write his own way when he asks you to spell something. One is to assure him that any way he spells the word is fine:

- "Write it your way. I like to know how you figure out spelling."
- "You're a writer who uses his own spellings. I like seeing you do that."

Clarifying questions may assist his efforts to spell his own way:

- "Say that word. What sounds do you hear?"
- "What letter do you think makes that sound?"

These questions are deliberately phrased to ask about a child's knowledge and thinking, not about a correct answer. Clarifying questions give you the opportunity to understand a child's system. By contrast, "What letter makes that sound?" or "What letter says *buh*?" imply a correct answer that an adult knows but a child may not.

You have many options in your replies to your child's answers. If your child names a letter other than the one that makes the sound he is trying to spell, you are not compelled to correct him at that moment. It is appropriate to say "Write that down" in situations where his enthusiasm for the project, his hurry to finish and do something else, or his feeling of competence as a writer are more important than telling him the correct sound. You might decide instead to play with that letter sound later by finding it in an alphabet book at reading time or looking around the room to locate all of the things that start with that letter, making a game of the experience.

Sometimes answering a question directly is the most appropriate response. If he is confused about two letters and asks "Is a *t* or a *d* in that word?" or "Is *c* the right letter?" it is possible to reply to the question and still encourage his choice of spelling:

- "In books that word starts with *t*. You are writing your own spelling, so you decide if you want to use *d* or *t*."
- "*S* is the right letter, but *c* also makes that sound in some words."

In any of these situations, support for his self-image as a writer, confidence, and initiative are the criteria for your reply. You know from his responses to your clarifying questions and from his writing which letter sounds he does not know. Play games with these at other times: while riding in the car, walking together, during bathtime, or reading a story.

Have a Go

Have a Go is a process used by New Zealand and Australian educators that encourages children to try out their own spellings before asking someone for the standard spelling.[5] Youngsters "have a go" at spelling words their own way, sometimes writing two or three different invented spellings of the same word before choosing one. If they want to, they can then check their invented spellings with sources of information about conventional spelling: other children, adults, dictionaries, and printed text.

Looking through a dictionary inspired one six-year-old to begin writing his own. Here is his definition of the word "shooting star" [The shooting star only comes at night. It is a star that goes very high. And if you are lucky you can find one.]:

The shoting star only comse at nihgt. It is a star that gos varye ih. and ifyour licy you can fide one.

Play with a Dictionary or Thesaurus

There are games you can play using a dictionary and, for older children, a thesaurus to support the process of learning spellings. In these games, the dictionary (or the thesaurus) is the rulebook.

WHAT COMES BEFORE? WHAT COMES AFTER?

This is a simple game. If you are enthused and curious about words, children will be too. Think of a word and look it up in the dictionary. Look at the word that comes before and after it. Have you or your child ever heard of either one? Would you ever use either in your conversation? Is there a word that particularly interests you or your youngster that you want to tell to other people? A child's interest in words could be sustained by playing this game once or twice a week.

THAT WORD DOES NOT EXIST!

To assist your child in acquiring a wide vocabulary and to teach what synonyms are, try the game That Word Does Not Exist! Pick a word and pretend that it does not not exist any longer. Think of other words that mean the same thing. After you have listed as many as you can, look in a thesaurus to see if there are any you have missed. Incorporate some of these synonyms into your conversations and look for them in stories that your child writes, reads, or tells.

Support Phonetic Spelling

At some point children want to know if their writing can be read by others, so they ask, "What does this say?" If it is scribbles, squiggles, shapes, or forms other than letters, your response is limited. Admit that you do not know how to read this writing and ask your child to read it to you so you will know what it says. If the text is composed of letters, there are two ways to reply to the question. State that you don't know but would like to know if he would read it to you. Or read the sounds of the letters that he has written. Use these responses interchangeably to introduce different learning experiences for your youngster and to enlarge his knowledge of symbols for both writing and reading.

Reading the letter sounds may initiate all kinds of questions about words, spelling, and symbols, because hearing what the letters create gives clues about the way they form words.[6] It is also a way to enjoy a laugh together if a child thinks the letter sounds are funny. Telling children that you would like to but do not know how to read their writing gives them the power to tell you something that you do not already know. Explain that sometimes children write their ideas and other times they experiment and play. Ask the child if there is a message or a story or if it is for experimenting. This assures that it might be either and that you approve of both. Remind them that as they continue to write and learn about letters, you will be able to read their writing.

If a youngster does not ask you what his letters say, it probably means that he is enjoying his writing and is content with his spelling. It is important to support what he is doing by not intervening. He will ask you when he wants information. To volunteer it before he asks may raise doubts and might take away some of the joy and excitement of inventing written language.

When your child asks you what letter makes a certain sound, occasionally refer to an alphabet chart on display or an alphabet book close by so he sees how to use these references himself. Point out the letter and picture together: " 'Man' starts with the same letter as 'monkey'—*m*."

If your child is attempting to identify more than the beginning consonant sound in a word, try a technique suggested by Lucy Calkins: "Stretch the word like a rubber band so you can hear the sounds. Say it slowly and listen for the different sounds."

Saying a word aloud more slowly than in regular speech sometimes makes it sound as if there are more sounds than there really are. If you are saying it slowly, try not to make "swimm-ing" sound like "suh-wim-ing."

The process of listening and writing, listening again, and writing more is quite a mental feat for a young child. Do not worry about the appearance of extra letters in these spellings. As a child continues to write and learn about spelling, extra letters regularly appear in some words and disappear from others. When a child realizes that silent letters are part of many words, he will add some to his spellings—not always in the correct place and not always the correct letter.

Play with Letter Sounds

In the game *Change-a-Word,* you and your child play with letter sounds by changing a word in as many ways as you can think of together:

end
ending
ends
bend
bends
bending
mending

To start, you or you child writes the chosen word in standard spelling. Then you help your child make changes by answering his questions about what letters to add and delete to make new words. The list of changes can be as few or as many as you have time for. Help your child return to the top of the list and circle the original word all the way through the list of changes.

You might enjoy the game *Invented Spelling Hangman* when your child knows many letter sounds. It is challenging for both an adult and a child. Invented Spelling Hangman is played like regular Hangman. To begin, you or your child thinks of a word, makes a line on the page for each of its letters, and draws a picture like the one below:

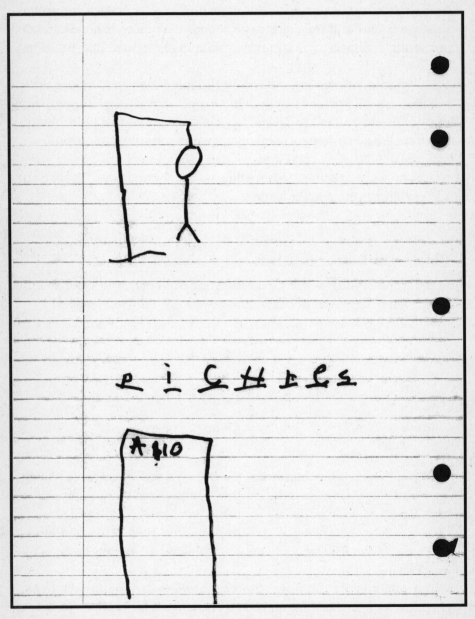

Hangman game with invented spelling of "pichres" [pictures]

Whoever thinks of the word asks the other player to start guessing letters that might be in the word. If the guess is right, the letter is written in its correct spot on the line under the picture. If the guess is wrong, the letter is written at the bottom of the page and a body part is added to the drawing of the hanged man. This game is a race to see if the player guessing letters can figure out the word before the drawing of the hanged man is completed.

Adults must work to figure out a child's invented spelling just as a child seeks to understand an adult's standard spelling. When your child's spelling of "foot" is f-a-t, you will be wrong if you say "fat." Discussing the spellings of words after the game is over adds to your child's knowledge of standard spelling. He can see how close or how far his invented spellings are from the standard spellings of the words.

In order for both of you to enjoy playing this game, your child must know the sounds of the letters, for these are the only clues you and he have to help you figure out what the word might be. If a child uses random letters to spell the words, the game has no clues to help you to make guesses. Give this game a go and find out what it is like to try to guess a word spelled in a child's spelling. Kids love to win, so good luck!

Use Oral Spelling

Oral spelling by parents is a useful way to promote knowledge of conventional spelling. Beginning with some often-used and important words such as "Yes" and "No," you can proceed through many others that your child will also regularly see in print. For example, include a spelling in your reply to a question:

- "*Y-e-s*, you may go outside."
- "*N-o*, Brendan is taking his turn first."

Identify these words in books and text and on signs so your child will recognize them in print. As she is able to spell them, introduce new ones:

- "Stop" or "go": "*S-t-o-p* running in the living room." "It's time to *g-o* to the store!"
- "In" or "out": "Let's go *i-n*." "Let's go *o-u-t*."
- "Mom" or "Dad": "Go ask *M-o-m* if she is ready."
- "cat" or "dog": "The *c-a-t* wants to come in the house."

One youngster used a group of words he had learned from oral spelling to create a story titled "The Days from Heaven."

Today is Friday. Today is Isday. Today is Catday. Today is Stopday. Today is Noday. Today is Inday. Today is Outday.

HANDWRITING

Handwriting enables people to communicate using symbols; legible handwriting makes comprehension easier. It should not be synonymous with writing, however. Writing is the communication of ideas, opinions, and information through pictures, letters, and words. Handwriting need not prevent children from expressing their ideas. Take dictation or tape children's stories. Make children's writing and handwriting two different things.

A great deal of time is usually spent in school having children practice one of many handwriting systems. The intention is that children not struggle to write letters or use extra strokes that make printing awkward or time consuming. Standardization of letter formation is the goal. Yet for all of the time spent practicing standardization, it is a person's unique handwriting that is used in courts of law as a means of identifying individuals.

Handwriting practice should focus on fluidity and ease of letter formation. If a child writes letters from the bottom up, quickly and legibly, without using extra strokes that make formation awkward, do not change it to the usual top-down formation. Certainly a child's handwriting should be legible; it can still have individuality and flair.

Play opportunities that use large and small arm and hand muscles build strength for handwriting. Pushups that babies do when they lie flat on their stomachs and move themselves up to look around and get ready to crawl initiates the beginning of the development of the muscle strength that is necessary for handwriting. Building with small Lego bricks or blocks, forming clay or Play Doh, making sand buildings, and using the thumb and first finger in pincer motions exercise small muscles.

First and foremost, handwriting depends on developing large arm and small hand muscles. When Austin Palmer designed his handwriting method a century ago, he expected that young children would stand, not sit, and that they would write at a board, in large print, to first develop the muscles of the upper arm. It was never his intention that children sit at a table or desk to write in small lines on paper before they strengthened their upper arms. Yet that is the way handwriting is taught today.

To help a child develop fluidity of motion with handwriting, hang a chalkboard or large piece of paper on a wall for practicing letters. Colored chalk or water for "paint" on the chalkboard, felt-tip markers or tempera paint for the paper are inviting ways to practice forming letters. The handwriting of all six children in one family we know draws compliments from other people. The large chalkboard that they had in their home is credited with developing each one's handwriting. No one asked them to practice, experiment, or write, but the chalkboard itself was fun to use and usually full of writing.

Handwriting reversals produce anxiety in some educators and parents who wonder whether a child is manifesting some kind of learning disability because of backward letter formation. Many children write letters backwards and some continue to do so for a long time. This is not permanent, irreversible, or a definite sign of a learning problem. For many, many children, it is part of the process of developing handwriting.

A common phenomenon occurs when children write from the right-hand side of the paper and move to the left—which makes great sense in Hebrew but is the opposite of the convention in English. You will see that this writing that goes across the page from right to left is perfect mirror writing, which adults could not do as easily if they tried. Young children, on the other hand, do not believe that writing must go in one direction only, or that letters have to face to the right to be considered correct. Many are able to write from right to left as easily as from left to right till they realize that one direction is conventional.

Even then, children as old as nine, ten, and eleven may still evidence mirror writing, especially in situations where they are trying to write something on the right-hand side of the paper. A child making a map was attempting to write the name of a place close to the right-hand margin. He reversed the letters in perfect mirror writing going from right to left and fit it in where he wanted it. He did not usually do this in his other writing, but it served his purpose well in the particular situation.

If you want to introduce letter formation and practice it with your child, here is one method you might use. It groups letters made in a similar fashion. Their names give clues about their formation.

- letters that originate from *C*: *c o a g q d e C O G Q*
- mountain letters (they start at the bottom and go up and down): *N M A*
- down, up, and over letters (the stroke is fluid, down, up, over): *r n m h b B*
- twins (capitals and lower case look the same and start at the top): *S s P p J j K k U u V v W w X x Y y Z z*
- stick letters: *i I l L E F H T t*
- stick letters with curves: *D R f*

If the letter *C* includes top and bottom curves, it becomes the base of many other letters that all begin with *C*. We call *C* the "magic letter" because there are so many others that are formed from it. Children are surprised to find that this is so.

Many youngsters confuse lower case letters that look similar, especially when written by hand: *b* and *d*, *p* and *q*, *g* and *q*, *g* and *d*. Show them that *d* is a *c* first with a straight line transforming it, as in the progression of letters in the alphabet song: *c, d*. Lower case *g* and *q* start with *c* but finish differently: *g* has a curved tiger tail and *q* has a quirky foot.

TRAFFIC SIGNS FOR WRITERS AND READERS

Writing conventions are like traffic signs. Authors use them to direct readers through a text. Conventions signal readers to pause, stop, go, answer a question, or pay attention. They help to convey meaning. Without them, understanding a text would be too difficult.

Young children can learn how to use the traffic signs of written language in the same way that they learn about traffic signs on streets and highways. Through questions and conversations, children inquire about stop lights and other signs they see because they want to know their meanings and purposes. They discover that traffic signs tell drivers and pedestrians how to act so as to prevent accidents.

A similar process takes place with interpersonal communication. By the age of six, most children know and use "traffic signs" in their oral speech. They recognize how particular words and expressions get the same reactions from many different listeners. "What," "where," "how," "who," and "why" all indicate questions to be answered. As they get older, children learn how a pause or an inflection of voice designates what is being said: For example, the same phrase can be used to challenge someone ("What do you mean!") or invite more discussion ("What do you mean?").

Thinking of writing conventions as traffic signs for writers and readers is a way to give youngsters the language they need to think and talk about language. As children recognize writing conventions and talk about them by name, the purpose for using them in their own writing becomes clearer.[7] Through daily family conversations you have already provided your children with language needed to talk about all sorts of things. In Bob's family, where his father, grandfathers, and uncle worked for the railroad, he learned railroading terms that other people might not know or use in their conversation: narrow gauge, gandy dancer, iron horse, high green.

In many homes kids discuss names and information about dinosaurs with precision and understanding because family members actively support their interest. They learn vocabulary—paleontologist, era, extinct, reptile, and the long names of different dinosaurs—as easily as the commonplace words they use in daily conversation. Other children acquire different words that are particular to their family's interests. Robby, whose father was in the heavy construction business, knew the names of large earth-moving equipment before he was four years old. "Look, there's a front-end loader" made complete sense to him.

A comma, dash, semi-colon, colon, period, question mark, exclamation point, quotation mark, paragraphs, capitalization, complete sentences, and dialogue can be interesting and fun for youngsters to learn. But a child must know what a question is and be able to recognize the difference between a question and a comment before she can begin to figure out when and where to use a question mark or a period in her text. The idea of adding emphasis or calling attention to something must be understood before a youngster will be able to use an exclamation point appropriately.

Learning about punctuation can begin before a child starts to understand what concept each mark represents. One mother we know points out the question and exclamation marks occasionally as she reads to her two-year-old. She uses the sounds that Victor Borge has made famous with his performances and recordings or oral punctuation. Now when her daughter sees these marks in print she says, "Make your sound,

Mommy, make your sound." That is exactly what you can do too in explaining punctuation to your child. By following Borge's formula— attaching a funny noise to each mark—children laugh, enjoy, and remember what they hear.

The traffic signs of print can be named and discussed when a child sees them, asks about them, and when you point them out. Most of the information that young children need to know about conventions is straightforward. For your reference and answers to other questions about conventions, we recommend *The Elements of Style*, by William Strunk Jr. and E. B. White. This succinct and occasionally witty explanation of rules and style has informed many people about writing for decades.[8] *You Kan Red This!: Spelling and Punctuation for Whole Language Classrooms, K–6*, by Sandra Wilde, offers many resources for parents, teachers, and children and strategies for teaching conventions.

ENJOYING AN EDITING KIT

A home-made *Editing Kit*, as part of or a companion to a Writing Box, can enliven learning about conventions for school-aged children. Editing and revising need not be arduous parts of children's writing. They can be enjoyable puzzles to work out together. One way to make the process fit for a child is to construct an Editing Kit in a shoebox.

Begin by making versions of the old-time visors worn by newspaper printers. Any visor that you have will do. Put a sign on the front of it that says "Editor." Or pin a sign on your child's shirt. One of our colleagues has a T-shirt he wears while writing with "Edit" on the front and "Revise" on the back. When the two of you put the visors on, they signal that you are editing. By focusing on just one convention at a time, you can relax as you assist your child in rereading and making changes in his writing that will help an audience to read and understand it.

Show children how authors signal breaks in a piece of writing. Most writing has a beginning, middle, and end. It starts with a title or greeting and continues on through a series of pauses and transitions to its conclusion. Short breaks within sentences are marked by a comma, dash, semi-colon, colon, period, question mark, or exclamation point. Paragraphs and headings alert the reader to other kinds of transition: a different character is speaking; there is a new point of view or new information; or the author has shifted voice.

For your Editing Kit, make a series of cards displaying the different conventions of punctuation; add one for capitalization and another for paragraphing. Take out only the ones you will be working on at a given time—for instance the question mark, the exclamation point, or the period. When going through a child's own writing, help him locate where a particular mark should be placed by reading a piece aloud and demonstrating how the text would sound with the inclusion of different punctuation. After putting in the punctuation, take a look at capitalization or save that for another editing session.

Included in our Bookcase are titles of entertaining and instructive books to look at in conjunction with editing activities. You and your child will see demonstrations of conventions in your reading together. Point them out occasionally so that they become familiar features of written language for your child to notice. This is an easy way to introduce them. They will emerge in your child's writing and you can comment when you see them.

A Note to Teachers

This Note to Teachers answers a number of questions we are regularly asked about Writing Boxes, whole language learning, parent-teacher cooperation, and educational change. We hope parents too will read this, because inspiring children's writing involves home and school working together to enable children to express themselves as confident and capable writers and thinkers.

CAN I USE THE IDEAS IN THIS BOOK IN MY CLASSROOM?

Our ideas and activities can be used easily and effectively in classrooms as teachers link writing to the many other things that children do with support from interested adults. In the book we set forth a proven formula of learning for youngsters: pursuing their own interests, taking risks, expressing ideas, making mistakes, and acquiring new competencies through their own approximations and efforts. The goal is to encourage them to continue to be playful, self-directed learners who choose interests and topics to explore because they like to do so. Teachers facilitate this learning by supporting children's curiosity and self-confidence, providing new and challenging experiences, answering questions, praising efforts, and helping individuals to find answers. As you consider what ideas to try with individuals or groups of students, follow the leads of children as to which work best. Our Young Writers' Bookcase offers many options for connecting writing with reading in your curriculum. Through the use of the proven formula in classrooms, you will foster children's developing literacy in and out of school.

WHAT IF MY SCHOOL CANNOT AFFORD WRITING BOXES FOR EVERY STUDENT?

Writing Boxes for every student may not be a viable option for many schools because of cost. As an alternative, consider creating a limited number of classroom-based Writing Boxes for children to use in school and sign out for evenings or weekends. Even on a limited basis, children will explore writing and drawing with the materials—in some cases trying things they had not done before.

Costs for Writing Boxes are adjustable. The package of materials we gave to each student the first year of our project was less than $25, container included. Other teachers have fashioned Boxes to fit their budgets. Some have used cardboard or plastic shoeboxes to send home paper, pencils, and felt-tip markers. Others have assembled three to six more elaborate Writing Boxes that students sign out for home use.

Explore the possibility of initiating partnerships with businesses and agencies in your area interested in supporting collaborative home-school literacy education efforts. Various merchants may be interested in contributing a particular item. A copy firm might offer scrap paper and might even glue it into note pads, or they might bind children's books at reduced costs. A stationery store might provide notebooks, a department store might give tape or gluesticks. A bank might donate pencils and pencil sharpeners. Since many firms are besieged by requests, seeking only outright donations may not be as successful as suggesting other ways that members of outside organizations might work with the school—perhaps as tutors or school volunteers—and how materials might be provided as part of a larger school improvement effort.

Add new items to your classroom Writing Boxes periodically. Parents too may add new materials. Consider sending home your own explanations of invented spelling, process writing, reading aloud, and other concepts related to children's writing. These might accompany the Writing Box or be sent as separate materials for parents to read. Suggest some writing activities for parents to do with their youngsters. We found that evening meetings—with childcare provided—for families were appreciated by many adults who wanted an opportunity to ask questions and share experiences.

Other educators have designed their own materials to link children's home writing with school: A Young Writers' Backpack, a Writing Suitcase, a Traveling Diary that accompanies a stuffed animal. Book backpacks—and a variation of this idea, math bookbags—include notebooks for students and family members to write in and send back to the classroom. Excellent ideas for highlighting children's writing as a connector between home and school are not limited to those we have described thus far. How you might create your own version is of great interest to us, and we encourage your efforts.

WHAT IS A WHOLE LANGUAGE PHILOSOPHY OF TEACHING AND LEARNING?

Whole language educators believe that school curriculum can utilize the naturally occurring ways children learn outside of school. A prevailing assortment of workbooks, basal readers, spelling and language texts is replaced by more interactive materials that involve children in thinking, observing, and questioning. Classroom teaching focuses on "lots of reading and writing, risk-taking to try new functions for reading and writing, focusing on meaning" through the use of children's literature, children's writing, poetry, songs, chants, and rhymes.[1]

Teachers using a whole language framework in their classroom view reading as the creation of meaning, rather than as the memorization of words, and process writing as an integral part of children's language learning. They avoid instructional methods that separate skills, preferring to combine phonics, spelling, handwriting, sight-word memorization, and comprehension together as part of the study of written language. They group students in many different ways, but not according to the traditional delineations of advanced, less advanced, and least advanced learners.

Whole language teachers view themselves as learners as well as instructors. They acknowledge that children know enormous amounts before entering school and that they will continue learning in countless social settings that involve family, peers, media, and individual play. They are kidwatchers, continually assessing children's knowledge in daily interactions. Their observations inform planning for each child and for the class.

Cooperation is stressed. Children teach each other by working together. Groups of students compare ideas, solve problems collectively, and share the knowledge they learn from each other. In order to help children continue to be the curious, questioning, goal-setting learners they were before entering school, whole language classrooms enlarge rather than restrict choices and opportunities to solve problems. Children make decisions about books they want to read, topics they want to write about, questions they want to answer, and projects they want to conduct.

HOW ARE WRITING AND READING DIFFERENT IN WHOLE LANGUAGE CLASSROOMS?

Whole language educators view writing and reading, defined as constructing and communicating meaning through symbols and text, as best learned through genuine communications in authentic situations. As Kenneth Goodman remarked: "In authentic experiences, the participants have real, personal purposes for participation. The language used is real, relevant to the purposes and context, and comprehensible."[2] Filling in the blanks on workbook pages or skill sheets or memorizing lists for weekly spelling tests are mechanical processes that blunt a child's motivation for learning. These activities lack authenticity and relevance for a child. Young authors, like other writers, require individual choice and personal decision-making to feel committed to a process of communicating their thoughts and ideas.

Children learn how pictures, words, tone of voice, gestures, movement, and facial expressions all communicate messages to others. Through transmitting their own messages using their own natural language, expressed and written in the ways they can, children understand why people write and how to use writing for their own purposes. They develop their abilities as communicators and learn conventions of print. Teachers regard every youngster's writing as important, no matter how it looks. They know that children's writing evolves in form and incorporates conventions as children understand them. They assist students in gaining further knowledge of communication by discussing language, writing with them, and encouraging children to write for many purposes.

Students write regularly, often daily, in invented spelling, strings of letters, wiggly lines that look like cursive writing, or standard conventions of print. Some leave spaces between their words, others put dots or lines between words to mark beginnings and ends, some draw complete circles around the words. They use punctuation as they become familiar with its purpose. The adjunct skills of handwriting, spelling, and sentence construction are invented, practiced, and learned by each youngster as part of his own writing—not as isolated pieces that must be learned before trying to communicate. Children see standard conventions of print modeled in the teacher's writing, in charts around the room, in books and printed materials, and learn about them from each other and through mini-lessons about writing.

WHAT ARE SOME WAYS FOR PARENTS TO BECOME INVOLVED IN THE SCHOOL?

Most schools are understaffed and need parents and other community members to contribute to education as volunteers, tutors, or mentors. Many small-group activities and hands-on projects are easier for a teacher to conduct with the help of other adults in the room. Volunteers allow teachers to try new and creative activities with students. At the Scenic Hills Elementary School in Springfield, Pennsylvania, teachers and parents have created partnerships that highlight children's writing. There is a drop-in writing center, called the "Scenic Hills Publishing Company," that is completely staffed by parent volunteers. Its goal is to "help students write, edit, revise, illustrate, and publish as many books as possible." Designated parents called "Mystery Readers" visit classrooms to read to the students. Teams of parents and first- and fourth-graders create "Buddy Books" or "Me Books" based on holiday themes.[3]

A different kind of publishing network exists as well. Parents assemble, type, or bind books at home with materials sent from school. Their children return the finished work. Although some of these parents never have the opportunity to visit school during the day, they still contribute to the writing and publishing process.

Parent volunteers, even a few times a year, make important contributions to children's learning when they read aloud to individuals and small groups, work in computer labs, staff the school library, attend field trips, assist youngsters with science experiments and other kinds of hands-on learning projects, or spend time with children who benefit from a one-on-one relationship with an adult. This does not mean that parents should become personal in-school tutors to their children. In fact, it is probably better for all concerned if parents serve as aides to an entire classroom or school and see their youngsters in a new environment.

WILL PARENT INVOLVEMENT IN SCHOOLS MAKE A DIFFERENCE IN MY TEACHING?

Parent involvement in children's learning opens the way for partnerships between schools and families, and such cooperation makes it possible for you to reach more of your students and understand more about each of their individual interests. Collaboration requires support and trust among the partners. Working together must be based on mutual respect and a willingness to address complex issues of learning. All partners must have substantive roles to play and a genuine voice in decision-making in whatever activity they do together. Byrd Jones and Robert Maloy have described successful collaborative arrangements as "interactive partnerships" in which ideas, resources, and people move back and forth between home and school. "Goals and objectives are not specifically defined in advance, but emerge and shift as they negotiate the terms of their mutual efforts."[4] Cooperation replaces criticism as adults look for ways to improve schools for all students.

Together, teachers and parents can change any curriculum area, including how writing is taught in schools. You need not be intimidated by the fact that a child's parents have different beliefs and assumptions about how children learn. No one strategy or approach works with every child every time. In education, every day is a new experiment. Differing viewpoints are a strength: Hearing another perspective can lead to parents and teachers trying new ideas with children that neither would have thought of by themselves.

HOW CAN I BEST EXPLAIN MY EDUCATIONAL GOALS AND EXPECTATIONS TO PARENTS AND INVITE THEIR ASSISTANCE?

You do not want classroom practices to ostracize children because learning activities at home differ from instructional practices in school. It is important to explain why you encourage invented spelling, allow students to write about their own topics, introduce different writing genres, enjoy language play and games, and read aloud from children's books to inspire new ideas. Work with parents toward the common goal of having each child become an enthusiastic reader and confident writer concerned with expressing ideas rather than focusing primarily on correct spelling, punctuation, and form. This is best accomplished through communication and collaboration.

Teachers have many different ways to send information to parents and invite their help and comment: in newsletters, parent conferences, and homework assignments. For instance, with the same $300 that some classrooms spend to buy consumable math and reading workbooks for students (that must be reordered every year), some teachers purchase a set of inviting predictable readers to send home in plastic bags as home reading books for students. Many teachers send home monthly packets of poetry, songs, rhymes, and jokes so children will have familiar text to read, sing, and enjoy with parents.

Working with teachers of low-income minority students in inner-city schools in Alabama, Professors Gary and Maryann Manning have observed the responses of parents to the once-a-week letters that a teacher sends home with students. The difference in this approach is that children also write their own weekly letter to parents about something they are learning or doing. Blank stationery accompanies these letters so that parents can write back. What happened during the first year of this innovative approach to linking home and school? Every parent wrote back at least twice during the year.[5]

Homework assignments might be bags of math games to be played at home, bags of books to read, or bags of paper and crayons so children can write books. One teacher sends home packets of games and activities for children and calls them "homeplay" instead of homework. There are many games in the "Math Their Way" series and in Peggy Kaye's books for parents (see pages 295–298).

Children might write a weekly newpspaper or newsletter in invented spelling using their illustrations. They may want to include questions to be answered in surveys from which to construct charts. They might send copies to parents and other relatives living outside the home. A classroom diectory, written and illustrated by the students, with information about what areas exist in the classroom, the procedures for using them, and the schedule of the week might be sent home as part of an explanation of your curriculum.

IS THERE ANOTHER WAY TO CONNECT WRITING AND READING IN SCHOOL WITH FAMILY ACTIVITIES?

Young children write more when teachers find ways to build connections between the writing they do in school and the writing they do at home. We used a Writing Box. Irene Tully developed another successful idea: a "Book Bag." A collection of reading materials is placed inside portable knapsacks for students to sign out and take home for a specified length of time—usually a week. Each Book Bag contains books about a specific theme and a spiral notebook in which children and adults share their responses to the materials they have read. Selecting from among the books, children read alone or with other family members, usually a parent. Afterward, whoever wants to may write their ideas in the notebook. In this way the comments of many different children, parents, and other adults are preserved from family to family and travel with the bag. These journals serve as cumulative records of responses.[6]

HOW CAN I USE HOMEWORK TO PROMOTE ENJOYABLE LEARNING IN FAMILIES?

Homework need not be a source of confrontation between you and families. In many homes in which one or both parents work, time for family activities is tight. For many, using time to do homework that requires filling in the blank with right answers or practicing spelling lists means that reading a book, playing a language game such as Hangman, or writing a story or letter together will not happen.

Suggest that parents use children's homework to explore new ideas or engage in enjoyable learning activities. For example, instead of a homework assignment that requires a child to correct punctuation and capitalization mistakes, parents and children might write a story together, checking their work when finished for punctuation and capitalization. In this way a child's own writing is a basis for learning about the conventions of print.

Even if parents do not know the correct rules of usage, children can take home examples of first and second drafts of their own writing to review. They can bring letters or stories written at home to school and become "Punctuation Detectives" with your help, searching to find punctuation that needs to be included. Since making mistakes is an important way that people learn, the process of correcting them need not be embarrassing for teacher, parent, or child.

There are many effective ways to modify or supplement a school assignment and turn it into a family learning experience. For instance, worksheets can be converted into games to sign out and play at home. A chart or short written report can inform you about which books read at home a child likes best. Helping parents find ways to incorporate homework assignments into the regular pattern of writing that exists in the home satisfies two learning goals: Families regard writing as an important and pleasurable form of individual self-expression, and they encourage attention to authentic writing instead of workbook exercises.

HOW CAN I FIND OUT WHAT CHILDREN ARE WRITING AT HOME?

Parent-teacher conferences are opportunities to discuss writing. At home, youngsters may be creating complex and creative stories, letters, or nonfiction. These may remain undiscovered unless home writing becomes part of your discussions with parents. Inquire about writing and how students choose to spend their free time. As children's interests shift and change, incorporate their latest pursuits into class discussions and projects.

Suggest that parents share samples of children's home writing with you, so that you can see what is being done outside of school. Compare work done in school and at home and decide together on some strategies to promote further writing or to practice certain skills. In this way home and school function as a team.

Ask parents to help keep you informed by maintaining writing logs: periodically collecting samples of their youngster's writing, dating each, and putting them in a folder or notebook. Make copies of these for your records. A video log is also a possibility if the equipment is available. Children might enjoy being videotaped reading stories they have written in order to demonstrate to you what they are doing at home. Younger siblings and friends may want to watch these too.

Another way to initiate teacher-parent dialogue about home writing is to include the child in your conferences. Then everyone has an investment in a successful outcome. Although conferences with a child present are not always easy, particularly if there is some difficulty in school that you wish to discuss with a parent, bringing samples of writing from home to the conference opens a way to talk about a child's imagination and capability with language. This gives you a chance to discuss directly how writing is being taught in school to help avoid confusion that might result if home writing activities focus attention only on correct conventions, rather than the joy of writing and communicating ideas. If parents are stressing correctness in writing, suggest that older children try the first and second draft strategies that many authors use: Freely write draft number one in their one spelling and punctuation and then revise draft number two with encouraging assistance from parents.

HOW HAS THE WRITING BOX PROJECT CHANGED SHARON'S TEACHING?

As we were preparing to send this book to the publisher, Sharon participated in a roundtable discussion titled "How What I Know Affects What I Do" at the 1991 National Council of Teachers of English Conference. She told teachers and researchers how the Writing Box and parent involvement in children's learning have changed her teaching methodologies and her beliefs about learners. Neither she nor Bob expected that their efforts to inspire writing at home would transform so many parts of her teaching.

Today Sharon's classroom is very different from that of a few years ago. More willing to follow the lead of the children than impose a predetermined curriculum on the class, she finds that every day is a search for the blend of enjoyment and relevance that makes learning engaging. For one boy this means bringing the *Boston Globe* sports section to school daily during basketball season in order to connect his math and reading to something he is passionate about learning. For one girl it is making sure that she has time on the computer to continue writing her adventure story about an American Indian woman. Parents' knowledge informs Sharon about what children are doing at home that can be incorporated into school activities.

Writing connects children's personal interests with all of the academic subjects that school is responsible for teaching: math, science, reading, social studies, geography, creative thinking. We hope that you will find this book useful as you consider what you believe about children's learning and examine how your beliefs affect what you do in your classroom. Perhaps some time in the future a requirement for teachers will be that we become classroom researchers pursuing knowledge and information with children—not dispensing answers or putting knowledge into them, but helping them acquire information and draw understanding from it for themselves.

CAN I MAKE A DIFFERENCE IN CHILDREN'S EDUCATION BY PROMOTING CHANGE IN MY CLASSROOM?

The opportunity to write this book came about because of changes in Sharon's teaching practices and in our thinking about children's learning as a result of introducing something new into the classroom: the Writing Boxes. The ensuing effects continue as we try out the formula for success with students' learning, see our results, and talk with and read about changes other educators are making with their students. As we observe children demonstrating their desire to succeed and see the positive benefits of supportive assistance from interested adults, Sharon's classroom practices and methodologies evolve into new ways of enabling children to reach their potentials.

You may be teaching in a school that is not yet using many of the ideas and approaches championed in this book. Working with colleagues to create schoolwide improvement initiatives, partnerships with outsiders, a positive climate for change, and more professional roles for teachers takes time and the development of trusting relationships. If you are aware of new initiatives and ideas that affect your teaching, and you discuss these with colleagues, you will promote thinking about teaching methodologies and theories of learning in your school. If teachers or parents are interested in investigating children's learning and thinking, then whole language, process writing, parent involvement, and classroom research are vehicles for doing so.

Ronald Edmonds and other researchers of "effective schools" have identified some characteristics of organizations that promote successful learning for all children: positive school leadership, agreement on goals and objectives, high expectations for students, a safe and orderly climate, and continual monitoring and feedback on student achievement.[7] Many effective-schools advocates also include parent involvement as an essential condition for improving schools and promoting learning for all youngsters. Effective schools are created through collaboration, self-examination, and commitment to make each child a successful learner in everyone's mind. Within a schoolwide focus or commitment to effectiveness, every teacher can contribute to a positive organizational climate that brings about improved educational outcomes for children.

Notes

A NOTE TO PARENTS

1. Jonathan Kozol, *Illiterate America* (New York: New American Library, 1985), 4.
2. Hudson Institute, *Workforce 2000: Work and Workers for the Twenty-First Century* (Indianapolis, IN: Hudson Institute, 1989).
3. John O'Neil, "New Curriculum Agenda Emerges for '90s," *ASCD Curriculum Update* September 1990: 2.
4. Phyllis Coons, "Study Sees Parents as Key to Success of 8th Graders," *The Boston Sunday Globe* 2 Sept. 1990: 33, 36.
5. For more information about the first year of the project, see Sharon A. Edwards and Robert W. Maloy, "The Writing Box: Promoting Kindergarten and First Grade Children's Writing at Home," *Contemporary Education* LXI. 4 (1990): 195–199.

CHAPTER 1: WATCHING YOUNG WRITERS

1. John Holt, *Learning All the Time* (Reading, MA: Addison-Wesley, 1989), 152.
2. Benjamin S. Bloom, ed., *Developing Talent in Young People* (New York: Ballantine Books, 1985), 3–4, 512.

3. Bloom 509.

4. Lucy McCormick Calkins, *The Art of Teaching Writing* (Portsmouth, NH: Heinemann, 1986), 47.

5. Vivian Gussin Paley, *The Boy Who Would Be a Helicopter: The Uses of Storytelling in the Classroom* (Cambridge, MA: Harvard University Press, 1990), 10.

CHAPTER 2: CREATING A WRITING BOX

1. S. J. Rich, "The Writing Suitcase," *Young Children* 40 (1985): 42–44.

2. D. Ray Reutzel and Parker C. Fawson, "Traveling Tales: Connecting Parents and Children Through Writing," *The Reading Teacher* 44.3 (1990): 222–227.

3. Linda Leonard Lamme, *Growing Up Writing: Sharing the Joys of Good Writing* (Washington, DC: Acropolis Books, 1984), 19–21.

CHAPTER 3: WRITING PROCESSES FIT FOR A CHILD

1. Kenneth S. Goodman, Lois Bridges Bird, and Yetta M. Goodman, *The Whole Language Catalog* (Santa Rosa, CA: American School Publishers, 1991).

2. Marlene Barron. *I Learn to Read and Write the Way I Learn to Talk: A Very First Book About Whole Language* (Katonah, NY: Richard C. Owen Publishers, 1990), 9.

3. Elizabeth Royte, "E. O. Wilson: The Ant Man," *The New York Times Magazine* 22 July 1990: 16–21, 38–39.

4. Dorothy S. Strickland, "The Child as Composer," in *The Whole Language Catalog*, 20.

5. Donald Graves, *Writing: Teachers & Children at Work* (Portsmouth, NH: Heinemann, 1983), 227, 226, 229.

6. Kenneth S. Goodman, Yetta M. Goodman, and Tucsonans Applying Whole Language TAWL, *A Kid-Watching Guide: Evaluation for Whole Language Classrooms* (Tucson, AZ: University of Arizona, 1984).

7. Mike Whiteford, *How to Talk Baseball* (New York: Dembner Books, 1987), 36.

8. Robert Kegan, *The Evolving Self: Problem and Process in Human Development* (Cambridge, MA: Harvard University Press, 1982), 26, 28.

9. Thomas Gordon, *Discipline That Works: Promoting Self-Discipline in Children* (New York: Plume Books, 1989).

10. Wendy Bean and Chrystine Bouffler, *Spell by Writing* (Portsmouth, NH: Heinemann, 1991).

11. Graves 55.

CHAPTER 4: INSPIRING YOUNG WRITERS

1. Aileen Fisher, "So You Want to Be a Writer?" in *The Whole Language Catalog*, 125.
2. Jon Winokur, ed., *Writers on Writing* (Philadelphia: Running Press, 1990), 7.
3. Catherine E. Snow and Anat Ninio, "The Contracts of Literacy: What Children Learn from Learning to Read Books," in *Emergent Literacy: Writing and Reading*, William H. Teale and Elizabeth Sulzby, eds. (Norwood, NJ: Ablex Publishing Corporation, 1986), 121.
4. Gordon Wells, *The Meaning Makers: Children Learning Language and Using Language to Learn* (Portsmouth, NH: Heinemann, 1986).
5. Sandra Wilde, "A Proposal for a New Spelling Curriculum," *The Elementary School Journal 90* 3 (1990): 275–289.
6. Bill Carter, "Children's TV, Where Boys Are King," *The New York Times* 1 May 1991: 1, C-18.
7. Vivian Gussin Paley, *Boys & Girls: Superheroes in the Doll Corner* (Chicago: University of Chicago Press, 1984), 1, 3.
8. Jim Trelease, *The New Read-Aloud Handbook* (New York: Penguin Books, 1989), 125.

CHAPTER 5: WRITING IS ALL IN THE FAMILY

1. George Dennison, *The Lives of Children: The Story of the First Street School* (New York: Random House, 1969), 92.

CHAPTER 6: PLAYING WITH LANGUAGE THROUGH WORDS, PICTURES, AND GAMES

1. Iona Opie and Peter Opie, *The Lore and Language of Schoolchildren* (New York: Oxford University Press, 1959), 1.
2. D. C. Denison, "The Interview," *The Boston Globe Magazine* 9 June 1991: 8–9.
3. Wells 156.
4. Paley 39.
5. Kenneth Koch, *Wishes, Lies and Dreams: Teaching Children to Write Poetry* (New York: Harper and Row, 1970), 2, 5–6.
6. Howard Gardner, *Artful Scribbles: The Significance of Children's Drawings* (New York: Basic Books, 1980), 5–6, 11, 15.

7. Mary Melonis, personal communication.
8. Arthur N. Applebee, Judith A. Langer, and Ina V. S. Mullis, *Who Reads Best?* (Princeton, NJ: Educational Testing Service, 1988).
9. M. Thomas Inge, *Comics in the Classroom* (Washington, DC: Smithsonian Institute Traveling Exhibition Service, 1989), 2, 5.
10. Joan Skolnick, Carol Langbort, and Lucille Day, *How to Encourage Girls in Math & Science* (Palo Alto, CA: Dale Seymour Publications, 1982), 28, 84–88.

CHAPTER 7: EXPRESSING IMAGINATION

1. Peter Elbow, *Writing with Power: Techniques for Mastering the Writing Process* (New York: Oxford University Press, 1981), 11, 340, 341.
2. Barbara A. Bode, *Dialogue Journal Writing as an Approach to Beginning Literacy Instruction* (Orlando, FL: Educational Resources Information Center, 1988), 9.

CHAPTER 8: USING WRITING MACHINES

1. Lucy Howard and Ned Zeman, "Periscope: Computerland," *Newsweek* 8 April 1991: 8.
2. Patricia Marks Greenfield, "Video Screens: Are They Changing the Way Children Learn?" *The Harvard Education Letter* March–April 1990: 1.
3. Office of Technology Assessment, *Power On! New Tools for Teaching and Learning* (Washington, DC: Government Printing Office, 1988).
4. Greenfield 2.
5. Sherry Turkle, *The Second Self: Computers and the Human Spirit* (New York: Simon & Schuster, 1984), 93, 68, 92.
6. Seymour Papert, *Mindstorms: Children, Computers, and Powerful Ideas* (New York: Basic Books, 1980), 11–12, 218.
7. Anne Wright, "Teaching Writing While Jumping Through New Technological Hoops," *English Journal* 77.7 (1988): 37.
8. Office of Technology Assessment 10, 12.
9. William V. Costanzo, "Media, Metaphors, and Models," *English Journal* 77.7 (1988): 29.
10. For more information about speech-based software, see Charles Parham, "Computers That Talk," *Classroom Computer Learning* 8.6 (1988): 26–31.
11. For more about print programs see Beth Lazerick, "Software Workshop: Great Getting-to-Know-You Activities Using Print Programs, Databases, and More," *Instructor* 100.2 (1990): 84–87.

12. For more on graphics see Susan Mernit, "Getting into Graphics," *Instructor* 101.6 (1991): 109–110.

13. Barry Owen, *Personal Computers for the Computer Illiterate: The What, When, Why, Where, and How Guide* (New York: Harper Collins, 1991), 55.

14. Michael W. Apple, "The New Technology: Is It Part of the Solution or Part of the Problem in Education?" *Computers in the Schools* 8.1/2/3 (1991): 44.

15. Patricia B. Campbell, "The Computer Revolution: Guess Who's Left Out?" *Interracial Books for Children Bulletin* 15.3 (1984): 5.

CHAPTER 9: INTRODUCING CONVENTIONS OF PRINT

1. For more information about spelling see Richard E. Hodges, *Learning to Spell* (Urbana, IL: ERIC Clearinghouse on Reading and Communication Skills and National Council of Teachers of English, 1981); Richard J. Gentry, *Spel . . . Is a Four-Letter Word* (Portsmouth, NH: Heinemann, 1987); Charles Read, *Children's Creative Spelling* (New York: Chapman & Hall, 1986).

2. Charles Read's research has shown how children reason about spelling. They create systems that are different from adults' perceptions of how spelling is figured out. One of the ways he found children spell is based on the placement of their tongue to produce some beginning sounds of words.

3. Marie Clay, *Writing Begins at Home: Preparing Children for Writing Before They Go to School* (Portsmouth, NH: Heinemann, 1987), 6.

4. Sandra Wilde, "A Proposal for a New Spelling Curriculum," 275–289.

5. Andrea Butler and Jan Turbill, *Towards a Reading-Writing Classroom* (Rozelle, Australia: Primary English Teaching Association, 1984), 3.

6. Judith A. Schickedanz, *Adam's Righting Revolutions: One Child's Literacy Development from Infancy Through Grade One* (Portsmouth, NH: Heinemann, 1990).

7. Yetta Goodman, personal communication.

8. William Strunk Jr. and E. B. White, *The Elements of Style* (New York: Macmillan, 1979).

A NOTE TO TEACHERS

1. Kenneth S. Goodman, *What's Whole in Whole Language* (Portsmouth, NH: Heinemann, 1986), 49.

2. *The Whole Language Catalog*, 281.

3. Anthony D. Fredericks and Timothy Y. Rasinski, "Whole Language and Parents: Natural Partners," *The Reading Teacher* 43.9: 692–694.

4. Byrd L. Jones and Robert W. Maloy, *Partnerships for Improving Schools* (Westport, CT: Greenwood Press, 1988), 11.

5. Gary and Maryann Manning, "Whole Language Success Stories with African American Inner-City Primary Students," paper delivered at the NCTE Annual Convention, Seattle, 22 Nov. 1991.

6. Irene Tully, telephone interview, 15 Dec. 1991.

7. Ronald Edmonds, "Programs of School Improvement: An Overview," *Educational Leadership* December 1982: 4–11.

A Young Writers' Bookcase

Welcome to our Young Writers' Bookcase, a selection of books pertaining to most of the major writing ideas and activities in chapters 4 through 9. It includes fiction, nonfiction, and poetry books. We provide the title, author, illustrator, publisher, date of publication, whether it's a hardcover or paperback, and a short annotation for each entry. A bullet (•) indicates a book that is currently out of print, but it may be available in a library or used-book store. The Bookcase is intended as a starting point to help you find other titles for your young writer.

Instead of offering a general age-level recommendation for each entry, selections within each category are arranged from least to greatest amount of text. Children's interests are truly the factor that decides what they want to hear, read, and research, not their age. A book enjoyed by many six- to ten-year-olds may be also exactly right for a four-, five-, eleven-, or twelve-year-old. Authors, illustrators, and publishers have responded to the likes and interests of children by producing a wide assortment of inviting books that appeal to a range of ages. Poetry, jokes, songs, picture books, chapter books, journals, diaries, magazines, and anthologies all inspire children's writing.

CHAPTER 4: INSPIRING YOUNG WRITERS

A Kiss for Little Bear, by Else Holmelund Minarik, pictures by Maurice Sendak (Harper & Row, 1968, paper): Little Bear paints a picture to send to his grandmother, which occasions several adventures leading to writing and a surprise ending

Amanda's Book, by Kerry Westell, art by Ruth Ohi (Annick Press, 1991, paper): Young Amanda cuts things out for her scrapbook, creating great confusion in the world, and then decides to write in a notebook instead.

Good Books, Good Times!, selected by Lee Bennett Hopkins, illustrated by Harry Stevenson (Harper & Row, 1990, hardcover): A collection of poems about the delights of reading.

From Picture to Picture Book, by Ali Mitgutsch (Carolrhoda Books, 1986, hardcover): How a picture book is created, from the initial ideas of a writer through all the stages of publishing.

How a Book Is Made, by Aliki (Harper & Row, 1988, paper): From author to editor and then to all of the people who make books, written in a comic-book style.

• *Little Bear's Pancake Party*, by Janice, pictures by Mariana (Lothrop, Lee & Shepard, 1960, hardcover): Reading is a necessity, as Little Bear discovers in this and a second book, • *Little Bear Learns to Read the Cookbook*.

Morris Goes to School, by Bernard Wiseman (Harper & Row, 1983, paper): Morris the Moose's first day of school is full of funny experiences.

Petunia, by Roger Duvoisin (Knopf, 1989, paper): Believing that keeping a book close to her will enable her to read brings unexpected results to Petunia.

Nicholas at the Library, by Hazel Hutchins and Ruth Ohi (Annick Press, 1990, paper): Nicholas has a great adventure at the library when he disappears into books with the librarian.

The Tale of Thomas Mead, by Pat Hutchins (Morrow, 1988, paper): The funny misadventures of Thomas Mead, who gives the same reply, "Why should I?" each time he is told that he ought to learn to read.

The Wednesday Surprise, by Eve Bunting, illustrated by Donald Carrick (Houghton Mifflin, 1989, paper): Anna teaches her grandmother to read without anyone in the family realizing what she is doing.

The Day of Ahmed's Secret, by Florence Parry Heide and Judith Heide Gilliland, illustrated by Ted Lewin (Scholastic, 1991, paper): As he goes about his daily job in the busy city of Cairo, a young boy anticipates the moment he can tell his secret to his family: that he can write his name.

Leonardo da Vinci: The Artist, Inventor, Scientist in Three-Dimensional Movable Pictures, by Alice and Martin Provensen (Viking, 1984, paper): The life and discoveries of the fifteenth-century inventor.

A Grain of Wheat: A Writer Begins, by Clyde Robert Bulla (David R. Godine, 1985, paper): A writer's autobiography concentrating on his childhood and how he decided to become an author.

Astrid Lindgren: Storyteller to the World, by Johanna Hurwitz (Viking Penguin, 1991, paper): The creator of Pippi Longstocking and other tales describes her childhood and the beginning of her writing career.

Starting from Home: A Writer's Beginnings, by Milton Meltzer (Viking Penguin, 1988, paper): Author of more than seventy books and five times nominated for a National Book Award, Milton Meltzer recalls how he became a writer.

Where Do You Get Your Ideas? Helping Young Writers Begin, by Sandy Asher, illustrated by Susan Hellard (Walker & Co., 1987, hardcover): Suggestions for writing and ideas for arranging the material.

CHAPTER 5: WRITING IS ALL IN THE FAMILY
Letters, Greeting Cards, and Postcards

The Jolly Postman or Other People's Letters, by Janet and Allan Ahlberg (Little, Brown, 1986, hardcover): The Three Bears, Cinderella, Hansel and Gretel's Witch, the Giant from Jack and the Beanstalk, and other fictional characters receive letters, messages, and cards. A sequel is available, titled *The Jolly Christmas Postman*.

Dear Mr. Blueberry, by Simon James (Macmillan, 1991, hardcover): Emily writes to her teacher, Mr. Blueberry, when she needs help with the whale in her pond.

A Letter to Amy, by Ezra Jack Keats (Harper & Row, 1984, paper): Peter writes a letter to invite Amy to his birthday party.

Arthur's Pen Pal, by Lillian Hoban (Harper & Row, 1982, paper and cassette): Arthur corresponds with a pen pal named Sandy, thinking she is a boy.

Dear Daddy, by Philippe Dupasquier (Viking Penguin, 1987, paper): Sophie describes her life in letters to her sea-voyaging father.

Jenny's Journey, by Sheila White Samton (Viking Penguin, 1991, hardcover): A young girl writes a letter to a friend who has moved.

Anna's Secret Friend, by Yoriko Tsutsui, illustrated by Akiko Hayashi (Viking Penguin, 1989, paper): When Anna moves she has no friends, till surprises begin arriving at her house and a letter gives her some clues.

Onion Tears, by Diana Kidd (Franklin Watts, 1991, hardover): A Vietnamese child who is having problems adjusting to her new American school writes a letter to her animal friends.

A Letter to the King, story and pictures by Leong Va, translated from the Norwegian by James Anderson (Harper & Row, 1988, hardcover): First written in Chinese over two hundred years ago, this story tells of a young girl who acts heroically to save her father's life by writing a letter to the king. The text is in English and Chinese.

Messages in the Mailbox: How to Write a Letter, written and illustrated by Loreen Leedy (Holiday House, 1991, hardcover): Ideas for writing all types of correspondence, with illustrations of students in Mrs. Gator's classroom trying each one.

Dear Mr. Henshaw, by Beverly Cleary, illustrated by Paul O. Zelinsky (Dell, 1983, paper): Leigh Botts begins writing letters to Mr. Henshaw, a children's author, in the second grade and continues throughout elementary school. A second book, *Strider*, is a diary of Leigh's experiences with a stray dog.

Brother Eagle, Sister Sky: A Message from Chief Seattle, paintings by Susan Jeffers (Dial, 1991, hardcover): Beautiful pictures highlight the famous words of an Indian chief spoken at a treaty meeting in the 1850s.

Notes, Lists, Menus, and Signs

I Read Signs, by Tana Hoban (Morrow, 1987, paper): Photographs of signs that we usually see in the city.

Harriet Reads Signs and More Signs: A World Concept Book, by Betsy and Giulio Maestro (Crown, 1984, paper): Harriet the hippo reads the neighborhood signs on her way to visit a friend.

Feathers for Lunch, by Lois Ehlert (Harcourt Brace Jovanovich, 1990, hardcover): A rhyming book describing a cat's desired menu.

Love from Aunt Betty, by Nancy Winslow Parker (Putnam, 1983, hardcover): Aunt Betty's recipe bakes a birthday cake that is one-of-a-kind.

The Outside Inn, by George Ella Lyon, illustrated by Vera Rosenberry (Franklin Watts, 1991, hardcover): Question-and-answer rhymes describe a nature menu.

•*The Forgotten Bear*, by Consuelo Joerns (Scholastic, 1978, paper): A teddy bear left alone on an island at the end of the summer sends a rescue note in a bottle.

Lucy Is Lost, illustrated by Ed King (Checkerboard Press, 1991, paper): Find Lucy and other things listed on each page in different spots in the world.

Miss Poppy and the Honey Cake, by Elizabeth MacDonald, illustrated by Claire Smith (Dial, 1989, hardcover): Miss Poppy must borrow the ingredients for a cake recipe from her exasperated neighbors.

Malke's Secret Recipe: A Chanukah Story, by David A. Adler, illustrated by Joan Halpern (Kar-Ben Copies, 1989, paper): Malke makes the best latkes in town but never shares her recipe till one Chanukah night, when Berel the shoemaker discovers it.

The High Rise Glorious Skittle Skat Roarious Sky Pie Angel Food Cake, by Nancy Willard, illustrated by Richard Jesse Watson (Harcourt Brace Jovanovich, 1990, hardcover): A young girl finds the secret ingredient of her grandmother's angel food cake with a little help from three angels.

Trips, Outings, and Errands

The Snake: A Very Long Story, by Bernard Waber (Houghton Mifflin, 1978, paper): A snake goes on a long journey, only to find out he ends up exactly where he has started.

City—Country: A Car Trip in Photographs, by Ken Robbins (Viking Penguin, 1985, paper): Photographs fill the pages with a brief text describing what a child sees from the backseat during a car trip.

Up in the Air, by Myra Cohn Livingston, illustrated by Leonard Everett Fisher (Holiday House, 1989, hardcover): A poem about flying on a passenger jet, with illustrations that look down onto the land from the plane.

Gila Monsters Meet You at the Airport, by Marjorie Weinman Sharmat, pictures by Byron Barton (Viking Penguin, 1990, paper): A young boy moving out West meets another moving back East, and they describe their stereotypical ideas of their new homes to each other.

Three Days on a River in a Red Canoe, by Vera B. Williams (Greenwillow, 1986, paper): A nine-year-old girl narrates this journal of a canoe trip with her mother, aunt, and cousin that includes drawings of their adventures, animals seen along the way, maps, a recipe, and camping instructions.

Dinosaurs Travel: A Guide for Families on the Go, by Laurene K. Brown and Marc Brown (Little, Brown, 1988, hardcover): A family of dinosaurs demonstrates how to get ready for a trip.

Your Best Friend, Kate, by Pat Brisson, illustrated by Rick Brown (Bradbury Press, 1989, hardcover): While on her vacation through the Southeastern United States, Kate writes letters and postcards to her friend Lucy. In *Kate Heads West*, the two girls write to relatives and friends as they travel together through Oklahoma, Texas, New Mexico, and Arizona.

Rehema's Journey: A Visit in Tanzania, by Barbara A. Margolies (Scholastic, 1990, hardcover): A nine-year-old girl leaves her home in the mountains and learns about her country while traveling with her father. Her journal includes many photographs.

Let's Go Traveling, by Robin Rector Krupp (Morrow, 1992, hardcover): Rachel Rose is a world traveler who writes a diary, draws maps and illustrations, and describes her journey in cards and letters.

Write How You Feel

• *I Was So Mad*, by Mercer Mayer (Golden Books, 1983, paper): A little boy gets mad at his family and decides to run away.

One of Three, by Angela Johnson, pictures by David Soman (Franklin Watts, 1991, hardcover): The youngest of three sisters describes what it is like being the littlest.

Feelings, by Joanne Brisson Murphy, illustrated by Heather Collins (Black Moss Press, 1985, paper): A young boy describes his responses to different events and experiences in his life.

Feelings, by Aliki (Morrow, 1986, paper): Vignettes, tales, and comics of youngsters expressing their feelings in words and actions.

Nathaniel Talking, by Eloise Greenfield, illustrated by Spivey Gilchrist (Writers and Readers, 1988, hardcover): A young African American boy describes his world, his family, and his strength of belonging.

The War Began at Supper: Letters to Miss Loria, by Patricia Reilly Giff, illustrated by Betsy Lewin (Dell, 1991, paper): Children in a second-grade classroom write out their fears and questions.

The Way I Feel. . . Sometimes, by Beatrice Schenk De Regniers, illustrated by S. Meddaugh (Ticknor & Fields, 1988, hardcover): A collection of poems describing young children's feelings.

Siblings and Friends

Waiting for Baby, by Tom Birdseye, illustrated by Loreen Leedy (Holiday House, 1991, hardcover): A young boy anticipates the activities he will enjoy with his younger sister when she is old enough.

Sisters, by David McPhail (Harcourt Brace Jovanovich, 1984, paper): Two sisters who are very different from each other also share something in common.

Amelia Bedelia's Family Album, by Peggy Parish, pictures by Lynn Sweat (Avon, 1989, paper): Amelia Bedelia's family is pictured, with information about each member.

The Journey Home, by Alison Lester (Houghton Mifflin, 1991, hard-cover): A brother and sister fall through a hole they dig, land at the North Pole, and must figure out how to get home again.

Best Friends, by Steven Kellogg (Dial, 1990, paper): Left in the neighborhood alone for the summer while her best friend is away, a young girl finds a new friend before welcoming back her old.

Matthew and Tilly, by Rebecca C. Jones (Dutton, 1991, hardcover): Matthew and Tilly's friendship shows acceptance of and joy in differences.

CHAPTER 6: PLAYING WITH LANGUAGE THROUGH WORDS, PICTURES, AND GAMES

Wordplay

CDB!, by William Steig (Simon & Schuster, 1968, paper): Sentences and phrases are written with letters representing words and syllables.

A Little Pigeon Toad, by Fred Gwynne (Simon & Schuster, 1988, paper): English idioms are pictured literally. Two other humorous books by the same author are *The King Who Rained* and *A Chocolate Moose for Dinner*

Easy as Pie, by Marcia and Michael Folsom, illustrated by Jack Kent (Houghton Mifflin, 1985, paper): A guessing game with English-language idioms.

Amelia Bedelia, by Peggy Parish, illustrated by Fritz Siebel (Harper & Row, 1983, paper): Amelia Bedelia interprets language literally, which makes for very funny predicaments. Eleven other titles in the series.

Frank and Ernest, by Alexandra Day (Scholastic, 1988, paper): Frank and Ernest answer a job ad and learn a new vocabulary working in a diner.

Word Works: Why the Alphabet Is a Kid's Best Friend, by Catherine Berger Kaye (Little, Brown, 1985, paper): For older children, this book is a wealth of fun and challenge with wordplay.

Storytelling

Emma's Vacation, by David McPhail (Viking Penguin, 1991, paper): Tired of all of the busy activities they do on their vacation, Emma suggests that she and her family swing in a hammock and tell stories to each other for fun.

Three up a Tree, by James Marshall (Dial, 1986, paper): Lolly, Spider, and Sam sit in their treehouse, competing to be the best storyteller. *Four on the Shore* introduces these three and their stories.

Two Ghosts on a Bench, by Marjorie Weinman Sharmat, illustrated by Nola Langner (Harper & Row, 1982, hardcover): Two ghosts tell stories to each other while haunting a park bench.

The Stories Julian Tells, by Ann Cameron, illustrated by Ann Strugnell (Knopf, 1989, paper): Each chapter in this book is another interesting adventure in the life of a young African American boy. First in a series of four books about Julian.

Tell Me a Mitzi, by Lore Segal, pictures by Harriet Pincus (Farrar, Straus & Giroux, 1982, paper): Mitzi tells humorous stories about her family. *Tell Me a Trudy*, by the same author, offers three more stories about a different family.

Coyote Stories for Children: Tales from Native America, adapted by Susan Strauss, illustrated by Gary Lund (Beyond Words Publishing, 1991, paper): Four oral stories from Southwestern Indian peoples.

A Story, a Story, an African tale retold and illustrated by Gail E. Haley (Macmillan, 1988, paper): An African American storyteller tells how most African folktales came to be called Spider stories.

A Wave in Her Pocket: Stories from Trinidad, by Lynn Joseph (Houghton Mifflin, 1991, hardcover): Tantie tells stories of her African heritage and her life on Trinidad.

Make-Believe Tales: A Folk Tale from Burma, retold and illustrated by Joanna Troughton (Peter Bederick Books, 1991, hardcover): Four animals challenge a traveler to a tale-telling contest.

Rhymes

Carrot/Parrot, by Jerome Martin (Simon & Schuster, 1991, hardcover): Flaps transform different words into rhymes. Also see *Mitten/Kitten*.

I Saw You in the Bathtub and Other Folk Rhymes, by Alvin Schwartz, pictures by Syd Hoff (Harper & Row, 1989, paper): Funny rhymes with funny illustrations.

Mother, Mother, I Want Another, by Maria Polushkin, illustrated by Diane Dawson (Crown, 1978, paper): A mother mouse misunderstands what her baby means by "Mother, mother, I want another."

Bringing the Rain to Kapiti Plain, by Verna Aardema, pictures by Beatriz Vidal (Dial, 1981, paper): A tale told in rhyme of an African plain during a drought and a young herdsman who shoots an eagle feather into a cloud.

Arroz Con Leche: Popular Songs and Rhymes from Latin America, selected and illustrated by Lulu Delacre (Scholastic, 1989, paper): Songs and rhymes in English and Spanish, with music included.

Tail Feathers from Mother Goose: The Opie Rhyme Book, by Iona and Peter Opie (Little, Brown, 1988, hardcover): A richly illustrated collection of many heretofore unpublished versions of well-known children's rhymes.

The Calico Book of Bedtime Rhymes from Around the World, edited by Mary Pope Osborne, illustrated by T. Lewis (Contemporary Books, 1990, hardcover): Poems about bedtime from many countries and cultures.

Maxi, the Hero, by Debra and Sal Barracca, pictures by Mark Buehner (Dial, 1991, hardcover): Maxi the dog rides with Jim the taxi driver and becomes a hero when he catches a thief.

Riddles and Jokes

Tickle Yourself with Riddles, by the Electric Company Staff, funny pictures by Michael Smollin (Random House and Children's Television Workshop, 1988, paper). See also *Tickle Yourself Again with Riddles* by the same authors.

Old Turtle's Riddle and Joke Book, by Leonard Kessler (Greenwillow, 1986, paper).

Fishy Riddles, by Katy Hall and Lisa Eisenberg, illustrated by Simms Taback (Dial, 1983, paper). Also see *Buggy Riddles*.

The Riddle Book, by Roy McKie (Random House, 1978, paper). Also see *The Joke Book*.

It Does Not Say Meow and Other Animal Riddle Rhymes, by Beatrice Schenk De Reginers, illustrated by Paul Galdone (Houghton Mifflin, 1983, paper).

Music and Songs

Lizard's Song, by George Shannon (Greenwillow, 1981, hardcover): Lizard composes his own original songs, but teaching one to Bear proves to be an unexpected adventure that produces more songs.

Ben's Trumpet, by Rachel Isadora (Greenwillow Books, 1979, paper): As he listens to jazz from the Zig Zag Club on his way home from school, young Ben imagines what he could do with a trumpet of his own.

Nate the Great and the Musical Note, by Marjorie Weinman Sharmat and Craig Sharmat, illustrated by Marc Simont (Dell, 1990, paper): Nate tracks down a note written in the form of a riddle.

I Like the Music, by Leah Komaiko, illustrated by Barbara Westman (Harper & Row, 1989, paper): A grandmother and granddaughter compare their musical tastes.

Poetry

Catch It If You Can, compiled by Brian Thompson, illustrated by Susie Jenkin-Pearce (Viking Penguin, 1989, paper): Funny poems and illustrations.

More Surprises, selected by Lee Bennett Hopkins, illustrated by Megan Lloyd (Harper & Row, 1987, paper): A short book of short poems about all kinds of funny, interesting things by different poets.

Ride a Purple Pelican, by Jack Prelutsky, pictures by Garth Williams (Greenwillow Books, 1986, paper): Poems include the names of many different states.

Where the Sidewalk Ends, by Shel Silverstein (Harper & Row, 1974, hardcover): Humorous poems that children from preschool to sixth grade love to hear and read. See *A Light in the Attic*, by the same author.

Dancing Teepees: Poems of American Indian Youth, selected by Virginia Driving Hawk Sneve, art by Steven Gammell (Holiday House, 1989, paper): Poetry drawn from Native American stories, chants, and tribal songs.

Honey I Love, by Eloise Greenfield, illustrated by Leo and Diane Dillon (Harper & Row, 1988, paper): Poetry especially for young African American children. See also *Night on Neighborhood Street* and *Under the Sunday Tree*.

Eric Carle's Animals Animals, poems compiled by Laura Whipple, illustrations by Eric Carle (Putnam Books, 1989, hardcover): The poems in this brightly illustrated book are from a variety of sources: the Bible, Shakespeare, Japanese Haiku, Pawnee Indians, sayings about the weather, and contemporary poets.

Frederick, by Leo Lionni (Knopf, 1987, paper): A mouse enhances his family's winter wait for spring with his poetry.

What I Did Last Summer, by Jack Prelutsky, pictures by Yossi Abolafia (Greenwillow, 1984, hardcover): A young boy narrates poems about his family's and his friends' adventures during a summer.

Beans on the Roof, by Betsy Byars, illustrated by Melodye Rosales (Dell, 1988, paper): In this short chapter book, the Bean family all begin writing poetry on the roof of their apartment building.

Drawing

The Rebus Treasury, compiled by Jean Marzollo, illustrated by Carol Devine Carson (Dial, 1989, paper): Familiar songs and Mother Goose rhymes in words and pictures.

Read-a-Rebus: Tales & Rhymes in Words & Pictures, by William H. Hooks, Joanne Oppenheim, and Betty Boegehold, illustrated by Lynn Munsinger (Random House, 1986, paper): Rhymes and stories that invite many rereadings.

Bear Hunt, by Anthony Browne (Doubleday, 1990, hardcover): Bear draws himself out of a series of dilemmas with a pencil.

Blackboard Bear, story and pictures by Martha Alexander (Dial, 1969, paper): When told he cannot play with the older boys, a little boy draws his own playmate. The first of four stories in this series.

Harold and the Purple Crayon, by Crockett Johnson (Harper Collins, 1959, paper): A young boy draws everything he needs for his very own adventure.

If You Take a Pencil, by Fulvio Testa (Dial, 1982, hardcover): Look at the stories you can draw with a pencil. A second book is *If You Take a Paintbrush: A Book of Colors*.

Matthew's Dream, by Leo Lionni (Knopf, 1991, hardcover): A visit to an art museum inspires a young mouse to become a painter.

Cherries and Cherry Pits, by Vera B. Williams (Greenwillow, 1991, paper): As she draws her pictures of people on the subway train and other events in her daily life, a young African American girl tells her stories aloud.

All I See, by Cynthia Rylant, pictures by Peter Catalanotto (Franklin Watts, 1988, hardcover): A young child is inspired by a man who paints whales.

The Art Lesson, by Tomie dePaola (Putnam, 1989, hardcover): A boy who loves to draw goes to school excited about art and is disappointed with the assignments he is given in class.

Mrs. Mary Malarky's Seven Cats, by Judy Hindley (Franklin Watts, 1990, hardcover): A young boy draws the cats vividly described to him by a babysitter.

Diego, by Jeanette Winter, text by Jonah Winter (Knopf, 1991, hardcover): In beautiful small illustrations with simple text, the story is recounted of how the famous Mexican painter Diego Rivera grew to be an artist.

Linnea in Monet's Garden, by Christina Björk, illustrated by Lena Anderson (Farrar, Straus and Giroux, 1987, hardcover): Linnea's journal entries introduce the French impressionist Monet by combining fiction and fact.

Comics

The Wish Card Ran Out!, by James Stevenson (Greenwillow Books, 1981, hardcover): With a magic wish card, a young boy tries to get his brother back.

Bumble Cat: How She Came to Be, by Phyllis Forbes Kerr (Houghton Mifflin, 1985, paper): A shy young kitten dons a bee costume and performs feats of heroism.

Wonder Kid Meets the Evil Lunch Snatcher, by Lois Duncan, illustrated by Margaret Sanfilippo (Little, Brown, 1990, paper): Brian and his friends become the superheroes from their favorite comics.

Tommy Traveler in the World of Black History, by Tom Feelings (Writers and Readers, 1991, hardcover): While reading historical accounts of important African Americans, Tommy's imagination propels the information into a comic-book format.

The Essential Calvin and Hobbes, by Bill Watterson (Andrews and McMeel, 1988, paper): One of the collections in book form of the popular Calvin and Hobbes comic strips.

The Adventures of Tintin: Explorers on the Moon, by Hergé (Little, Brown, 1976, paper): One in a series of comics, unique in the arena of children's books, that has been of great interest to youngsters for decades. There are numerous other titles.

The Tintin Games Book, by Hergé (Little, Brown, 1990, paper): A book of games featuring Tintin, his dog Snowy, and other familiar characters from the comic series.

Maps

This Is the Way We Go to School: A Book About Children Around the World, by Edith Baer, illustrated by Steve Björkman (Scholastic, 1990, paper): Children in many countries are pictured going to school.

As the Crow Flies: A First Book of Maps, by Gail Hartman, illustrated by Harvey Stevenson (Bradbury Press, 1991, hardcover): A set of maps drawn from the individual perspectives of different animals.

My Camera at the Zoo, by Janet Perry Marshall (Little, Brown, 1989, hardcover): Through the lens of a child's camera, we see the zoo that is mapped on the inside of the book. See also *My Camera at the Aquarium*.

Puzzle Island, by Susannah Leigh, illustrated by Brenda Haw (Usborne Publishing, 1990, paper): A young pirate and his pet parrot must follow the hidden clues on each page to find a treasure. *Puzzle Town* and *Puzzle Farm* are also in the series.

The Big Mile Race, by Leonard Kessler (Dell, 1983, paper): Turtle and his friends plan and map a race.

My World & Globe: An Interactive First Book of Geography, by Ira Wolfman (Workman, 1991, paper): Kids inflate and decorate their own globe with stickers of people, places, animals, and plants.

The Great Round-the-World Balloon Race, by Sue Scullard (Dutton, 1991, hardcover): On the anniversary of the first manned flight in 1783, balloonists from fifty-seven countries compete in a modern-day 2,300-mile race around the world.

The Great Kapok Tree: A Tale of the Amazon Rain Forest, by Lynne Cherry (Harcourt Brace Jovanovich, 1990, hardcover): A young man attempting to cut down a tree in the rain forest takes a short nap and thinks better of his decision.

Bananas: From Manolo to Margie, by George Ancona (Houghton Mifflin, 1982, paper): A book in photographs that traces the journey from banana tree to supermarket shelf.

Where in the World Is Geo? A Child's First Atlas, illustrated by Susanna Ronchi (Barron's Educational Services, 1991, cardboard): Games introduce facts about the continents.

Graphs and Charts

When Sheep Cannot Sleep: The Counting Book, by Satoshi Kitamura (Farrar, Straus and Giroux, 1986, paper): A unique counting book whose index is a number chart.

How Many Trucks Can a Tow Truck Tow, by Charlotte Pomerantz, illustrated by R. W. Alley (Random House, 1990, paper): A counting book in song.

From One to One Hundred, by Teri Sloat (Dutton, 1991, hardcover): The numbers proceed from 1 to 10 and continue to 100 by tens. A picture key on each page tells which items to count to find the number illustrated.

How Much Is a Million?, by David M. Schwartz, pictures by Steven Kellogg (Scholastic, 1985, paper): Marvelosissimo the Mathematical Magician explains the concept of a million to a group of children in intriguing ways. *If You Made a Million* is a second book by this author.

What Did You Eat Today?, by David Drew (Rigby, 1987, paper): In small or big book format, these feature charts and graphs of information about science and math. Other titles are *Creature Features* and *The Book of Animal Records*. Order by catalog (800-822-8661) from Rigby.

The King's Chessboard, by David Birch, illustrated by Devas Grebu (Dial, 1988, hardcover): A king learns a lesson about geometric and arithmetic progression.

Anno's Mysterious Multiplying Jar, by Masaichiro and Mitsumasa Anno (Putnam, 1983, paper): This book begins simply and evolves into a mathematical puzzle of immense dimensions. Others are *Anno's Math Games*, *Anno's Math Games II*, *Anno's Counting House*, and *Anno's Hat Tricks*.

The I Hate Mathematics! Book, by Marilyn Burns, illustrated by Martha Weston (Little, Brown, 1975, paper): Math activities for kids who think they don't like mathematics.

Writing Games

The Secret Birthday Message, written and illustrated by Eric Carle (Harper & Row, 1986, paper): A young boy must solve a coded message of words and pictures to find a secret surprise: his birthday present.

I Spy at the Zoo, by Maureen Roffey (Macmillan, 1987, paper): The old game of I Spy in a storybook. The same author has also written *I Spy on Vacation*.

Crossword Mysteries: Daring Detective Challenge #1, by Helene Chirinian, illustrated by Neal Yamamoto (Price Stern Sloan, 1990, paper): A mystery story accompanies every crossword puzzle. Also see *Amazing Maze Adventures: Trip to the Lost Planet*, by the same author and illustrator.

Fun with Hieroglyphs, by Catharine Roehrig (Viking Penguin and the Metropolitan Museum of Art, 1990, hardcover): A child's introduction to hieroglyphic writing in a package that includes a book, stamps, ink pad, and information charts. Fun with Hieroglyphs stationery is also available.

Autographs! I Collect Them!, by Michael K. Frith (Random House, 1990, paper): Different categories of autographs with space for all of them.

Upside-Downers, by Mitsumasa Anno (Putnam Books, 1988, hardcover): This clever book can be read by two people on either side, or one reader can rotate it in circles.

CHAPTER 7: EXPRESSING IMAGINATION

Stories

Here Comes the Cat!, by Frank Asch and Vladimir Vagin (Scholastic, 1989, paper): "Here comes the cat" appears in Russian and in English on each page of this story with engaging illustrations.

Sesame Street, My Stories, illustrated by Maggie Swanson (Western Publishing, 1991, paper): This large-size book provides ideas and space for story-writing on every page.

Dinosaur Beach, by Liza Donnelly (Scholastic, 1989, paper): A young boy rides on the back of a dinosaur and spends a day at a dinosaur beach.

Time Train, by Paul Fleischman, illustrated by Claire Ewart (Harper & Row, 1991, hardcover): A class of elementary-school children and their teacher board a train in New York City destined for Dinosaur National Monument in Utah to see and play with living dinosaurs.

The Stone-cutter: A Japanese Folk Tale, by Gerald McDermott (Viking Penguin, 1975, paper): A stone-cutter seeking ultimate power goes through a series of magical transformations.

The Terrible EEK: A Japanese Tale, as retold by Patricia A. Compton, illustrated by Sheila Hamanaka (Simon & Schuster, 1991, hardcover): A conversation between a father and his son results in a misunderstanding that creates a most unexpected adventure.

• *The Goose Who Wrote a Book*, by Judy Delton, pictures by Catherine Cleary (Carolrhoda, 1982, hardcover): Goose has written a story that she revises according to each of her reader's reactions, with a surprising result.

Galimoto, by Karen Lynn Williams, illustrated by Catherine Stock (Mulberry Books, 1990, paper): A young boy collects enough wire to build a wonderful toy.

Alistair's Time Machine, by Marilyn Sadler, illustrated by Roger Bollen (Prentice Hall, 1989, paper): Determined to win first prize in a science fair, Alistair builds a time machine.

A Trip to Mars, by Ruth Young, illustrated by Maryann Cocco-Leffler (Franklin Watts, 1990, hardcover): A young girl writes down space facts discovered while dreaming about a journey to the planet Mars.

Toad Is the Uncle of Heaven, by Jeanne M. Lee (Holt, Rinehart and Winston, 1989, paper): A Vietnamese folktale in which a toad struggles to live through a drought.

The Three Astronauts, by Umberto Eco and Eugenio Carwi, translated by William Weaver (Harcourt Brace Jovanovich, 1989, paper): Astronauts from the USA, Russia, and China land on Mars simultaneously and learn a lesson about the differences and similarities of "alien" life forms.

The Flame of Peace: A Tale of the Aztecs, by Deborah Nourse Lattimore (Harper & Row, 1987, paper): A boy named Two Flint seeks the magic flame that will bring peace to his beautiful city.

Ka-ha-si and the Loon: An Eskimo Legend, by Terri Cohlene, illustrated by Charles Reasoner (Watermill Press, 1990, paper): A young boy considered lazy by his family and tribe becomes a hero with help from the Loon. Facts and pictures of the Eskimo peoples accompany the legend.

Borreguita and the Coyote, by Verna Aardema, illustrated by Petra Mathers (Knopf, 1991, hardcover): A lamb must outwit a coyote many times in this Mexican folktale.

Personal Experience Stories

Louise Builds a Boat, by Louise Pfanner (Franklin Watts, 1990, hardcover): Louise designs and builds her own boat, christened the *Clementine*, to sail around the world and visit her friends. Hidden messages appear in the mast flags.

A Country Far Away, by Nigel Gray, pictures by Philippe Dupasquier (Franklin Watts, 1988, paper): The parallel experiences of two boys, one living in an American city and the other in a rural African village.

Sam Goes Trucking, by Henry Horenstein (Houghton Mifflin, 1989, paper): Photos of Sam's day trip with his father in a big Mack truck.

Dancing with the Indians, by Angela Shelf Medearis, illustrated by Samuel Byrd (Holiday House, 1991, hardcover): An African American family attends the yearly pow-wow of the tribe that harbored their great-grandfather from slavery.

How Many Stars in the Sky?, by Lenny Hort, paintings by James E. Ransome (Morrow, 1991, hardcover): A young African American boy and his father, neither of whom can sleep, set out together to count the stars in the sky.

Watch the Stars Come Out, by Riki Levinson, illustrated by Diane Goode (Dutton, 1985, hardcover): A grandmother tells her granddaughter of her own mother's journey by boat to a new country.

Cowboy Dreams, by Dayal Kaur Khalsa (Clarkson N. Potter, 1990, hardcover): The author describes her longing to be a cowboy and how she tries to fulfill this dream while living in the city.

Arthur Meets the President, by Marc Brown (Little, Brown, 1991, hardcover): Arthur the Aardvark writes an essay and wins a trip to meet the president of the United States.

Family Pictures: Cuadros de familia, by Carmen Lomas Garza (Children's Book Press, 1990, hardcover): The author describes in English and Spanish her experiences growing up in a Hispanic community in Texas.

"All About" Books

Trucks, (Aladdin Books, 1991, hardcover): The Eye-Openers series for younger children includes large print, a few facts on each page, and photographs. Other titles include *Pets*, *Zoo Animals*, and *Farm Animals*.

What's Inside? Shells (Dorling Kindersley, 1991, cardboard): One in a series of nonfiction books featuring large pictures and short text that explain what's inside various things.

Eyewitness Juniors: Amazing Butterflies & Moths, written by John Still, photographed by Jerry Young (Knopf, 1991, hardcover): A series with information and photographs. Other titles describe birds, mammals, snakes, spiders, cats, frogs and toads, lizards, poisonous animals, crocodiles and reptiles, fish, and monkeys.

New Questions and Answers About Dinosaurs, by Seymour Simon, illustrated by Jennifer Dewey (Morrow, 1990, hardcover): Information about dinosaurs in a reference format for beginners.

How Is a Crayon Made?, by Oz Charles (Simon & Schuster, 1988, paper): An account of how crayons are produced at a factory.

The Kids' Cat Book, by Tomie De Paola (Holiday House, 1979, paper): Patrick goes to Granny's for a free kitten and learns all about cats.

Hermit Crabs, by Sylvia A. Johnson, photographs by Kazunari Kawashima (Lerner Publications, 1989, paper): Color photos and text provide an introduction to hermit crabs. Includes an index and glossary.

Amazing Animal Senses, by Ron and Atie van der Meer (Little, Brown, 1990, cardboard): Pictures and movable flaps describe how animals use their senses.

The Seven Natural Wonders of the World: A Pop-Up Book, by Celia King (Chronicle Books, 1991, cardboard): Short explanations accompany the seven pop-ups of natural wonders. *The Seven Ancient Wonders* is also available in a pop-up format.

The Usborne Book of Facts and Lists (Omnibus Edition), by Lynn Bresler, Neil Champion, Anita Ganeri, and Struan Reid (Usborne, 1987, paper): Up-to-date information about the earth, countries of the world, the weather, and space, illustrated in cartoons and pictures.

Air, Light & Water, by Mary-Jane Wilkins, illustrated by Chris Forsey (Random House, 1991, paper): Facts about air, light, and water in a question-and-answer picturebook.

Natural Wonders: Stories Science Photos Tell, by Vicki Cobb (Lothrop, Lee and Shepard, 1990, hardcover): Thirteen photographs with accompanying stories that explain the science concepts behind them with clarity and simplicity.

Explorabook: A Kid's Science Museum in a Book, by John Cassidy and The Exploratorium (Klutz Press, 1991, paper): Hands-on science activities involving magnetism, illusions, light waves, biology, and physics.

"All About Me" Books

The ME Book, by John E. Johnson (Random House, 1979, hardcover): An All-About Me book for the youngest readers.

My Book About Me by Me, Myself, with help from my friends Dr. Seuss and Roy McKie (Random House, 1969, cardboard): Pages to record information, write, draw, collect autographs, and express feelings.

Three Names, by Patricia MacLachlan, pictures by Alexander Pertzoff (Harper & Row, 1991, hardcover): A young boy writes about his great-grandfather and a dog named "Three Names."

Fictional Characters

The Missing Tarts, by B. G. Hennessy, illustrated by Tracey Campbell Pearson (Viking Penguin, 1989, paper): An adventure with Mother Goose characters ensues when the queen's tarts are stolen.

Anno's Journey, by Mitsumaso Anno (Putnam, 1981, paper): Fictional characters appear in real places around the world.

Harry and the Terrible Whatzit, by Dick Gackenbach (Ticknor & Fields, 1977, paper): A young boy confronts his fears and solves the problem of a monster in the basement.

Jessica, by Kevin Henkes (Viking Penguin, 1989, paper): A young girl creates a fictional friend.

The Sandman, by Rob Shepperson (Farrar, Straus and Giroux, 1989, paper): Fun and adventure for a young boy when the Sandman arrives at night.

Lily Takes a Walk, by Satoshi Kitamura (Viking Penguin, 1991, paper): A little girl's dog sees many fantastic creatures on their walks together.

Super Cluck, by Jane O'Connor and Robert O'Connor, illustrated by Megan Lloyd (Harper Collins, 1991, hardcover): A boy and his mother wrote this book together, creating Super Cluck, a chicken who hatches on earth after accidentally arriving from outer space.

The Story Cloud, by Cooper Edens, ilustrated by Kenneth Leroy Grant (Simon & Schuster, 1991, hardcover): A boy is invited into a story cloud and embarks on an adventure filled with the fictional characters from fairy tales, nursery rhymes, and classic children's stories.

Journals

Ever Wondered? For Explorers, Inventors, and Artists of All Ages, by Paul Owen Lewis (Beyond Words Publishing, 1991, paper): By creating amusing possibilities from information normally taken for granted, this book can be a starting point for "I Wonder" Journals.

Teddy Bear's Scrapbook, by Deborah and James Howe, illustrated by David S. Rose (Macmillan, 1988, paper): A little girl is shown a scrapbook containing photographs of different occupations and interests in her teddy bear's life.

Nature All Year Long, by Clare Walker Leslie (Greenwillow, 1991, hardcover): Monthly entries describe what is occurring in nature during the seasonal changes in New England.

Linnea's Almanac, by Christina Björk, drawings by Lena Anderson (Farrar, Straus and Giroux, 1990, hardcover): Linnea keeps a monthly journal of her activities with plants and nature. See also *Linnea in Monet's Garden* (page 271).

The Burning Questions of Bingo Brown, by Betsy Byars (Viking Penguin, 1990, paper): Bingo forms questions about his classmates and school at the pencil sharpener during journal-writing time.

Crinkleroot's Guide to Walking in Wild Places, by Jim Arnosky (Bradbury Press, 1990, hardcover): Crinkleroot chronicles the plants, animals, and natural features he sees on his walks through the woods.

Pedro's Journal: A Voyage with Christopher Columbus, August 3, 1492–February 14, 1493, by Pam Conrad (Boyd's Mill Press, 1991, hardcover): A cabin boy aboard the *Santa Maria* describes Columbus's first voyage in a journal.

Homes in the Wilderness: A Pilgrim's Journal of Plymouth Plantation in 1620, by William Bradford and others of the Mayflower Company, edited by Margaret Wise Brown (Linnet Books, 1988, paper): Settlers describe a strange new continent and their daily lives in this modern version of the original English entries.

Writing Down the Days: 365 Creative Journaling Ideas for Young People, by Lorraine M. Dahlstrom (Free Spirit Publishing, 1990, paper): Journal-writing activities for every day of the year.

Versions of Books

Deep in the Forest, by Brinton Turkle (E. P. Dutton, 1976, paper): A wordless picture book about a baby bear who wanders into the cabin of a mother, father, and a girl who looks like Goldilocks.

ROLL OVER!, by Mordicai Gerstein (Crown, 1984, hardcover): The old rhyme about ten in the bed and the little one said, "Roll over."

In a Dark, Dark Wood: An Old Tale with a New Twist, by David A. Carter (Simon & Schuster, 1991, hardcover): A surprise awaits in a box on a shelf in a dark house.

The Teeny Tiny Woman, as retold by Jane O'Connor (Random House, 1986, paper): The tale of a little woman who finds a bone but has to give it back to its rightful owner.

Quick as a Cricket, by Audrey Wood, illustrated by Don Wood (Child's Play, 1982): Versions of old sayings.

The Frog Prince, Continued, by Jon Scieszka, illustrated by Steve Johnson (Viking, 1991, hardcover): The prince married the princess but did not live happily as a frog, so he set off to find a solution, and the funny story begins.

The Missing Mother Goose, by Stephen Krensky, illustrated by Chris Demarest (Doubleday, 1991, hardcover): Original versions of seven Mother Goose rhymes.

Jim and the Beanstalk, by Raymond Briggs (Putnam, 1989, paper): A giant is toothless and unkempt till he meets the boy who climbs the beanstalk.

Pig Pig and the Magic Photo Album, by David McPhail (Dutton, 1989, paper): While posing to have his picture taken, Pig Pig ends up in many misadventures every time he yells "cheese."

Diaries

UFO Diary, by Satoshi Kitamura (Scholastic, 1991, paper): A description of a day on earth by a visitor from another planet who is never seen but whom we learn about from the diary.

The Mouse's Diary, by Michelle Cartlidge (Lothrop, Lee & Shepard, 1981, paper): A little mouse describes two weeks of her life during the Mouse-field School summer term.

Happy Birthday to Me! A Four-Year Record Book for Birthday Boys and Girls, by Dian G. Smith (Scribner's, 1988, paper): Book for recording the details of celebrations and information about a child's growth and development.

An Owl in the House: A Naturalist's Diary, by Bernd Heinrich and Alice Calaprice (Little, Brown, 1990, hardcover): An account of a family's activities when an owl lives in their house.

Cassie's Journey: Going West in the 1860s, by Brett Harvey, illustrated by Deborah Kogan Ray (Holiday House, 1987, hardcover): The journey from Illinois to California, based on the diaries of women pioneers.

The Diary of a Church Mouse, by Graham Oakley (Macmillan, 1987, hardcover): Humphrey the mouse writes about the daily activities of the animals living in Wortlethorpe Church, including Sampson the cat.

Tree in the Trail, written and illustrated by Holling Clancy Holling (Houghton Mifflin, 1942, paper): The chronicle of a young sapling that grows and becomes many things.

Newspapers and Magazines

Dylan's Day Out, by Peter Catalanotto (Franklin Watts, 1989, hardcover): A wordless picture story about Dylan the dalmatian out loose for a day without his owner knowing it.

•*Headline*, by Malcolm Hall, illustrated by Wallace Tripp (Coward, McCann & Geoghegan, 1973, hardcover): A family of pack rats lives in the printing room of a newspaper and causes problems for the printers.

The True Story of the 3 Little Pigs! By A. Wolf, by Jon Scieszka, illustrated by Lane Smith (Viking Penguin, 1988, hardcover): An account of the classic story from the point of view of the wolf.

Audio- and Videotapes

The Broccoli Tapes, by Jan Slepian (Putnam, 1989, hardcover; a paperback is available from Scholastic): A sixth-grader audiotapes her adventures during a five-month visit to Hawaii.

CHAPTER 8: USING WRITING MACHINES

• *Flicks*, by Tomie De Paola (Harcourt Brace Jovanovich, 1979, hardcover): Five silent movies that end in surprising ways.

Lights! Camera! Action! How a Movie Is Made, by Gail Gibbons (Harper & Row, 1985, paper): The process of movie production, including writing the script.

The Bionic Bunny Show, by Marc Brown, illustrated by Laurence K. Brown (Little, Brown, 1985, paper): The behind-the-scenes story of the making of "The Bionic Bunny Show" in a cartoon format.

My First Computer Book, by David Schiller and David Rosenbloom, illustrated by Tedd Arnold (Workman, 1991, paper with computer disks): An introduction to computers featuring Bialosky the Bear, with paint, music, story, and mystery game software for Apple II machines. Another book covers IBM PCs and compatible computers.

Meet the Computer, by Seymour Simon, illustrated by Barbara and Ed Emberley (Harper & Row, 1985, paper): Colorful pictures and diagrams offer an overview of how a computer works.

How to Talk to Your Computer, by Seymour Simon, illustrated by Barbara and Ed Emberley (Harper & Row, 1985, paper): Introduction to computer language of BASIC and LOGO.

The Ultimate Collection of Computer Facts and Fun: A Kid's Guide to Computers, by Cindra Tison and Mary Jo Woodside (SAMS, 1991, paper): Facts, pictures, and games to introduce children to computers.

The TV Kid, by Betsy Byars, illustrated by Richard Cuffari (Viking Penguin, 1976, paper): An introverted boy seeks refuge in the world of television. Also see *The Two-Thousand Pound Goldfish*, by the same author.

CHAPTER 9: INTRODUCING CONVENTIONS OF PRINT
The Alphabet

David McPhail's Animals A to Z (Scholastic, 1989, paper): Each page has a capital letter and an illustration of an animal and other objects that begin with that sound.

Albert's Alphabet, by Leslie Tryon (MacMillan, 1991, hardcover): A letter to Albert from the school principal occasions a day of building alphabet letters for the playground.

Puffin First Picture Dictionary, by Brian Thompson, illustrated by Celia Berridge (Viking Penguin, 1988, paper): A beginner's pictionary, with capital and lowercase letters on every page.

Alphabet Times Four: An International ABC, by Ruth Brown (Dutton, 1991, hardcover): An alphabet book with words for each letter in four languages: English, Spanish, French, and German.

Idalia's Project ABC, by Idalia Rosario (Holt, 1981, hardcover): An urban alphabet book in English and Spanish.

Q Is for Duck: An Alphabet Guessing Game, by Mary Elting and Michael Folsom, pictures by Jack Kent (Ticknor & Fields, 1980, paper): Riddles about the letters in the alphabet for children to solve.

Jambo Means Hello: Swahili Alphabet Book, by Muriel Feelings, illustrated by Tom Feelings (Dial, 1981, paper): Introduces the twenty-four letters used in the Swahili alphabet in African pictures and words.

Ashanti to Zulu, by Margaret Musgrove, illustrated by Leo and Diane Dillon (Dial, 1976, paper): Each letter describes a different African people whose name begins with it.

Spelling

Clowning Around, by Cathryn Falwell (Franklin Watts, 1991, hardcover): A clown plays with letters to achieve word spellings.

Pat the Cat, by Colin and Jacqui Hawkins (Putnam, 1983, hardcover): A rhyming flapbook that incorporates many words spelled with "at" in the story. Part of a series of flapbooks by these authors.

Alphabet Soup, by Kate Banks, pictures by Peter Sis (Knopf, 1988, hardcover): Each time a boy and his bear need help, the boy puts a spoon into his alphabet soup and with the letters spells out the solution to their problem.

Punctuation

How Many Babies on the Farm?, a lift-the-flap book by Robert Crowther (Simon & Schuster, 1990, paper): To answer each counting question, lift a flap. Another book by the same author is *Who Lives on the Farm?*

Where's My Cheese?, by Stan Mack (Pantheon Books, 1977, hardcover): A funny story told in a question-and-answer format.

Why Is the Sky Up?, by Joyce and James Dunbar (Houghton Mifflin, 1991, paper): A preschooler asks his parents for answers to many questions about science and nature.

The Amazing Voyage of Jackie Grace, by Matt Faulkner (Scholastic, 1987, paper): Almost all the punctuation in this story is exclamation points—with good reason!

Parts of Speech

Merry-Go-Round: A Book About Nouns, by Ruth Heller (Grosset & Dunlap, 1990, hardcover): Capitalization, plurals, and spelling in rhymes.

Other titles by this author include *Kites Sail High: A Book About Verbs, A Cache of Jewels and Other Collective Nouns*, and *Many Luscious Lollipops: A Book About Adjectives*.

Taxi: A Book of City Words, by Betsy and Giulio Maestro (Houghton Mifflin, 1989, hardcover): City nouns—*parks, skyscraper, theater*, and many others—are described as a taxi does its job during a busy work day.

Riddle Roundup: A Wild Bunch to Beef Up Your Word Power, by Giulio Maestro (Houghton Mifflin, 1989, paper): Puns, homonyms, and homographs make these riddles. Others in the series are *What's a Frank Frank? Tasty Homograph Riddles,* and *What's Mite Might? Homophone Riddles to Boost Your Word Power*.

Wacky Summer Fill-Ins, by Melissa Hartley (Scholastic, 1990, paper): Stories with missing nouns, verbs, adjectives, and adverbs.

The King's Cat Is Coming!, by Stan Mack (Pantheon Books, 1976, hardcover): An alphabet book in which each letter is an adjective or adverb describing a cat

Publishing
Gorgeous Books
at Home

"This is a special day," one kindergartner announced as he walked by Sharon on his way out of school. "I published a book!"

In his class, as in many others, young children are published authors. Their writing is assembled into books with title pages, publication dates, and information about the author featured on the last page. These books become part of the classroom (or school) library till the students take them home at the end of the year or leave a copy for the school to keep.

Recognize that children are young authors. Publish their writing at home. Publication emphasizes children's choices. From the size of the book and its cover design to how the writing appears on the page, a youngster's decisions are integral to publishing. Books can be made as informal or as elaborate as you wish: cardboard or paper covers; pages sewn, ringed, or stapled together, with text typed or handwritten.

A youngster's writing can be sent, displayed, or included in a book exactly as it is written, without changes.

If you are expecting someone to read it who might need some interpretation, a conventionally spelled text can be transcribed onto the child's paper or written on another sheet.

Six-year-old Paul's version of a children's rhyme [Rain, rain, go away, come back another day. Rain, rain, go away, come back another day. Rain, rain, go with me. I'll go get an umbrella today. Please go with me, will ya?]

A conventionally spelled version may appear by itself—as with Joshua's Valentine poem on page 62. The purpose and the audience will determine which form of publication seems most appropriate.

Also ask your child which she would prefer: having both texts appear or only one. If she wants a standard version of the text to accompany her own, print in large, block print letters or type on a computer or typewriter (preferably in a large print size if it is an option). Having both on the page makes it possible for her to compare them and comment about what she sees. Her writing may provide clues to help her read the conventional text. If she wants only the conventional spelling, when you have finished typing or hand-printing it, she adds the illustrations. Finally, she might include a short section for the end of the book titled "About the Author."

The title, date of publication, town, and state may appear on the title page of the published work. Try making up a name for your home publishing company and include it too. You might also make multiple copies of the finished book to send to others, keeping the original as part of the child's library of self-authored books.

Parents promote children's own book-making by organizing materials so youngsters can find and use them. A supply of paper in many different sizes to be stapled or ringed together allows choices about size and length. Different colors for covers and pages is a way to attract a young writer's attention. Regardless of the colors, a supply of paper that does not run out is a necessity. Lined and unlined paper appeal to children at different times. With paper cut into different sizes, a child can make a book at any time without an adult's help if he is old enough to use a stapler or to put papers on a ring. If not, then you might assist him to complete the necessary steps. Paper for book publishing can be kept together in pocket folders, or in an expanding cardboard file with different sizes in each pocket.

Old wallpaper sample books, available free at many paint and wallpaper stores, are a source of beautiful book covers. The wallpaper samples can be cut to cover different-sized pieces of cardboard. Wrapping paper, scrap, construction, or drawing paper also make fine book covers. Typewriter or homemade labels displaying the title are affixed to the front cover. Use whatever materials you have at hand that your child likes.

The quickest and easiest ways to make a book are to sew, staple, or ring pages together or put them into plastic covers. Children old enough to do so can punch holes in pages and weave a string through them to hold pages together. They can also staple pages or put them on rings that open and close.

BINDING BOOKS WITH STRING

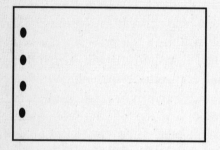

Using a paper punch, make holes in the left-hand side of the pages and front and back covers of the book.

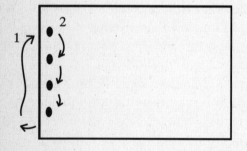

Measure string or yarn twice the length of the side of the book plus five or six more inches. Insert it from the back through the top hole. Go through each hole as shown and then tie the string that remains at the top to the string at the bottom.

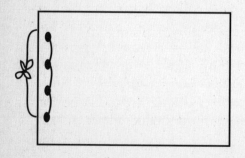

Make sure the string is taut but also that the pages of the book turn easily.

BINDING HARDCOVER BOOKS

Bound books are the most formally published. They take time to make, but they are attractive. Two pieces of the same size cardboard can be transformed by covering them with wallpaper or contact paper. After the cardboard is covered, pages are sewn together and glued to the inside of the cover. Here are the directions for this elegant book-making procedure.

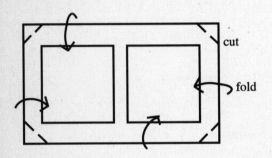

Place two pieces of the same-size cardboard onto contact paper, leaving an inch border around the cardboard and in the middle between them. Before attaching the cardboard to the contact paper, cut off the ends of the four corners as shown. Fold the contact-paper border over the cardboard smoothly.

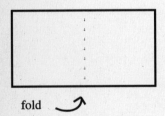

Fold in half sheets of paper (sized to fit into the cardboard covers) to the desired thickness or to the number of pages you need to publish a story. Add extra folded sheets to be the title page in the front and the "About the Author" page in the back. Poke holes in the fold with a needle to make sewing them together easier.

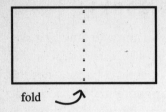

fold

Measure a piece of construction paper to fit the inside of the cardboard covers, fold it in half, and sew it with the pages. This piece of paper will be glued to the inside of the cover to hold the paper pages inside the book.

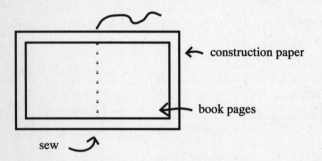

← construction paper

book pages

sew

Sew the pages twice: once from top to bottom and then back up from bottom to top. Knot the string securely and glue the construction paper to the inside of the cardboard covers. Open and close the book as you press the construction paper in place to achieve the right flexibility between cover and inside paper.

Resources for Parents and Children

ANTHOLOGIES OF CHILDREN'S BOOKS FOR PARENTS

There are a number of excellent books that parents can use to select additional books to read with their children.

Hart-Hewins, Linda, and Jan Wells. *Real Books for Reading: Learning to Read with Children's Literature*. Portsmouth, NH: Heinemann, 1990.

Jett-Simpson, Mary, and The Committee on the Elementary School Booklist, eds. *Adventuring with Books: A Booklist for Pre-K–Grade 6*. 9th ed. Urbana, IL: National Council of Teachers of English, 1989.

Kimmel, Margaret Mary, and Elizabeth Segel. *For Reading Out Loud: A Guide to Sharing Books with Children*. Revised ed. New York: Dell, 1991.

Kobrin, Beverly. *Eyeopeners! How to Choose and Use Children's Books About Real People, Places, and Things*. New York: Penguin Books, 1989.

Trelease, Jim. *The New Read-Aloud Handbook*. New York: Penguin Books, 1989.

Yaakov, Juliette, with the assistance of Anne Price. *Children's Catalog*. 16th ed. New York: H. W. Wilson, 1991.

GENERAL INFORMATION ABOUT CHILDREN, LEARNING, AND EDUCATION

Harste, Jerome C., Virginia A. Woodward, and Carolyn L. Burke. *Language Stories and Literacy Lessons*. Portsmouth, NH: Heinemann, 1984.

Kaye, Peggy. *Games for Reading: Playful Ways to Help Your Child Read*. New York: Pantheon Books, 1984.

Koch, Kenneth. *Rose, Where Did You Get That Red? Teaching Great Poetry to Children*. New York: Vintage Press, 1973.

Kohl, Herb. *Book of Puzzlements: Play & Invention with Language*. New York: Schocken, 1986.

————. *Mathematical Puzzlements: Play & Invention with Mathematics*. New York: Schocken, 1987.

Kozol, Jonathan. *Savage Inequalities: Children in America's Schools*. New York: Crown Publishers, 1991.

Lightfoot, Sara Lawrence. *Worlds Apart: Relationships between Families and Schools*. New York: Basic Books, 1978.

Livingston, Myra Cohn. *Ways to Begin Writing Poetry*. New York: Harper Collins, 1991.

Paley, Vivian Gussin. *Wally's Stories*. Cambridge: Harvard University Press, 1981.

————. *Bad Guys Don't Have Birthdays: Fantasy Play at Four*. Chicago: University of Chicago Press, 1988.

Taylor, Denny. *Family Literacy: Young Children Learning to Read and Write*. Portsmouth, NH: Heinemann, 1983.

White, Burton L. *The First Three Years of Life*. New, revised ed. New York: Prentice-Hall, 1990.

WRITING RESOURCES FOR CHILDREN

Burnie, David D. *How Nature Works: 100 Ways Parents and Kids Can Share the Secrets of Nature*. Pleasantville, NY: Reader's Digest, 1991 (hardcover). Hands-on science activities to do at home.

Cole, Joanne, and Stephanie Calmenson. *The Laugh Book: A New Trea-*

sury of Humor for Children. Illustrated by Marylin Hafner. New York: Doubleday, 1986 (hardcover).

The Lincoln Writing Dictionary for Children. New York: Harcourt Brace Jovanovich, 1988 (hardcover). Included in this volume are 35,000 entries, 750 illustrations, and quotations from famous writers.

Morley, Diana. *Marms in the Marmalade*. Minneapolis, MN: Carolrhoda, 1984 (hardcover). Where do words come from? The fun of words that do not make sense.

Pollack, Pamela, ed. *The Random House Book of Humor for Children*. Illustrated by Paul O. Zelinsky. New York: Random House, 1988 (hardcover). Thirty-four funny stories from Mark Twain, Judy Blume, Issac Bashevis Singer, Louise Fitzhugh, and other well-known writers.

Schiller, Andrew, and William A. Jenkins. *Roget's Children's Thesaurus for Ages 8–12*. New York: Harper & Row, 1991 (hardcover). Word choices with an introduction for how young writers can use the thesaurus.

Stoll, Donald R., ed. *Magazines for Children*. Educational Press Association of America and International Reading Association, 1990. Annotated listing of over 120 magazines written and published for young readers.

SOFTWARE RESOURCES FOR FAMILIES

The following organizations provide newsletters for computer-users and make available low-cost and public-domain software written by teachers and others. Contact them directly for more information:

The Boston Computer Society
One Center Plaza
Boston, MA 02108
617-367-8080

CUE Softswap
P O Box 271704
Concord, MA 94527
415-685-7289

Berkeley Macintosh Users' Group
(BMUG)
1442A Walnut Street #62
Berkeley, CA 94709-1496
415-459-BMUG

Educorp
7434 Trade Street
San Diego, CA 92121
800-843-9497

MASSCUE (Massachusetts
Computer-Using Educators)
P. O. Box 82-188
Wellesley, MA 02181

Scholastic Software Club
Scholastic, Inc.
P. O. Box 7503
2931 E. McCarty Street
Jefferson City, MO 65102
800-541-5513

Home versions of school software are available at discounts for club members.

Judy Salpeter's *Kids & Computers: A Parents' Handbook* (Carmel, IN: Sams/Prentice-Hall Computer Publishing, 1992) is a useful reference book on new technologies and software programs for home use.

References

Banks, Ann. *Me and My Stepfamily: A Kid's Journal*. New York: Puffin Books, 1990.

Barron, Marlene. *I Learn to Read and Write the Way I Learn to Talk: A Very First Book About Whole Language*. Katonah, NY: Richard C. Owen Publishers, 1990.

Bean, Wendy, and Chrystine Bouffler. *Spell by Writing*. Portsmouth, NH: Heinemann, 1991.

Bloom, Benjamin S., ed. *Developing Talent in Young People*. New York: Ballantine Books, 1985.

Buckleitner, Warren. *Survey of Early Childhood Software*. Ypsilanti, MI: The High/Scope Press, 1991.

Butler, Andrea, and Jan Turbill. *Towards a Reading-Writing Classroom*. Rozelle, Australia: Primary English Teaching Association, 1984.

Calkins, Lucy McCormick. *Lessons from a Child*. Portsmouth, NH: Heinemann, 1983.

Chouinard, Carole, and Randall Baer. *Making Fun Family Videos*. Kansas City, MO: Andrews and McMeel, 1991.

Clay, Marie. *Writing Begins at Home: Preparing Children for Writing Before They Go to School*. Portsmouth, NH: Heinemann, 1987.

Dennison, George. *The Lives of Children: The Story of the First Street School*. New York: Random House, 1969.

Durkin, Dolores. *Children Who Read Early*. New York: Teachers College Press, 1966.

Edmonds, Ronald, "Programs of School Improvement: An Overview." *Educational Leadership* December 1982: 4–11.

Elbow, Peter. *Writing with Power: Techniques for Mastering the Writing Process*. New York: Oxford University Press, 1981.

Gardner, Howard. *Artful Scribbles: The Significance of Children's Drawings*. New York: Basic Books, 1980.

Gentry, Richard J. *Spel . . . Is a Four-Letter Word*. Portsmouth, NH: Heinemann, 1987.

Goodman, Kenneth S., *What's Whole in Whole Language*. Portsmouth, NH: Heinemann, 1986.

Goodman, Kenneth S., Lois Bridges Bird, and Yetta M. Goodman. *The Whole Language Catalog*. Santa Rosa, CA: American School Publishers, 1991.

Gordon, Thomas. *Discipline That Works: Promoting Self-Discipline in Children*. New York: Plume Books, 1989.

Graves, Donald. *Writing: Teachers & Children at Work*. Portsmouth, NH: Heinemann, 1983.

Holt, John. *Learning All the Time*. Reading, MA: Addison-Wesley, 1989.

Hopkins, Lee Bennett, ed. *Pass the Poetry, Please!* Revised, enlarged, and updated edition. New York: Harper & Row, 1987.

Jones, Byrd L., and Robert W. Maloy. *Partnerships for Improving Schools*. Westport, CT: Greenwood Press, 1988.

Kegan, Robert. *The Evolving Self: Problem and Process in Human Development*. Cambridge: Harvard University Press, 1982.

Koch, Kenneth. *Wishes, Lies and Dreams: Teaching Children to Write Poetry*. New York: Harper and Row, 1970.

Kozol, Jonathan. *Illiterate America*. New York: New American Library, 1987.

Lamme, Linda Leonard. *Growing Up Writing: Sharing the Joys of Good Writing*. Washington, DC: Acropolis Books, 1984.

Newman, Judith. *The Craft of Children's Writing*. Portsmouth, NH: Heinemann, 1985.

Office of Technology Assessment. *Power On! New Tools for Teaching and Learning*. Washington, DC: Government Printing Office, 1988.

Opie, Iona, and Peter Opie. *The Lore and Language of Schoolchildren*. New York: Oxford University Press, 1959.

Owen, Barry. *Personal Computers for the Computer Illiterate: The What, When, Why, Where, and How Guide*. New York: Harper Collins, 1991.

Paley, Vivian Gussin. *Boys & Girls: Superheroes in the Doll Corner*. Chicago: University of Chicago Press, 1984.

———. *The Boy Who Would Be a Helicopter: The Uses of Storytelling in the Classroom*. Cambridge: Harvard University Press, 1990.

Papert, Seymour. *Mindstorms: Children, Computers, and Powerful Ideas*. New York: Basic Books, 1980.

Read, Charles. *Children's Creative Spelling*. New York: Chapman & Hall, 1986.

Schickedanz, Judith A. *Adam's Righting Revolutions: One Child's Literacy Development from Infancy Through Grade One*. Portsmouth, NH: Heinemann, 1990.

Shermer, Michael. *Teach Your Child Science: Making Science Fun for the Both of You*. Los Angeles: Lowell House, 1989.

Skolnick, Joan, Carol Langbort, and Lucille Day. *How to Encourage Girls in Math & Science*. Palo Alto, CA: Dale Seymour Publications, 1982.

Strunk, William, Jr., and E. B. White. *The Elements of Style*. New York: Macmillan, 1979.

Turkle, Sherry. *The Second Self: Computers and the Human Spirit*. New York: Simon & Schuster, 1984.

Wells, Gordon. *The Meaning Makers: Children Learning Language and Using Language to Learn*. Portsmouth, NH: Heinemann, 1986.

Wilde, Sandra. *You Kan Red This! Spelling and Punctuation for Whole Language Classrooms, K–6*. Portsmouth, NH: Heinemann, 1992.

Wolfman, Ira. *Do People Grow on Family Trees? Genealogy for Kids and Other Beginners*. New York: Workman Publishing Company, 1991.